Trauma and Transformation

at Ground Zero

Trauma and Transformation

at Ground Zero

A Pastoral Theology

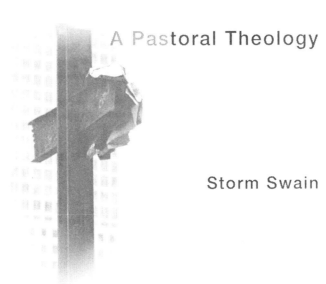

Storm Swain

Fortress Press
Minneapolis

TRAUMA AND TRANSFORMATION AT GROUND ZERO
A Pastoral Theology

Unless otherwise noted, scripture quotations are the author's own translation or from the New Revised Standard Version Bible, copyright © 1989 by the Division of Christian Education of the National Council of Churches of Christ in the USA, and are used with permission.

"Terce" (p. 1), "Lauds" (p. 19), "Matins" (pp. 39–40), "Sext" (p. 83), "Vespers" (pp. 144–45), and "Compline" (p. 182), from *A Book of Hours for the World Trade Center* (Glasgow: Glasgow City Council, 2006), are copyright © Stephen R. Harding and used by permission of the author.

Jim Cotter, "Prayer at Night" (pp. 35–36), 1981, *Prayer at Night's Approaching*, 2001, Cairns Publications; also in forthcoming *Praying the Dark Hours*, 2011, Canterbury Press in association with Cairns Publications.

Interior photos are FEMA News Photos and are used following FEMA usage guidelines.

Author photo: © 2011 Br. Hal Weiner, O.U.M. All rights reserved

Cover design: Laurie Ingram
Cover and title page image: USA-New York City-Ground Zero © David Howells/Corbis
Book design: James Korsmo / Timothy W. Larson

Library of Congress Cataloging-in-Publication Data

Swain, Storm.
 Trauma and transformation at Ground Zero : a pastoral theology / Storm Swain.
   p. cm.
 Includes bibliographical references (p.   ) and indexes.
  ISBN 978–0–8006–9805–8 (alk. paper)
1. Pastoral theology. 2. Suffering—Religious aspects—Christianity. 3. September 11 Terrorist Attacks, 2001—Religious aspects—Christianity. 4. Psychic trauma—Religious aspects—Christianity. 5. Church work with disaster victims. 6. Trinity. I. Title.
 BV4330.S98 2011
 259'.6—dc22   2011015062

The paper used in this publication meets the minimum requirements of American National Standard for Information Sciences—Permanence of Paper for Printed Library Materials, ANSI Z329.48-1984.

Manufactured in the U.S.A.

Contents

Preface

Undertaking any endeavor where one seeks to be true to the profound task of holding the stories of those who have worked at the face of trauma, and the story of God within that, is a humbling task. I have found none more so than this work, which seeks to describe a model of pastoral care that is integrally connected both to the story of the God in whom that care is grounded and to the stories of those who suffer the realities of our world as well as those who care for them.

In the pages of this book you will find the description of a trinitarian pastoral theology reflected in the experience of the chaplains at the 9/11 Temporary Mortuary (T. Mort.) at Ground Zero, which offers a model of pastoral care as "Earth-making/Pain-bearing/Life-giving." This model has its roots in at least two different locations yet transcends them. *A New Zealand Prayer Book—He Karakia Mihinare O Aotearoa* was published the year that I decided to discern a sense of vocation as priest by going to seminary. Within the pages of that prayerbook was a version of Jim Cotter's rewrite of the Lord's Prayer, describing God as "Earth-maker, Pain-bearer, Life-giver," which is the model that will be described in this book. In the years that followed I was witness to the way that image has captured and transformed the imagination of pastors, parishioners, and liturgists both in this country and in many places around the world. It is an image that seems to speak so well to the relationship of God to humanity in a theologically sound yet down-to-earth way. It is an image that plays with me particularly as I have encountered the tougher parts of my ministry as a psychiatric chaplain, where "pain-bearing" seems often to be a more prominent part of the vocation of pastoral care than anything else. Over the years I have found myself working out this theology of pastoral care initially on paper table napkins, over coffee, and living it out in the ministry with those incredible individuals who trusted me enough to share their stories and traumas. I am deeply indebted to Jim Cotter for the rich incarnational connections between God and humanity implied by this description of the economic Trinity, which has wound its way around my heart for over twenty years.

The seeds for this book, however, began to take shape at another point of discernment. I had just entered the doctoral program at Union Theological Seminary, and was preparing to race from a staff meeting at the Cathedral of St. John the Divine in New York City to my first class on "Aggression," when the first plane hit the first World Trade Center (WTC) tower on September 11, 2001. In the months that followed I was witness both to the trauma experienced by those who "lost" families, friends, and colleagues in the WTC and the transformative love of those who cared for the traumatized. I was deeply moved by the work of the men and women of the police and fire departments, corrections services, American Red Cross, other uniformed services, chaplains, and volunteers with whom I was privileged to work alongside and at times to care for at the Armory & Pier 94 Family Assistance Centers, Respite 3, and the Disaster Mortuary. This encounter with suffering and the response to it on the scale we experienced it in New York was transformative for me.

Therefore, when I wished to explore what love lived out in reality looks like, it was to this disaster I returned. In seeking to explore this experience I sought to find a group of clergy who had responded likewise, but in an area of disaster spiritual care of which I had not been a part. I am indebted to the clergy who ministered as chaplains at the T. Mort. whose stories are the music behind the theological words that frame this discussion of pastoral care and theology. Through their participation these chaplains showed a commitment to the ongoing development and under-standing of disaster spiritual care, while holding with immense care and respect the "sacred stories" of their encounters with those individuals who worked on recovery at Ground Zero in New York. I particularly am grateful to the thirty-three chaplains who were generous enough to share their experience with me in questionnaire and those who were interviewed. I especially want to thank Barry Bates, Linda Smith Criddle, Emile Frishe, Doniel Kramer, Ed Martin, John Moody, Leroy Ness, Denise Mantell, Andrew Osmun, Joe Parrish, Lawrence Recla, Mindy Rosengarten, Roger Ross, Rob Schwartz, Tom Synan, Herb Trimpe, Justus Van Horton, and William Wrede. Beyond my own reflection on their experience and theological framing of it, it is their profound stories that provide the constant music behind and within my words. As you will see, the framing of this experience as trinitarian is entirely my own and may differ radically from the theological perspectives of many of the chap-lains, but their courage and care in sharing their experience has made such theo-logical reflection possible and this book would be impoverished without it. I also wish to thank my colleagues and friends, Mitties De Champlain, Tom Faulkner, Elizabeth Maxwell, Deb Tammereau, and Pippa Turner, whom I didn't interview, but whose collegial support and ministry at the T. Mort. I found inspiring.

There is another group of individuals whose particular story is not repre-sented on these pages but whose ministry was foundational for the 9/11 chaplaincy response. The story of the formation of the chaplaincy at the T. Mort. includes the ministry of those from the Spiritual Care Aviation Incident Response team (SAIR) who managed at a metalevel, after the first few days, the spiritual-care disas-ter response. I particularly want to thank SAIR team member Daina Salnitis for her calm, clear, well-grounded leadership at the FACs and D. Mort. after 9/11, particularly regarding ministering to first responders on the job. For those particu-larly interested in the life cycle of a disaster and how such a coordinated response moves from the outstretched hands, hearts, and minds of local clergy to a voluntary ministry that can maintain such a level of care over nine months, you will find an addendum to this book on the Fortress Press Web site (http://fortresspress.com/store/item.jsp?clsid=283303&productgroupid=0&isbn=0800698053).

I am indebted also to the generosity of a number of other individuals and organizations. My deepest thanks goes to the Rev. Julie Taylor of Disaster Chaplaincy Services—NY who provided access to the DCS-NY 9/11 Chaplaincy Archives and who valued my efforts to begin to tell a portion of the 9/11 chaplaincy story in New York. I continue to be humbled by the generosity of FDNY Chaplain Father Christopher Keenan and the Franciscan brothers of Harlem for their support. My enduring gratitude also goes to Peter Gudaitis of New York Disaster Interfaith Services who enabled me to undertake the interviews at NYDIS, overlooking Ground Zero in New York. The generosity of Paul Myhre, Associate Director, and the Wabash Center for Teaching and Learning in Theology and Religion cannot be underestimated in the completion of this project. Thank you, all.

My thanks goes also to the midwives of an earlier draft of this book, Dr. Harry Fogarty, Dr. Melvyn Hill, and Dr. Christopher Morse, but most gratefully to Dr. Ann Belford Ulanov. Above all I am grateful for Dr. Ulanov for modeling "joy" as an academic and a practitioner, and it has been the gift of who she is as much as what she has done that has contributed to my formation as a scholar and pastoral psychotherapist.

My thanks goes also to the Congregation of Saint Saviour at the Cathedral Church of St. John the Divine in New York City, where I was ministering as Canon Pastor while undertaking the research for this book and was the community that held me in my own disaster response after 9/11. The ministry and care of the then-wardens, Chris Johnson and Sandra Schubert, and the vestry have been formative in my thinking about how this model functions in congregational ministry. I wish to thank also Margaret Klench, Dr. Mary-Jane Rubenstein, and Elizabeth Salzer for their care and friendship. I am grateful to my colleagues in ministry at the cathedral, particularly for those days after 9/11 where we really got to experience the church being church in response to those who had walked out of the towers, up the island and into the cathedral, those that came to be anointed when words could not contain the suffering, those first responders and Muslim students who came seeking a safe space to cry and to pray, and that community that welcomed the stranger as neighbor reaching out in love. I particularly want to thank Dean James A. Kowalski who supported me as both a priest and as an academic, and whose encouragement to write gave me the push I needed.

During the writing of this book I have also been immensely grateful for the support of both colleagues and students at The Lutheran Theological Seminary at Philadelphia, who have worked with me with grace, understanding, and patience. The vocation to teach is a constantly humbling one, and I am privileged to experience it in a place that places emphasis on public theology not as an academic exercise but as a living, engaged practice both inside and outside the church and with such excellent students as to give me hope for the church's ability to care and respond well in the future.

I wish to acknowledge also the friends and colleagues who are a part of the fabric of my being whose care and encouragement during this process and its formation made a huge difference to my life and well-being: Karen O'Malley, the Rev. Erice Fairbrother, Dr. Lilian Larsen, and Tamara Walker. I lift both glass and prayer in thanks to you.

There are two other individuals whose presence has made a huge impact on the completion of this work. My son Theo lived through this both *in utero* and after birth. His first four-syllable word was "dissertation." As I sought to balance ministry, the academy, and motherhood he reminded me what is life giving in the midst of it all. Finally, my thanks go to the Rev. Stephen Harding, my husband whose incredible care and continuous support made this possible. That this support was provided in a context of academic and professional boundaries reflecting on a ministry of which he had been a part, and that before it was finished the only parts of the book he read were the words he had written, simply increases my respect and gratitude to him all the more. The addition of his poetry to this work gives an immanency and quality to the experience of the chaplains that is an immeasurable gift. Stephen, I am profoundly grateful for it and for all that you have done for me.

I humbly dedicate this to the chaplains of the Temporary Mortuary at Ground Zero, to the other 9/11 chaplains, and to all those who worked on recovery, who over nine months sought to bring those who were lost "home." May God's peace be with you all.

The Trinity

As a Pastoral Model in the Face of Trauma

Terce

Clear early morning, checking email, voicemail,
making a list for the day on call.
The news of the first, then the second.
Forget staff meeting and go across First Avenue
to see with my own eyes the smoke from the towers
and then to the Emergency Room.

Mood of adrenaline and positive testosterone:
determination and resolve that everything will be done.
Shock, particulate inhalation, reliving of trauma,
hearing thuds as the bodies hit the ground; the blackness
that descended for five minutes and
left all present searching for air.
Trauma freshly lived, noise, concern
tears from the survivors; sobs and fear of being
left alone in a place where the lights went out
before the building fell, retriggered by a power surge.
The uncertainty of the living, families' terror
and prayers that all might be safe.
Calling one's loves, hoping to hear their voice
and dreading their not answering.

The white parietal bone of the skull
innocently visible against the black bag
and the black of charring
naked, vulnerable,

A surge of people, ash caked and wet
Disaster, V., and a number, on their chart
noise intensifying, chaos controlled and diverted

Operating rooms cleared for survivors, beds
opened up for them, plans made, teams mobilized—
at 12:30 the flow of admissions trickles to an end.

It takes a while to realize that these are the survivors.
There aren't any more.[1]

It was 8 P.M. on a New York Friday night, ten days after September 11, 2001. I had just arrived at "D. Mort," the Medical Examiner's Morgue, to do my first shift there as a chaplain. There I was—an experienced Episcopal priest and fledgling disaster chaplain. I had been a hospital chaplain for eight years, working with suicidal and homicidal persons for six of those years. I had trained about fifty seminarians as a Clinical Pastoral Education (C.P.E.) supervisor, and had just started my second year of psychoanalytic training for my doctoral program. Now, for five of the last ten days, I had been serving families and working on multidisciplinary death notification teams at the 9/11 Family Assistance Centers (at the Armory and Pier 94). Five days before, I had preached to a cathedral congregation of over five hundred persons about Jesus standing with Mary and Martha after Lazarus had died, wondering aloud with them, "How close do we let ourselves come to the tomb?" So here I was, standing at the face of the tomb, realizing I did not know what to do. It was not that I did not know how to engage in pastoral crisis intervention, but I did not know what to do to process this event in myself.

It is in the face of such situations that our pastoral training and professional development either holds us or deserts us. It is in the most difficult moments of ministry we see what it is that holds us, sustains us, and enables us to be with others in their deep trauma. What is it that enables a forensic chaplain to sit and listen to a man who has killed his wife and children without being overwhelmed by horror in hearing the gruesome details that he shares in his dissociated state? How does a pastor not get caught up in her own anger in hearing the suicidal woman who secretly believes God has cursed her because a Sunday school teacher told her that God would do so if she left the church? How did the chaplains minister at Ground Zero, the smell of death pungent in their nostrils and fires continuing to burn underground, as they were called onto "the Pile" or into "the Pit" to bless a body or body part that may have belonged to a loved one of the person standing next to them, while hundreds of firefighters, police, and construction workers stood silent, helmets off, waiting to hear their prayers ring out over the site?

These are a few examples of the kind of suffering humans experience throughout their lives and that pastors, hospital and prison chaplains, pastoral psychotherapists, and disaster response chaplains encounter in their work every day. What does it mean to love in these instances? How do we minister in these contexts? The answer goes beyond an application of listening skills, of spiritual and religious interventions, to creating a fabric of meaning and a way of being with another. It is *not* that these questions are unique to situations of trauma in pastoral work; rather, it is that trauma highlights most clearly what the questions are and what spiritual resources we draw on in pastoral ministry every day. Over the days and months of 9/11 chaplaincy that followed, I realized that the pastoral model which I had reflected upon for a number of years was in fact my strongest resource in the face of such trauma. It was a model of the Trinity.

The Trinity as Pastoral Model

This book offers a trinitarian pastoral theology, grounded in the God of love, who is both Trinity and Unity. This trinitarian image of God is reflected in humans when lived out in relationship with others as the three movements described as *Earth-making*, *Pain-bearing*, and *Life-giving*. By engaging the psychoanalytic thought of D. W. Winnicott, this model of pastoral engagement is also expounded upon and reflected as relational spaces or movements of *Holding*, *Suffering*, and *Transforming*. These three movements in pastoral care and crisis intervention allow persons to work through trauma in a subjective intrapsychic and interpersonal way to get to a place of transformation. They are present in those pastoral caregivers who have found a way to hold, bear, and transform their experience so as to manifest resilience, post-traumatic growth, and connection to meaning and community, rather than the arousal and avoidance those with "secondary traumatic stress" (STS) experience or the sense of hopelessness and disillusionment of those with "compassion fatigue." To explore this we will examine the experience of a selective group of pastoral caregivers in the context of a particular trauma: the chaplains who worked at the Temporary Mortuary (T. Mort.) at Ground Zero in New York City after the terrorist attacks of September 11, 2001.

The September 11 WTC Disaster

On September 11, 2001, the United States of America suffered a disaster, the like of which had not been seen on these shores before. On that Tuesday morning, four passenger airplanes were hijacked by foreign terrorists and used as weapons of mass destruction inside the borders of the continental United States. First one airplane, then another, was flown into the separate towers of the 112-story World Trade Center (WTC) in New York City, exploding on impact, killing all on board and many in the towers. Another plane was flown into the Pentagon in Washington, D.C. The fourth plane, also bound for Washington, was crashed into a Pennsylvania field through the intervention of passengers who sought to overpower the terrorists before that plane, too, could be used as a weapon.[2] Despite the intervention of first responders and mass evacuation of thousands from the WTC, the disaster grew to

Image 1.1. An aerial view of Ground Zero (October 4, 2001). (Photo by Andrea Booher/FEMA News Photo.)

greater proportions than the initial impact when the two WTC towers collapsed, killing 2,490 civilians and 418 first responders[3] who sought to rescue them. Such a disaster had not only a traumatic impact on the individuals and families directly concerned, but an impact on the city, country, and arguably many parts of the world.

In the face of such a trauma, how does transformation happen? Under such circumstances, transformation is most often seen as "a return to normative and adaptive functioning." But what happens when a disaster is of such a magnitude that there is no possibility of a return to "normal"? For many the disaster of 9/11 was of such a magnitude. Beyond the immediate impact of the day of the terrorist attacks was the effect of the short-lived rescue period, and the long period of the recovery of bodies and body parts. For those outside New York and Washington, unaffected by personal relationships to those who had died, it may have been seen as a discrete event, largely localized to one day. In New York, for those involved in the recovery effort, 9/11 was not a day but a time-space that encompassed nine months. One chaplain noted this very fact when asked what was the worst thing about the experience: "One of the things that bothers me is the vast number of people who when they use the expression 9/11, think of an event that happened on one day or maybe two or three. The story of 9/11 that I am much more committed to tell . . . is the recovery effort. The aspects of nobility, commitment, and competence that went with that [are] not often told."

Even for those not involved in the recovery effort in New York, however, the impact of the day of the disaster was exacerbated by the potential trauma of the ongoing threat of terrorism, reinforced by the chemical terrorism of anthrax and the effect of the crash of Flight 587 due to a mechanical malfunction almost two months to the day after the terrorist attacks. "In a traumatized city, there were thousands of traumatized [responders] reacting just like everyone else, needing to give whatever they could."[4] It is in the context of a disaster where many felt traumatized—not only individuals directly involved but the whole city itself—that the chaplaincy response to 9/11 arose, where clergy sought to "give whatever they could" in the midst of their own possible trauma in the face of the disaster.

The T. Mort. Chaplains

The main role of the group of chaplains at the Temporary Mortuary (T. Mort.) at "Ground Zero" was "a ministry of presence and prayer." Although pastoral crisis intervention and pastoral care of those involved in recovery were important tasks, the T. Mort. chaplains' prime task was to be there to bless the bodies and body parts that were recovered on the site. In relation to the question of how one might move from a space of trauma to a space of transformation, I chose the example of these chaplains, not only because of their experience with pastoral care in crisis but due to their proximity to what can be described as "the horror" of Ground Zero—the recovery of often multiple body parts for each person killed—in the context of ministering to first responders recovering parts of people they may well have known.

Much of the time the chaplain on duty would be walking the perimeter of the site or sitting in the covered trailer of the T. Mort. and then, when called, would be taken to "the Pile" or, later, down in "the Pit" to bless the body, or part thereof, that had been recovered. If "the remains" were that of a member of service—a firefighter, police officer, FBI agent, Emergency Medical Technician (EMT), or paramedic—then the whole recovery crew would stop and participate in this ritual. Then the body or body part would be taken to the T. Mort. trailer and a medical examiner would make a preliminary examination. After being prayed over again, it would then be transferred to an ambulance, escorted by an honor guard if a member-of-service, and taken to the medical examiner's morgue. The chaplain would return to the trailer.

Over the nine months that the recovery site at Ground Zero was open, over sixty clergy worked as chaplains at the T. Mort. This represents approximately 6 percent of the 962 chaplains who volunteered for the American Red Cross (ARC) in some aspect of the disaster response, most working in the family assistance centers and respite centers. Almost three-quarters of these chaplains worked during both 2001 and 2002, many taking at least one shift a week for the entire nine months that the Ground Zero site was open. There is much that can be learned from these chaplains as to the ministry of pastoral response to disaster and how they were able to respond in the way they did. Of the clergy who worked the whole nine months, almost half came from the five boroughs of New York City, with 35 percent living in Manhattan. All of these chaplains would have been affected in some way by the 9/11 disaster, and those who were New York City residents additionally so by the ongoing mentality of living in a city still under the threat of terrorism and a city and country engaged in public mourning (or, one could argue, the refusal to mourn). How does one minister to the traumatized when one may be somewhat traumatized oneself? What helps? What hinders? What are the particular spiritual resources that enable clergy to continue in such a ministry? And what is the trauma really about?

Trauma and Resilience

Trauma theory has had two major trajectories: the *symptomatic*, which has focused on the symptoms of trauma, and the *analytic*, which has often focused on the mechanisms or meaning of trauma. Together these have come to outline the two strands of the current theories.

Much of the research on trauma, since the introduction in 1980 of the diagnosis "Post-Traumatic Stress Disorder" (PTSD) into the American Psychiatric Association's *Diagnostic and Statistical Manual of Mental Disorders III* (DSM-III), has centered around the effects of trauma in terms of its symptomology—arousal, avoidance, and intrusion—with little attention to the cause. However, PTSD is one of the few diagnoses in the DSM-III that posited a causative agent in its definition of a psychological disorder: a "stressor that would evoke significant symptoms of distress in almost anyone . . . that is generally outside the usual range of experience."[5] Beyond cause and effect, however, is another factor. In the assessment of trauma we need to take three factors into account. Psychologist Bonnie Green notes the variables of (1) an objectively defined event, (2) the person's subjective interpretation of its meaning, and (3) the person's emotional reaction to it.[6] Many people may experience the same external event; however, diagnosis in the DSM-IV fourteen years later recognized that only some may become traumatized to the extent that they exhibit PTSD, due to whether "the person's response involved intense fear, helplessness or horror."[7]

One can see these factors in the chaplains' experiences. One of the more experienced chaplains, a former military person, describes this cognitive process when first on site:

> Part of the way I deal with the stuff is the way the other first responders do. It's a cognitive mission orientation. What's the perimeter? What are the security issues? What are the jobs? What are the things going on? Where's this? Where's that? Where's help if you need it? Where are you able to help? What are the methods of egress? Where do the things end? What is the stability? Where is the equipment? Are we good to go? Who's where? What am I wearing? What does that match with? What's traffic? What IDs are necessary?

Another chaplain's first response shows a very different cognitive and affective process. "All I can say is that, for whatever reason, my inner sense was of devastation [on the one hand]. . . . But on the other hand, actually being able to do ministry."

Here one can see that if the event is interpreted as traumatic, the trauma is secondarily held up against the extant worldview of the individual (or culture). If one has a worldview that is inclusive of disasterous events, one is less likely to be traumatized by them. Religiously, a person's worldview that sees disaster as part of the karmic cycle or the reality of life in a "sinful and broken world"[8] may be able to mitigate trauma in a way that a worldview that says "God will protect me from all harm" may not. This can be seen in one chaplain's account about his relationship with God after 9/11:

> Oh, we had a tough time. We had a struggle. Yes, we did. I know I was the problem. I didn't let [God] get too close. It's because of the anger in me I think at that time too, taking on the anger of the area and the situation . . . the chaos and all of that. For me, I saw anger in all of that. There were no nice buildings there anymore. It was just twisted steel and rubble and all of that stuff. It was an anger scene for me in that sense, the destruction; it's not what it should be. Yes, I blamed God, yes, I cursed at God, I called Him names, apart from "God." He probably sat back and waited until I came to my senses. People brought me to my senses, people I was with. . . . And after a while, too, in the praying over the remains, I came to see that I'm wasting a lot of energy on that side. I've had my shouting match at Him, let go, move on.

In exploring trauma, it is therefore not enough to focus simply on the event but also on the interpretation of the event and the meaning it has to a person. Some events for most people may be of such a magnitude that they may overwhelm regardless; others, however, may bear them in a way that is surprisingly resilient. It is helpful therefore to discern what really is traumatic in a "traumatic event.'" Later we will see that Object Relations theory contributes to this discussion in its own understanding of what traumatizes.

Current theory about traumatic stress reflects this tension or balance of focus between internal and external, between environmental and personal, between impact, affect, and interpretation. In exploring the experience of the T. Mort. chaplains, it is the *subjective interpretation* of and *emotional reaction* to the external event to which we are attending. In exploring the subjective interpretation and affective life of clergy we need to look beyond a simple psychological exploration of coping skills, identity, purpose, values, and tools in ministry, to the spiritual resources and responses of the clergy. Even more so with clergy we must look to theology as well as psychology to frame our field of inquiry and interpretations.

Anecdotal evidence from the 1995 bombing of the Alfred P. Murrah Federal building in Oklahoma City, cited in all pastoral crisis intervention training[9] and now promulgated widely in the disaster community, "indicated that two-thirds of the local clergy [who worked in the recovery efforts] left Oklahoma City after the relief effort, and one-third of those left the ministry entirely."[10] The reality in New York appears to be very different, as this chaplain from the T. Mort. at Ground Zero relates:

> If I hear one more time statistics about Oklahoma City and how five years later, every religious leader is now running a candy store, or something. . . . I can't stand that statistic because my feeling is you have to examine that further. What kind of religious leader were they? What kind of leadership positions were they in? What kind of religious communities were they? Because I don't see that happening here at all! I'm not aware of anybody who has given up being a religious leader, not that I'm polling all of New York. But I for one am not somebody who walks away. I remember PBS had a show, something like, "Where's God in September 11th?" or something or other. And they had this one guy who was an Episcopal priest and (I've never heard of him before, I never saw him before, I don't even think he was from this diocese) and I felt sorry for him, because I thought, "This is somebody who's not going to be a priest." You know I hope he is, I hope he's doing fine. But in that story, he didn't know God anymore. And I thought, "God, I know God." I felt like I didn't know God before this. This just took me to a deeper level.

A survey conducted in a conference in New York on June 17, 2002, found—contrary to the often hypothesized opinion that intense exposure to a disaster experience increases risk of PTSD or, in the case of first and secondary responders, what is now being named as secondary traumatic stress (STS), "compassion fatigue," or "vicarious traumatization"—that clergy and other religious volunteers who worked at the high-exposure sites of ARC, which would have included the T. Mort. chaplains, showed lower levels of compassion fatigue and burnout than non-ARC religious volunteers who worked at other sites (such as St. Paul's Chapel).[11] In fact, those who worked for ARC only showed even lower levels of compassion fatigue than nonresponders! Why is that? What has enabled these clergy at T. Mort. to work and then, perhaps, in some way "work through" the disaster of 9/11?

Later findings from the above research[12] indicate that those chaplains who worked for ARC alone, with its holding frame of limited shift work and postshift "defusings" (approximately twenty-minute structured reflections on the shift), suffered less burnout. However, the chaplains at T. Mort. did not have the same resources for defusing as did the other ARC chaplains, and alternative explanations need to be explored. Another significant contribution to health, rather than burnout and compassion fatigue, seems to be the effect of C.P.E. training. Interestingly, while those responders who were hospital chaplains as well as T. Mort. chaplains suffered compassion fatigue, this appeared to be mitigated by significant compassion satisfaction.

In the disaster care environment, there is an increasing movement from a focus on pathology to a focus on health. A lot of attention has been paid to PTSD, and in the first two years after 9/11, also to STS, vicarious traumatization, and compassion fatigue. However, many organizations training for disaster care as well as the American Psychological Association are exploring "resiliency" to examine those factors that in the face of trauma enable persons to survive and even to grow.

What are the spiritual resources that enabled these clergy "to hold" the experience of being at Ground Zero with its sights, sounds, and smells, "to bear" the suffering of those first responders and others working in recovery and their own suffering, and to find something life giving in this experience that enabled them to be less compassionately fatigued even than those who had not volunteered? We will see in the latter chapters of this book that those chaplains who showed an ability to (1) hold the experience, (2) to bear their own pain and that of those they ministered to, and (3) who found in the face of the disaster that which was life giving were those who reported coming through the experience not traumatized but transformed. The 9/11 disaster is an extreme example, but I think it simply highlights the challenge of pastoral ministry in relation to human suffering that hospital and prison chaplains, pastoral psychotherapists and social workers, lay ministers and parish pastors face every day. What does it mean to love in these instances of crisis? How do we minister in these contexts? Through the work of the chaplains at the T. Mort. and the lens of a trinitarian theology we will begin to explore these questions.

One Spiritual Care Aviation Incident Response (SAIR) team member who functioned as a coordinator at the ARC Family Assistance Center during October 2001 reported at the end of his ministry there, "What an experience. It was the most sustained emotionally challenging event of my life." He went on to say, "I like the response a chaplain gave when asked, 'How are you doing?' He said, 'Ask me in five years.'" The reflections of the chaplains you will find in this book were collected through questionnaires, interviews, and the offering of the chaplains' own sermons, journals, and published comments approximately five years after the disaster. On a theoretical level one could question whether such research is too late after the disaster. However, several of those who had been chaplains commented that they do not think they could have participated any earlier. A couple said that they had not looked at their 9/11 material since 2002 and were not sure whether they were ready. One chaplain said, although it was almost five years later, that he could remember it clearly, because for him the experiences were contained in "*kairos* time—sacred time," not chronological time, so he could go back to it as if it were yesterday.

Through the generosity of Julie Taylor, executive director of Disaster Chaplaincy Services–New York, I had a list of sixty-seven chaplains who had been scheduled by ARC to work as chaplains at the T. Mort. between November 13, 2001, and June 10, 2002.[13] Of these, the records indicated that thirteen had only spent one shift at the T-Mort. They may of course have spent shifts previous to this as part of the significant ministry of the Archdiocese of New York who staffed the T. Mort. before that time, the Episcopal Church's ministry at Ground Zero from St. Paul's Chapel, or through another avenue. Of the 75 percent of the chaplains I was able to contact, although many more indicated a wish to do so, a little over half the total number of chaplains filled in the questionnaire and almost a third were interviewed. Those interviewed spanned the country from Massachusetts to Florida, and from as far away as Papua New Guinea.

The narrative reflections in these pages represent, in the words of one chaplain, "a precious gift." This gift entailed both risk and benefit, both of which can be seen in the response of a chaplain near the end of his interview:

> [When] I first filled out the questionnaire it was difficult. I could feel physical symptoms again. I could feel emotional upset. I'm feeling it in my voice now while I'm talking about it. So I thought about what would be the most healing thing. And I thought the most healing thing would be to go through this whole process. That again, like being at Ground Zero, if I couldn't find my way through this process and complete it, then I'm still holding stuff that I really need some help with. As soon as I came to that realization, it was okay. And I was wondering what was going to happen with the pictures [in the interview] and while they were poignant, and they brought me back to a lot of memories of what it looked like, it wasn't upsetting at all. I think I found a way to put this in its place. You know, it's not "forget it," it's not "be gone," it's not locked up in a room somewhere. But it's in a place, like the place that I reserved for the birth of my first grandchild or the place that I reserve for my father's funeral. It's in a place of my experience and my connections with the divine at that time and how I function and how I feel about it. And I'm pretty much okay with this. And I'm really glad that we did this.

Pastoral Theology

Any foray into pastoral theology has to negotiate the journey attending to at least two focal questions: (1) How do we do pastoral theology and be true to the doctrines that have been formed, received, and debated for at least two millennia now? and (2) How do we do pastoral theology and be true to the complexity that we are discovering more and more every day as we continue to plumb the depths of ourselves as bio-psycho-socio-spiritual beings in the context of the best and worst that humanity can do? Pastoral theology has often been critiqued as either simply *applied theology*—an application of doctrine to human life—or *practical theology*—an application of the skills of the human sciences to the pastoral arena. However, there appears to be an increasing focus in this discipline to move beyond these extremes to an integrated position with as much academic rigor and integrity as systematic theology while grounding it concretely in the real experience of pastoral care.

Clearly, the task of pastoral theology is much more sophisticated than a simple application from theology to pastoral practice or visa versa, but a true engagement between the knowledge and wisdom of theology and sound research grounded in the pastoral field drawing on the resources of other applicable disciplines. Theological reflection in pastoral theology may begin with pastoral experience or with a theological concept and its scriptural grounding. Much "classical" or what Carrie Doehring names as "premodern"[14] pastoral theology simply contains these elements. As such, it is an *intra*disciplinary reflection that, with rigor and sound scholarship, has validity in its own right in terms of its faith tradition.

Chapter 1 of this book is primarily just such an engagement in pastoral theology in attending to the formation of an economic model of the Trinity and exploring why it has relevance for pastoral practice. This chapter explores the thought of Augustine of Hippo in his reflections upon the Trinity and his consequent development of a theological anthropology of the *imago Dei* that sees the human mind as a reflection of the Trinity. Rather than seeing this "image" as something fixed, this book will explore it as an active concept, something that is activated by living relationship with an other but interpreted through our own being. I then offer a new model of the economic Trinity, that of English priest Jim Cotter, as one that is useful and applicable in pastoral practice. In addition, I will introduce the *inter*disciplinary elements through psychoanalyst D. W. Winnicott's contribution to an understanding of love. This interdisciplinary engagement between theology and the insights and instructive practices of psychoanalysis reflects the continuing development in the field of pastoral theology, which add a "modern" lens to the classic approach.[15]

Chapters 2, 3, and 4 are an outworking of this model of the economic Trinity, and each attend to one aspect of this trinitarian model. These chapters reflect this interdisciplinary correlation between theology and psychoanalytic thought, each following a definite structure: (1) theological thought, (2) psychological and psychoanalytic thought, and (3) a model of pastoral practice. Chapter 3 explores "Earth-making," correlating it to "Holding" and relating it to pastoral practice. Similarly, chapter 4 explores "Pain-bearing," correlating it to "Suffering"; and chapter 5 explores "Life-giving" and correlates it to "Transforming." Such correlation is not a simply an equating of Augustinian and trinitarian theology to Winnicott's thought but a reflection on the essence of each "part" of the Trinity and how we may see it manifest in his theory, thereby addressing the questions: How does Winnicott's thought contribute to an understanding of creating? How may pain-bearing be reflected in his theory? What is seen as life giving? It is my hope that both theologians and more secular practitioners will see that "Holding" is both a reflection of theological "Earth-making" in analytic thought, and also contributes a deeper, more grounded understanding to what is the principle and experience of creation and creativity as it relates to the human person. Likewise, "Suffering" can be seen intrapsychically not just as a pain to be borne but an achievement. "Transforming" is not simply a resurrection-like reality that happens to us, but also a way of being to which we can open ourselves as we engage in creative and life-giving ways.

Both models can be seen separately. Earth-making/Pain-bearing/Life-giving may speak primarily to Christian practitioners, while Holding/Suffering/Transforming speak to those involved in other fields. Each can stand alone in its own right. However, the insights of analytic theory can contribute much to theological understanding. Likewise, theology can often reflect on existential and religious questions that psycho-analytic psychology believes to be beyond the realm of the social sciences. Theology has no such constraint, yet it must be grounded in the reality of what humanity faces in the world every day. What this theological model offers to analytic thought is a coherence and cohesion that may not be evident otherwise. This model of the Trinity—Earth-making/Pain-bearing/Life-giving—includes both unity and multiplicity, grounded as a model of God's activity in the world. Holding/Suffering/Transforming has no such inherent overarching unity. Winnicott's thought is not trinitarian, despite his focus on the "third space" of illusion as a transitional space where person, culture, and religion connect and create. Theology, therefore, can contribute both this sense of unity and the understanding of the mutual indwelling of each of the model's three parts within the others.

For those of us working as pastoral caregivers these two models can be held in tension and mutually inform practice. As such, methodologically my pastoral theology is *theological reflection* on pastoral practice reframed as a relational model with an *interdisciplinary correlation* to the psychoanalytic Object Relations theory. The focus of interdisciplinary engagement between theology and Winnicott's psychoanalytic theory that this book takes is that of a *reflective* correlation grounded in *relationality*. This takes some further explanation as the terms can have multiple meanings.

Relationality

In my understanding, theology, in essence, is a reflection upon humanity's *relationship* with the divine, with God. Likewise, the human sciences reflect upon the human person's relation to him/herself and to the other, both intrapsychic and interpersonal.

My understanding of relationality is grounded upon an "I-Thou" understanding of the human person. Beyond creaturely instincts we are formed by and oriented toward our relations with others. One could say that for humanity there is no I without a Thou. Although humans may choose or be forced to live alone for a variety of reasons, our formation as humans is dependent upon being in relation with others and our psyches are constituted in terms of both inner and outer relationships. As such, from a psychoanalytic perspective I draw upon the British Object

Relations school, primarily upon the work of D. W. Winnicott. Winnicott denotes the formation of being as in and through our primary relationships, which becomes an internalized way of being (inner object relations) and is lived out externally in our relationship with objective others.[16] The "other" can relate to any object, from an objectively perceived other person, to a part of that relationship, to one's dog, to the universe, to the subjective "objects" that populate our inner world which may only have a partial relationship to the external other. Thus, relationality needs to be read as both intrapsychic and interpersonal, our relationship with those in both our inner and outer worlds. This psychoanalytic understanding both prefigures and exemplifies much that is becoming popular in postmodern theory about knowledge and what we perceive as truth.

Theologically, an understanding of relationality is grounded in the relations between God and humanity, in the incarnation, in creation, and in the ongoing ethic of love that points us toward the hope of our final destiny. It is grounded in the understanding of God as a being-in-relation, the three-in-one; the one who loves within the freedom of God's own interrelatedness. This understanding of relationality takes us beyond discussion of a ontology of being as static substance to a sense of a dynamic being as being-in-relationship, a being as constantly becoming. Increasingly contemporary theologians such as Leonardo Boff, David S. Cunningham, Stanley Grenz, and Pamela Cooper-White are focusing on relationality in both the doctrine of God and of theological anthropology. Grenz suggests that:

> The most innovative result of this conversation . . . has been the coalescing of theology with the widely accepted philosophical conclusion that "person" has more to do with relationality than with substantiality and that the term stands closer to their idea of communion or community than to the conception of the individual in isolation or abstracted from communal embeddedness. So widespread is the unease towards substantialist categories and so thorough has been the ascendency of relationality as central to the understanding of personhood that Ted Peters can conclude . . . "the idea of person-in-relationship seems to be universally assumed."[17]

Grenz indicates that in philosophy, anthropology, and both Protestant and Roman Catholic theology there has been a shift to conceive of "person" not as an individual but as a being-in-relationship. For Grenz this is applicable both to God and the human person. Likewise, Boff claims, "*Person* is indeed a being-in-oneself and hence means irreducible individuality, but this individuality is characterized by the fact of being always open to others. Person is thus a node of relationships facing all directions. Person is a being of relationships."[18]

In theology there have traditionally been two entry points into this understanding of personhood as being-in-communion. One is the incarnation, where in Jesus the relation of divine and human can be explored in the one "person."

However, we cannot stop at the incarnation as a model of imitation, for in the Spirit we, too, get drawn into this relation with the divine, which manifests as three-in-one, and are impelled to live out of this in relation to the world. The other theological concept that draws both of these together is that of the *imago Dei*, the "image of God" in humanity. Dietrich Bonhoeffer's epistemology is one that integrates both these conceptions. In expounding upon Bonhoeffer's early theology in *Sanctorum Communio*, John Godsey writes,

> Every human Thou is an image of the divine Thou, and it is God that comes and makes the other a Thou for me. Since behind every human Thou is the divine Thou, whose will is love, the I-Thou relation is the basic social category, and the person, God, and social being are intrinsically related. . . . the problem one faces in knowing another human is parallel to that of knowing God: the other must reveal itself. In this way, through an act of self-revealing love, the one who confronts us as a Thou becomes known as an I.[19]

Revelation both on a human and divine level is intensely relational. As pastoral caregivers we are called into this relationship where "the other must reveal itself." Such revelation can only happen in a relationship, pastoral or otherwise, where we are prepared not only to know the other as an objective Thou but, through empathic attunement, know the other as an I, that they may know themselves through an act of "self-revealing love" in a safe and trusted relationship. When we know the other as an I, we cease to judge their worst, which enables through this self-revelation their best—the image of the "divine Thou, whose will is love"—to lead them to love themselves, others, and even the divine Other in ways not previously experienced. However we describe this knowing, the journey is often one of suffering as we shine light on our psyches, allowing the reality of trauma and pain to be held in relationship rather than denied, repressed, or acted out in our own bodies and upon others. It is an understanding in "a post-modern approach"[20] that pastoral ministry is transformed by the unique story and contextual relationality of *each* of the participants, and their relation to God.

In this way relationality, as explored in this book, is translated into active, dynamic terms, such that God as Creator is not seen as a being that once created but as also creating—one who is continually in creative relation to all that is, was, and will be. Christian Scripture refers to this eternal perspective in the dialogue between Jesus and the Sadducees concerning the resurrection: "And as for the resurrection of the dead, have you not read what was said to you by God, 'I am the God of Abraham, and the God of Isaac, and the God of Jacob'? He is not God of the dead, but of the living" (Matt. 22:31-32; see also Mark 12:26-27; Luke 20:37-38).

A focus on the relationality of God and its connection to our relational selves calls for a dynamic active ethical relation to the world, a relationality as not just being but as becoming, where being and doing are caught up in active relationship, where in a relation of love we become what we are, the image of God. This relational reframing is a shift from a seemingly static and perhaps historical role to a relational function of being and doing in relationship. Hence, God the *Earth-maker* becomes *earth-making*, and so forth. In the following pages we will explore these relational functions in the context of active actual relationships both interpersonally and intrapsychically through the pastoral experience of the chaplains at Ground Zero. Focusing on relational *functions* has the advantage of retaining the distinctiveness of role in pastoral ministry while leaving open the possibility of mutuality between the persons. While we could argue that the chaplain *acted* as the Life-giver, theologically we can argue only God *is* such. As we will see, the reality was most often that in life-giving pastoral relationships the chaplains also found themselves transformed. In pain-bearing relationships with those involved in recovery they also found themselves cared for and their own pain held. As they made space for others they were moved by how others made space for them to be and do what they were called to do.

In the human sciences, it is the psychoanalytic theorists who have most profoundly reflected on the formation of self in relationship. Winnicott is, I believe, the psychoanalyst who more than any other focuses on the formative power of *primary* relationship, that which enables the developing formation of a "True Self," primarily through the "holding relationship"[21] of a primary caregiver to "her" child. This relationship is characterized by empathic attunement, a mirroring back to the infant what is interpreted of their personal reality, suffering the aggressive and libidinal impulses and providing a transformative space where the developing self may respond to the other (be it mother, other, or world) creatively and spontaneously. The thought of Winnicott can offer us both an interdisciplinary critique of the self-containedness of what has been termed Augustine's "theo-psychology"[22] and a complement to it, grounding it in interpersonal relations while attending to the intrapsychic dimensions.

Reflection

It is in this light that *reflection* is also seen. Reflection has two bases. First, it has to do with reflecting upon something, a conscious, sustained focus in relation to a particular topic, to see through to a deeper and broader understanding. Second, on a concrete level, reflection is about mirroring an image. At depth in the psychoanalytic world "mirroring" is seen as a *relational* connection between the affective life of one to another. This mirroring is not simply a parroting or mimicking, but an affective holding, handling, and representing of the experience of the other. For Winnicott this is grounded in our first relationship of care, which shows, in contrast to the likeness in the mirror, that a relational image can still be held in an unequal relationship if one takes the role of care for another. This deepens our understanding of "reflection," a word that I will use to denote mirroring. It, too, becomes less of a fixed concept and more of a relational one.

The theological thought of Augustine offers a similar reflection on mirroring in its distinction between image and likeness. When we think of one's *image* reflected in a mirror, what we are more accurately thinking of is one's *likeness*, the outward appearance only. Theologians from Irenaus and Augustine, to Luther and Calvin, to Barth and Bonhoeffer have made a distinction between image and likeness, the general argument being that in "the fall of Adam and Eve" humanity lost the created *likeness* to God, although the divine *image* in some sense remained. Augustine makes much of the use of the word *speculum*, from Paul's comment in 1 Corinthians 13:12 that "we see through a *glass* darkly, but then we will see face to face." Augustine notes that the word *speculum* denotes a mirror, rather than transparent glass. His understanding is that *we* are that which is reflected in the mirror through which we imperfectly see God. Here we can see that mirroring for Augustine is also a relational term, rather than simply a pictorial analogy.[23]

In seeking to reframe the concepts and images of both theology and psychoanalytic thought in a joint relational model, however, we move beyond what may be seen as analogous. Yet this falls short of what may be conceived of as substantial. In correlating theological and psychological concepts, we are not saying, "Here, this is like that (e.g., holding is like Earth-making)," but more, "Here, holding is *reflected* in Earth-making." When taken further to describe the relationship between God and humanity, this becomes not "Here, humanity is like God," but "Here, humanity *may be* participating in God participating in us." Such an integrative model can distinctly honor both disciplines and both humanity and divinity without limiting God's activity to what is perceived of as "theological" or "spiritual." Hence, what is described is in the realms of theological anthropology rather than simply pastoral practice. It would have been easy simply to say that the Trinity is a useful model for pastoral care and to explore it in practice. Yet, in the task of pastoral theology we are called to say why it is useful in the pastoral field, how it comes to be useful, and where it comes from.

Theologically, therefore, we move from simply *analogia trinitatis* to *imago trinitatis*, from analogy to living image. When looking for theological concepts reflected in psychological understanding, we are not looking for a simple likeness, but an image that has a life of its own that informs and extends the theological image. We can see how this gets lived out in the pastoral field in the reflections of one chaplain who was asked about the essence of his ministry at Ground Zero.

> The essence of my ministry? To use a word that we don't often use in Judaism, to "witness." For all the people that were doing the work down there, I and my colleagues were the witness for them. We were the ones that recorded their deeds, if only in our minds and our hearts. And we held them up when they began to get fragile and we were the ones that listened. And that's the one

skill and the one effort, listening. That was the heart of the ministry, listening, even if it was to listen to one word or no words. To just listen to the energy of the person. And they knew that they were being seen, that they were being heard, that they were being felt. *That whatever they were expressing was real because somebody else could mirror it back to them and that somebody was there willing to take some of their pain.* That was the ministry. . . . And so I began to understand the Christian concept of witnessing to really validate the presence of the person who was doing what the person was doing. And to validate the presence of soul that was represented by the toe bone that somebody found; to validate the work; to validate the heroism of people who could stay there day after day and do that. *To, in a very quiet way, sing their praises.* Not a big deal, but just to thank people for what they were doing, even if they said, "Don't thank me, we have to do this." But they got it. Somebody saw them and somebody was there to say, "Yeah, yeah, yeah. *We're here to hold you.* We're here to help. In any way that you can use us we're here to help you."

One can see even from this chaplain's description a reflection of the pastoral model I will come to describe:

1. *Earth-Making/Holding:* The holding and handling of the other and their story, what this rabbi names in his tradition as "recording their deeds," the space created by the relationship characterized by a listening and reflecting back (representing) that is not only a sensory and verbal skill but an affective and energetic engagement;

2. *Pain-Bearing/Suffering:* The chaplain notes the willingness to "take" or bear some of the pain of the other;

3. *Life-Giving/Transforming:* The implied effect of the chaplain validating, thanking, and even singing the praises of the workers.

This can easily sound like a theology of works, and we do not know in pastoral care whether it is our own efforts or the Spirit of God in us, yet we know that the call to love God in the other—naked, hungry, imprisoned, sick, and sinning—is that to which all believers have been called. So let us then turn to those who engaged in such a ministry of love to explore how this theology is reflected in the pastoral field. I choose here to examine a group of pastoral caregivers whose experiences exemplify the foundations of pastoral practice, the breadth of what pastoral ministry is in this post–9/11 world, and the challenge of holding oneself together in ministry in the face of trauma, be it that of others or our own.

* * * *

The theological reflections in these following pages are my own and may or may not reflect the theology of the chaplains themselves. Indeed, the chaplaincy at Ground Zero was rich and diverse, as were the interviewees, who were self-selecting. Those who wished to be interviewed were both male and female,[24] of a variety of Christian denominations, as well as Jewish rabbis and interfaith ministers. They ranged from those who had ministered at the T. Mort. for only a few days to those who had ministered for approximately forty days over nine months. I hope that this research may help prepare clergy for response to later disasters in a way that will help mitigate some of the adverse affects of the disaster by training and support, preparing clergy for a ministry that has heretofore not been a part of seminary curricula.

It is not a generalization to say that the chaplains at the Temporary Mortuary also ultimately felt blessed by being at Ground Zero. Whether they came from a Christian tradition, Jewish, Interfaith, or another faith perspective again and again the chaplains commented on a sense of the holy at Ground Zero and the privilege to participate in such a ministry. In many ways the environment was like 'Hell,' yet for many of the chaplains it was indeed sacred ground.

> Those nine months were extraordinarily difficult. Part of what made them bearable was the heroism and committed dedication of everyone involved in the rescue and recovery efforts. To have been able to be a part of that effort was inspiring and humbling. To have been able to be part of the united response to the attacks gave me a glimpse of the workings and the presence of God on earth. My weekly shifts at the various sites were sacred time. When I was brought on the site I felt the prayers of the world, focused there. It was sacred space, and to have been able to serve there was profoundly moving.[25]

I was profoundly moved by the chaplains who were generous enough to share their experiences of Ground Zero that others might gain from what touched them so deeply. Such an offering as part of the wider contribution to 9/11 oral history is gift in itself. So let us begin to unwrap such a gift as we begin to reflect on the pastoral ministry of love in the face of trauma.

chapter 1

The Trinity

From Immanent to Economic

Lauds
Coming in at three a.m.
Sleep deprived,
but adrenaline alert to say prayers at the morgue.

After four months almost a full body is found
only missing everything from
both knees down,
lying on his left side.

O the intimacy of this position,
as if he were curled up tenderly
against his lover
and the beseeching aspect
of this man's body:

The white parietal bone of the skull
innocently visible against the black bag
and the black of charring
naked, vulnerable,

seeking to be held
just one more time.[1]

The Pastoral Ethic of Love

Much pastoral theology focuses on pastoral care as an expression of the divine rule to "love one another *as* we have been loved," or, alternatively, ministration *to* the other *in* whom we see Christ, catching God's image in others, loving God through loving the other. Much of it is grounded in the theology of the incarnation, the movement of God to and for us in the person of Jesus, and in an understanding of humanity as *imago Dei*, the image of God, who is love. Here, pastoral care as a "ministry of presence" becomes less about one's own presence, and more about the presence of the divine. A chaplain describes this well:

> . . . I don't know if this is the essence of [the T. Mort. chaplaincy], but I think it was "the presence. . . ." I think it was first when people were talking about "the ministry of presence," when that became kind of a term that was being used, I was like, "A ministry of what?" Because I always associated it with clergy who just were there and never really did anything. I didn't understand what that was, but of course after this experience, I not only understood it, but used it. I would say the essence of it *was being God's presence.*

Who is this God who is present? Christian theology posits the trinitarian nature of the One God of Judaism due to belief in the incarnation—that Jesus of Nazareth was God incarnate. Gospel accounts describe Jesus' experience and teachings of God the Father and he promises them the gift of the Spirit. In John's Gospel he makes such claims as "I and the Father are one," "If you have seen me you have seen the Father," and he says that wherever two or three are gathered together he is there. Through Jesus' life, death, resurrection, and the experience of the early church, Christians came to believe in a God that is not only a unity of being but also a "unity in community": God as three in one—Trinity—Father, Son, and Holy Spirit. Hence, for Christians, the Trinity is a way of describing the being of God in both God's unity and multiplicity.

Through the incarnation God takes on what is not God, crossing the "gap" between Creat*or* and creat*ed* in the person of Jesus. In this unique person, existentially, humanity takes into itself the being of God, where God in Jesus is fully human and divine, "truly God and truly man," with all the bio-psycho-social manifestations of such, "like us in all respects apart from sin."[2] Thus, we are encouraged in incarnational theology not simply to see the hypostatic union of divine and human in the Son, as a one-to-one correlation, but to see the Trinity, the three-in-one, in the divinity. Incarnation takes us to Trinity, and perhaps back again.[3] In the incarnation and resurrection, God takes ontologically into Godself the being of humanity in the second person of the Trinity—the Son, Jesus. God is not only psychologically relevant because of the person of Jesus, a man with a psyche, but God is relevant to us from what we know of God in *Godself*, not simply in the tri-unity of being but the unity of the three persons of the Trinity *as love*, a state of being that we as humans experience in a way not shared by the animal kingdom.

Here the Trinity lends itself to a pastoral model for reasons arising from the nature of Trinity itself. These reasons relate to what is called in theological language the *immanent* and the *economic* Trinity. The immanent Trinity speaks of *who God is—theologia*, the relation of God as Trinity as God is *to Godself.* The economic

Trinity speaks of *what God does* in the world, the economy of salvation—*oikonomia*, of the relation of God as Trinity as God is *to us*. More will be said about these distinctions later. However, where psychology intersects with this theological distinction is through both the nature and the action of God where we are called to minister not only from the "how" of God, but the "who" of God, the God who not only calls us "to love as God loves us" but who *is* love itself.

God as Love

One of the most foundational figures writing both on the Trinity and its connection to human personhood is the great fifth-century theologian Augustine of Hippo. He writes in his treatise *Deus Trinitatis* (On the Trinity):

> For it is our contention that God is called love for this reason, that love itself is a substance worthy of the name of God, and not merely because it is a gift of God, such as where it said to God: "For thou art my patience" [cf. Ps. 71:5]; for it is not, therefore, said that the substance of God is our patience, but that it comes to us from Him, as it is read elsewhere: "For from him is my patience" [cf. Ps.62:5]. The speech itself of the Scriptures easily refutes any other interpretation. For such a sentence as "Thou, O Lord, art my patience" is said in the same sense as: "Thou, O Lord, art my hope" [cf. Ps. 91:9], and "My God, my mercy" [Ps. 59:17], and many similar texts. But it was not said: "O lord, my love," or "'Thou art my love," or "God, my love"; but it was said: "God is love" in the same sense as it was said: "God is spirit" [John 4:24].[4]

As a species distinctive for our ability to love, the understanding of God as love takes us not only to the heart of God but to the heart of the human person for whom love may be both a psychological and spiritual reality. If the love of God is not simply something that God does, but who God is, then the human ability to love may say something about the nature of God in us.

> [John,] in the following verses after speaking of the love of God, not that by which we love Him, but that "by which he first loved us, and sent his son as a propitiation for our sins"; and, hence, exhorts us to love one another, *so that God might abide in us*, then, because he had said in unmistakable terms that God is love, he wanted to speak more plainly on this subject at once: "In this," he said, "we know that we *abide* in him and he is us, because he has given us of his Spirit." Therefore the Holy Spirit, of whom he has given us, causes us to remain in God, and God in us. But love does this. He is, therefore, the God who is love.[5]

However, this abiding of God in us is reflective of the *unity* of God, God as love, rather than a trinitarian expression of God's comm-unity,[6] although theologians

such as Jürgen Moltmann argue that only the trinitarian nature of God can philo-
sophically justify the God whom we see on the cross that loves, suffers, and can
change.[7]

It is of note, however, that Augustine, in his reflections upon the Trinity, seeks
to retain the love of God as reflective of God's unity but through it to see the tri-
unity of God shining through, particularly in the *hypostasis* (person) of the Holy
Spirit: "One may object: 'I see love and I conceive it in my mind as best I can, and
I believe the Scripture when it says: "God is love, and he who abides in love abides
in God," but when I see it I do not see the Trinity in it.' But as a matter of fact you
do see the Trinity if you see love."[8]

Augustine sees that love has a triune character but seeks to make clear that even
though we can understand love in this way we must be careful to see love as reflective of God rather than God imposed upon our human idea of love.

> But what is love or charity, which the Divine Scripture praises and proclaims so highly,
> if not love of the good? Now love is of someone who loves, and something is loved with
> love. So then, there are three: the loved, the beloved, and love.[9]

> With regard to the question at hand, therefore, let us believe that the Father, the Son,
> and the Holy Spirit are one God, the Creator, and the ruler of all creation; that the
> Father is not the Son, nor is the Holy Spirit the Father or the Son, but that there is a
> Trinity of inter-related persons, and the unity of an equal substance. . . . We are now
> most eager to see whether this most excellent love is proper to the Holy Spirit, and if
> it is not so, whether the Father, or the Son, or the Holy Spirit itself is love, since we
> cannot contradict the most certain faith and the most weighty authority of Scripture
> which says: "God is love" [*1 John 4:16*]. Nevertheless, we should not be guilty of the
> sacrilegious error of attributing to the Trinity that which does not belong to the Creator,
> but rather to the creature, or is imagined by mere empty thought.[10]

In Augustine's argument about the Trinity as love, it is helpful to note several points
about the Trinity itself that are pertinent to our discussion. These are:

- Substance and relationship
- Distinction and connection between immanent and economic Trinity
- *Hypostasis*—personhood and appropriation of identity and function in the Trinity
- *Perichoresis*—mutual indwelling of the hypostases in the Trinity

Augustine does see the Trinity as unity and community, "being" in relationship.
Indeed, Augustine gives primacy of thought to God as unity, the "one God, the
Creator, and the ruler of all creation."[11] Although he is most confident of appropriating love to the Holy Spirit, rather than the Father or the Son, at other times he
sees love as the property of God in unity.

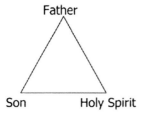

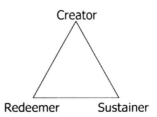

Fig. 1. The Immanent Trinity and the Economic Trinity

Augustine names the *immanent* Trinity in the scriptural terms as "Father, Son, and Holy Spirit," a description of *who* God is. The economic Trinity, however, God as God is *for us*, is commonly named with terms such as "Creator, Redeemer, and Sustainer," what God *does* in the world—the economy of salvation.

It is important to remember that for Augustine the immanent Trinity *does not* map onto the economic Trinity as a one-to-one correlation, the equation of Father with creation, Son with redemption, and Spirit with sustaining. For Augustine, God as Creator is reflective of God's unity and does not appropriate the act of creating to a particular *hypostasis* (person) of the Trinity. This also serves to retain an understanding of God's freedom from the world in God's essential being rather than God being bound to the world. Therefore, for Augustine immanent is not economic Trinity as regards parallel functions, yet immanent is economic Trinity as regards the unity of God.

The temptation to appropriate a specific function to a particular *hypostasis*, or person, of the Trinity is corrected by the understanding of the *perichoresis*, the mutual indwelling of each in the other, as unity in the Trinity. Therefore, each *hypostasis* of the immanent Trinity acts in ways that are creating, redeeming, and sustaining. Although the term *perichoresis* was attributed to Pseudo-Cyril, and fully explicated by John of Damascus some three centuries later, this mutual indwelling is constantly implied in Augustine's work. He therefore can move freely, it seems, between appropriating love to one *hypostasis* of the Trinity and claiming it as a reflection of the unity of God.

These concepts that relate to unity and community within the Trinity, though seemingly technical issues, all have a relationship to the pastoral field. People are more inclined to report experiencing God's presence (the unity of God), both in terms of felt presence and in the experience of community, and less likely to say, "I experienced the Spirit here in the community, God the Father here in my prayer, Christ here in the brokenness of the bodies." They will speak, rather, of the presence of God, feeling of holiness, essence of love, as does the following chaplain:

> **My remembrance is that most of the time I was there, I was experiencing the sense of the presence of God in that place. . . . And that is what I was more aware of than feelings of sadness. . . . There was a real sense of holiness in**

> that place. Destruction, yes, and all of that. But there was the way everybody was working together and cooperating with each other and supporting each other. There was a real sense of community and holiness. And that is what I remember rather than sadness or despair or anything like that. . . .
>
> For the most part, it was a very powerfully moving and uplifting experience for me. When I think back on it, I was impressed with the holiness of it all. And some of the experience of the closeness of God that I had there. That's, as I think about it, the overwhelming thing about it, not sadness, not fear or anything—the sense of holiness.

There is manifest in many of the chaplains' reflections a sense that God was not simply out there, or even over there, but that God was with them and in what they were doing, in the prayers they prayed and the pastoral relationships that developed. "But when I was afraid [before beginning the ministry], and I went into St. Paul's Chapel . . . and prayed and I just felt the Holy Spirit reaching out to me and saying 'You can do this. We'll do this together.' *That was a relational thing.*" When this chaplain went on to speak of the end of his ministry at the T. Mort., he came back to a similar relational point in discussing love. He noted that "a primary function of clergy and one of our most laudable goals is just [being] real. If it isn't real, you can't love it. Love is not hypothetical. You can only embrace reality, there's nothing else there."

Image of God as Love in the Human Person

For Augustine, Christ is not only the exemplar *par excellence* of how to love but he asserts that in the human psyche there is an image of the Triune God, who is love incarnate. However, this image is not a static "picture" of God but of a dynamic way of being and relating. Through the action of the Spirit we are drawn into the *renewal* of that image as we remember, understand, and choose to love God and each other.

Augustine reflects on many triads or trinities in the human person, inward and outward,[12] but he is clear that our relatedness to God is not about threeness or any superficial similarity but about the essence of God in Godself. "Certainly, not everything in creatures that is in some way similar to God is also to be called His image, but to that alone to which he himself is superior; for the image is only then an expression of God in the full sense, when no other nature lies between it and God."[13] He makes a distinction between what is a *likeness* to God in the human person and what is the *image* of God.

Augustine argues that the image of God in the human person must indeed be a trinitarian image. Reflecting upon the first creation story in Genesis, Augustine says, "If the Father did not make in His own image but in to that of the Son, why did he not say: 'Let us make man according to thy image and likeness,' but did say 'according to our image'—unless it be the image of the Trinity was made in man, so that man should in this way be the image of the one true God, because the Trinity itself is the one true God?"[14] The plural language used by God in the first Genesis creation story substantiates for Augustine that the image of God is a trinitarian image.

Augustine's eventual analysis of inward and outward trinities in the human person is a constant reflection on the analogies between human personhood and the Triune God, yet he is constantly careful to say that observant trinities *do not* constitute the image of God. He does, however, come to affirm that there is one trinity in the human person that is the image of God—the rational mind's *memory*, *understanding*, and *will*—that which can know God, which can understand God, and which can freely love God, even in God's unknownness. Augustine's conception of this threefold self that is an image of God arises from his questions of "Who loves that which he does not know?"[15] and "By what likeness or comparison with known things can we believe, so that we may also love the God who is not yet known?"[16] It is extremely important, therefore, when contemplating Augustine's conception of the person, to realize that it is *not* memory, understanding, and will as a deification of the rational mind that is the image of God, but that these are relational functions in the person which give the ability to love God. As such, even though Augustine's image can be read as self-contained and oriented to itself only, it is in essence relational, its object being God. This trinitarian image in the human person is grounded in the love of God and lived out in love of the "neighbor."

> Wherefore, this is the best known and principal commandment: "You shall love the Lord your God" [Deut. 6:5]. Human nature, therefore, has been so formed that never does it not remember itself, never does it not understand itself, never does it not love itself. . . .
>
> Hence, *he who knows how to love himself loves God*; on the other hand, he who does not love God, even though he loves himself, insofar as that is naturally implanted within him, is not unfittingly said to hate himself, since he does that which is opposed to himself, and pursues himself as if he were his own enemy. . . .
>
> But when the mind loves God and by consequence, as we have said, remembers and understands Him, then *with respect to its neighbor* it is rightly commanded *to love him as it loves itself*. For it no longer loves itself perversely but rightly when it loves God, by partaking of whom that image not only exists, but is also renewed so as not to grow old, reformed so as not to be disfigured, and beatified so as not to be unhappy.[17]

The human person's ability to hate oneself, and to love that which is not God or for God, is not a negation of the image of God for Augustine. However, for Augustine the image of God that is reflected in the human psyche is an image that is distorted through the fall, in the second creation narrative in Genesis where humans freely choose to disobey the God who created them (see Gen. 2:4b—3:24). Therefore, his Christian anthropology of the psyche as the image of God that we are all endowed with is not a static fact but has to be *restored* or *renewed* through the dynamic action of the self *in response* to the action of God. This can easily sound like a theology of works, that we become one with God by loving God through our own effort and energy, aside from the life and works of Christ. Yet, Augustine is careful to give primacy both to Christ's effectiveness, the work of the Spirit and grace, even as he charges us with the work of making progress ourselves in this renewal of the image of God in us.

> Whoever, then, is being renewed in the knowledge of God, and in justice and holiness of truth, by making progress day by day, transfers his love from temporal to eternal things, from visible to intelligible things, from carnal to spiritual things, and constantly endeavors to restrain and lessen the desire for the former, and to bind himself by love to the latter. But he does so in proportion to the divine help he receives, for the saying of God is "Without me you can do nothing" [John 15:5].[18]

This renewal of God's image, the Triune God of love, is that task to which we are called day by day, a task we effect both through the gift of grace and our own endeavors. One chaplain noted the power of such an understanding: "To recognize that who I am is really kept in the mind of God [was transformational]. If that's true and you're created in God's image, and we all are, then as you recall who anybody else is, the reality of that person is only in your mind—the mind of God." For Augustine, drawing on Paul's theology in 1 and 2 Corinthians, as beings who are a reflection of God we see this image reflected in ourselves "as through a glass darkly" (1 Cor. 13:12). This description for Augustine is that of the image of God in the human person as a mirror of God whose likeness is currently obscured. "'We see now through a mirror in an enigma, but then face to face' (cf. 1 Cor. 13:12). If we inquire what this mirror is, and of what sort it is, the first thing that naturally comes to mind is that nothing else is seen in a mirror except an image. We have, therefore, tried to do this in order that through this image, which we are, we might see Him by whom we have been made in some manner or other, as through a mirror."[19] This mirror, therefore, is a not a two-dimensional glass, but a relational picture that reflects the Triune God whose image is not so much a likeness but a reflection of the personhood of one being in the face of another.

This reflection of God that is currently obscured but will eventually be perfected in God, is to God as Trinity. In one respect only does Augustine say that the likeness is to Christ solely, in "reference to the immortality of the body. For in this too, we shall be like God, but only the Son, because he alone in the Trinity took a body, in which he died, rose again, and which he brought to higher things."[20] In this we are to see that embodiment is not to be disconnected from our eternal destiny and the Son's embodiment is taken into the experience of the Trinity, but that the love of Christ that was not a function of his embodiment is an expression of the Trinity as a whole. Yet it is through love manifest in the third hypostasis of the Trinity, the Holy Spirit, in whom we are taken beyond the Incarnate One into communion with the Trinity. "Love, then, which is from God and is God, is properly the Holy Spirit, through whom the charity of God is poured forth in our hearts, through which the whole Trinity dwells in us."[21] Here, although Augustine appears to concentrate on the immanent Trinity, his focus is on memory, understanding, and love as functions that need to be renewed and reoriented toward God rather than the nature of the psyche in itself. This shows us that the image of the Trinity in the human psyche is that of the *economy* of God, God as God is for us, as love is something that takes us beyond our own selves toward others. We can see this in one chaplain's reflections:

> It [blessing bodies and body parts] is what one does. And so what it's like is to be able to be part of *more than oneself* doing [this]. It's something of the same answer of what's it like to preside at the altar. . . . *I'm there as God's lightning rod*, so to speak, conducting God in the world, the world in God. And that, by the way, is a punning word, "conducting." Both as a conduit and director. Please note the instrument that a conductor plays—answer, *none*. The conductor doesn't play an instrument or sing or compose, at least, not in the act of conducting, and in that sense is the one least in charge. And in that sense, the less I'm in charge, the more I am.

This sense of being God's lightning rod, as "conduit and director," reflects on a place of self beyond self—"the less I'm in charge, the more I am." Yet it is a self that is in relationship, both to God and to those others in the music of pastoral care.

Augustine's focus on the inner self in seeming isolation from outer relationships may appear to show a disconnect in his theology between *theologia* and *oikonomia*, between nature and functioning in the world, through a lack of translation of this image in relationship with others. But his interpretation of the great commandment to love involves the threefold foci of God, others, and ourselves, yet grounded in the being of God. "Neither should we let this question disturb us, how much we ought to spend upon our brother, how much upon God—incomparably more upon God than upon ourselves, but as much upon our brother as upon ourselves—and we love ourselves so much more, the more we love God. We, therefore, love God and our neighbor from one and the same love, but we love God on account of God, but ourselves and our neighbor on account of God."[22]

Given Augustine's explication of love as triune, and the image of God in the self likewise, we will next turn to a field that grounds its theory of formation of the self in relationships, that of Object Relations psychoanalysis and primarily the thought of Donald Winnicott, to explore how love is reflected in that theory in a way which enables us to examine further theologically how we can see this lived out in practice.

When we begin from a theological perspective, we begin with the love of God that created us, redeemed us, and sustains us. "Beloved, since God loved us so much we ought to love one another . . . if we love one another, God lives in us and his love is perfected in us" (1 John 4:11-12). We loved because God "first loved us" (1 John 4:19). Jesus tells his disciples to "love one another as I have loved you" (John 15:12). Here, love is a response to being loved. The formation of what it is to be a Christian person is grounded in the relational matrix of the love of God, and the God who is love. Augustine, as we have seen, grounds his understanding of the psyche in the capacity to know, understand, and love God. Are these theological suppositions about the formation of the self in response to love any different from those of Object Relations psychoanalytic theory? Can we see these theological principles reflected in psychoanalytic thought? The answer is both no and yes.

Love in Object Relations Thought

Object Relations theory is essentially about internal and external relationship with self and others and the structures of the psyche that support such. It sees the formation of our self in our response to another "object," that is, an objective other. However, in this theory it is another person, not God, with whom the loving relationship is first established. Unlike theology, which can seem to focus on the "Father" God, even in trinitarian theology, Object Relations theory sees the genesis of love in the maternal relationship. According to Ronald Fairbairn, "The child's oral relationship with his mother in the situation of suckling represents his first experience of a 'love' relationship, and is, therefore, the foundation upon which all his future relationships with love objects are based. It also represents his first experience of a social relationship; and it therefore forms the basis of his subsequent relationship to society."[23]

When we have the foundation of such a relationship from our infantile experience with a person who loves us *enough* to empathize accurately and respond to our infantile needs, to suffer our libidinal and aggressive impulses without retaliation, and to give us both a containing relationship and space to develop, we are enabled to be who we have the potential to be. This potential becomes realized as creative, spontaneous persons grounded in a sense of the real, with an ability to relate to others not simply as extensions of ourselves but as persons in their own right. We become able to be with others and also alone, with a capacity for concern for others, able to trust, to believe, and to develop a moral relationship to the world that is not simply an application of law but an inner ethical compass which sees beyond our own needs and desires. We grow, in Winnicott's words, a "True self" that is in relationship. Most often this relationship is first with our mothers, or with those that take the role of primary caregiver in our early lives, be they female or male. Whatever the family configuration, psychologically, we can see a reflection of the theological assertion in the Christian Scriptures that we love because we are first loved, by God in Christ, and in psychoanalytic thought by our first relationship of care as we first come to being. In Object Relations theory, the creation of a human person is not a *fait d'accompli* of birth, but is absolutely dependent on a relationship of care, ideally of love, that will hold our selves not only in those first months of life, but will enable us to develop inner structures that we may hold ourselves together in the face of whatever life has to offer. Winnicott describes formation of the self in this way:

> There starts in the infant and continues in the child a tendency toward integration of the personality, the word *integration* tending to have a more and more complex meaning as time goes on and the child gets older. Also the infant tends to live in his or her own body and to build the self on the basis of bodily functioning to which belong imaginative collaborations that quickly become extremely complex and constitute the psychic reality specific to that infant. The infant becomes established as a unit, feels an I AM feeling, and bravely faces the world with which he or she is already becoming able to form relationships, affectionate relationships and (by contrast) a pattern of object-relationships based on the instinctual life. . . . Here is human nature unfolding itself. BUT, . . . maturational processes depend for their becoming actual in the child, and actual at appropriate moments, on a good enough environmental provision.[24]

This "good enough environmental provision" is through the love of a mother, parent, or parent-substitute who creates an environment of care and relationship of love in which the self can form in its own unique way.

Ann Belford Ulanov, writing on the thought of Winnicott, sees a relationship between the living out of this "mother love," and the *agape* of the theological or religious world. Using Winnicott's own gender-related terms,[25] Ulanov sees this "female-element love" as a personally mediated "holy intent":

> Female-element love conducts us to the power of loving that the religious term agape represents. Agape possesses no agenda; it seeks to promote life in its individual idiosyncratic forms so that each living thing fully fills out its nature and recognizes the same in others. The feminine mediates this holy intent. The capacity for illusion changes into a capacity for creative exchange between subjects that exist objectively for each other. The mother or the mother in the male facilitates a love that includes hate, where quiet love and erotic and excited or aggressive love accomplish fusion. Then the child can find a personal transformation of its own destructiveness of what is loved into imaginative work and creative living.[26]

Such facilitating love forms a space, or *spaces*, within the becoming self, that (1) enables the individual's unique, "idiosyncratic," creative nature to develop between their subjective experience and that which is objectively perceived, (2) contains and transforms aggression and its effects, and (3) opens the way to creative living both internally and in relation to the world.

Gradually, through the mother's empathic attunement, constancy, and mirroring, the child comes to experience life in three "areas": an inner area, and outer area, both of which are relatively constant, and a third area—the area of experience—which Winnicott names variously as a "transitional space" or "playspace." We experience this area in highly variable ways, it being at the border of inner and outer. This space is the space between mother and infant initially, between child and environment, and later between individual and the world. It is the space of illusion where we in our creating discover that which is external to us, infusing it with our own meaning. It is in this space that Winnicott locates cultural experience for the individual—the space of the arts, religion, and scientific endeavor. It is in this area of experience that the infant comes initially to recognize the mother as a "not-me" object and relate to her as an object other than the self. Here the space-holding and space-affording mother can be experienced as an "other" and the infant can experience itself as a "self."

Such a relational formation of the self can sound as ideal as the earlier assertions about Christian community; however, Winnicott was realistic about this experience of love on behalf of the mother. Such a mother, in his eyes, did not have to be ideal, but "good enough"; creating an "average expectable environment,"[27] able to consistently and accurately attune well enough to the infant's needs and being that the infant can go on being who she or he is without interruption.

At a later developmental stage, however, such interruption is part of the opportunity for growth as the infant learns to recognize, own, and express his or her needs as a separate being rather than have them met already by a mother who is so attuned to be merged with the developing child and able to meet those needs before she or he expresses them. Like the important theological distinction between God and humanity, although the "mother" may be seen as largely responsible for the creation of the child, as it develops within her body for the nine or so months of its prenatal life and she provides an environment and relationship of care after birth, it is important that both the mother and the child come to realize that it is a separate being with its own unique self. The response to the primary love is thus also not a *fait d'accompli* but an achievement that encompasses, as Augustine seemed to know, the ability to hate as well as love the same person (object). Winnicott sees this achievement as key in the development of a sense of responsibility and, again, highly dependent on the relationship with the primary caregiver:

> One stage in the child's development has especial importance. . . . At this stage to which I refer now there is a gradual build-up in the child of a capacity to feel a sense of responsibility, that which at base is a sense of guilt. The environmental essential here is the continued presence of mother or mother-figure over time in which the infant is accommodating the destructiveness which is part of his make-up. This destructiveness

becomes more and more a feature of his object relationships, and the phase of development to which I am referring lasts from about six months to two years, after which
the child may have made a satisfactory integration of the idea of destroying the object
and the fact of loving the same object. The mother is needed over this time and she is
needed because of her survival value. She is an environment-mother and at the same
time an object-mother, the object of excited loving. In this latter role she is repeatedly
destroyed or damaged. The child gradually comes to integrate these two aspects of the
mother and to be able to love and be affectionate with the surviving mother at the
same time. This phase involves the child in a special kind of anxiety which is called a
sense of guilt, guilt related to the idea of destruction where love is also operating. It is
this anxiety that drives the child toward constructive or actively loving behaviour in his
limited world, reviving the object, making the loved object better again, rebuilding the
damaged thing.[28]

Such ability to choose or respond in ways that are not loving, or even destructive,
in the theological world is reflective of living as sinful persons in a world where
we, as often as not, choose not to love our primary Other—God, other beings, or
ourselves. In Winnicott's understanding, however, the infantile need for destruction
in fantasy and its consequent desire for "reviving," "rebuilding," or "reparation" is
important developmentally and something that serves a *positive* function in the
psyche. This owning of human aggression and its contribution to the formation of
an ethical self is seen as a vital component of what it is to be human and something
that should not be denied or idealized. Perhaps a correlation between this dynamic
in relation to the primary caregiver and the infant can be seen to be reflected in
the religious relationship of repentance and forgiveness between the person and
the God of mercy who calls them to live out of a relationship of responsibility, the
one whose love does not depend on their actions, but nevertheless knows and calls
them to account for themselves also. Yet, there is no escaping the difference between
Winnicott's thought and theology here in its relation to destructiveness.

Unlike theology, which can often appear to see response to God as a free
choice, Object Relations theory sees our ability to be lovingly concerned and caring
for others as highly dependent on our experiences of care. Arguably, however, this
could also be asserted in Christian theology through the soteriological assertion
that God in Christ saved us because, in the end, we cannot save ourselves. Hence,
many theologies assert that Christian faith and love are not a choice but a gift of the
Holy Spirit. This, of course, begs the questions, Why does God not gift everyone
with the same faith? and, if it is a gift, why the so-often popular condemnation of
those who do not seem to have been given this gift, and who perhaps even practice
another faith?

A partial answer to this question comes from Winnicott's thought, and he
muses "it might even turn out that religion could learn something from psychoanalysis,"[29] when he explores the formation of the "God concept":[30]

It seems that although most religions have tended to recognize the importance of family life it fell to psycho-analysis to point out to the mothers of babies and to the parents of the very young the value—no, the essential nature—of their tendency to provide for each infant that which each infant needs by way of nurture . . .

To sum up this first stage of my simplified scheme for describing the developing human being: the infant and small child is usually cared for in a reliable way, and this being cared for well enough builds up in the infant to a belief in reliability; on to this a perception of the mother or father or grandmother or nurse can be added. To a child who has started life in this way the idea of goodness and of a reliable and personal parent or God can follow naturally.

The child who is not having good enough experiences in the early stages cannot be given the idea of a personal God *as a substitute for infant care.* . . . This is a first principle of moral education, that *moral education is no substitute for love.*[31]

Winnicott does not allow at this stage for an objective relationship with God, and could be argued to limit the freedom of God to the ability of the mother to love. At these early stages, love has to be concretely experienced in the care of the primary caregiver, the idea of goodness can follow, and later the connection of that to God. Otherwise, he appears to see God as an idea, a concept, the deity of a moral code with which the parents desire the child to comply but do not reflect in their own love and care of the child. Yet Winnicott locates the development of the belief in a *personal* God in that transitional space, the "third area," between the mother and child as subject and object, and later between the self and other "objects." Such space between what is imaginatively created, and what is found "lying around" in the world and takes on personal meaning, is the space in which the child, and later the adult, develops a sense of culture, art, and religion that is both objectively there but subjectively related to, rather than the compliant acceptance of a religion that provides a moral code but does not feel real. One chaplain reflected on this relationship between the real and the sacred when asked about what was life-giving about the ministry:

> I guess the sense of *the holy is in the real.* . . . I don't think it's possible to separate the holy from the real. But there's a lot of effort to try and do that. To sort of say, "Well, this is a 'religious experience' and this is something other." This whole business of the fear of secularism just drives me crazy. What are we afraid of? If we'd know more about what life is about really, then we wouldn't be so afraid of it.

It is worth noting that Winnicott's view of the life of "the healthy person" is a triad. Remembering that Augustine cautioned against assuming that triads were trinitarian, nevertheless, we can see some resonances. Winnicott notes:

My last word must be about the lives that healthy people live.

1. The life in the world, with interpersonal relationships as the key even to making use of the non-human environment.

2. The life of the personal (sometimes called inner) psychical reality. This is where one person is richer than another, and deeper, and more interesting when creative. It includes dreams (or what dream material springs out of). . . .

3. The area of cultural experience. Cultural experience starts as play, and leads on to the whole area of man's inheritance, including the arts, the myths of history, the slow march of philosophical thought and the mysteries of mathematics, and of group management and of religion.[32]

Winnicott's understanding of the person as embracing these three areas of life is something of a reflection of the unity and community in humanity, which we reflected on theologically, that of shared reality but also of inner imaginative appropriation and relatedness. What Winnicott adds to this theological understanding is reflected in Augustine's question of how we can love that which we do not know. Augustine's answer focuses on the mind that can remember, understand, and will to be in relation with the Other. Winnicott shows us, however, the development of the individual is more than simply the mind, but *a self* that can love and learns to do so in relationship with others, by being cared for by an other or others. Like the "ecclesial self," as Stanley Grenz says, it is "more than personal, it is shared identity."[33] It involves both a triadic multiplicity and an "indwelling," reminiscent of *perichoresis*. Here the person is both uniquely an individual and also a self constituted by being in relationship with others, and still yet includes that "third area" which Winnicott calls "cultural experience." Winnicott's healthy person is both integrated *and* differentiated, not an isolate but a self that is constituted by both inner and outer realities and the meaning formed by them, which is not solely personal but communal and even cultural. His understanding of the self reflects both an Enlightenment focus on the individual but also answers postmodern critiques of "the individual" as a construct that fails to take into account the formation by others and the contextual interrelationship with the world in which the developing individual is located.

In Winnicott's triad of life, between the individual's inner world and society and the world, this third area is the space of experience, which has important implications in our later exploration of disaster and trauma. Such space is highly variable, as it "depends on experience which leads to trust. It can be looked upon as sacred to the individual in that it is here that the individual experiences creative living."[34] Developed from the experience of a "good-enough" mothering relationship, the ability to engage creatively with whatever life has to offer (in a world that is not as constant as Winnicott would like to believe), is done through what Winnicott describes as "play." Rather than seeing this as a frivolous action, it becomes the deeply creative ability to be and do in relation to external circumstances and inner reactions. In a situation of trauma, however, it may be that what is needed is (an) other relationship(s) that provides the same sort of reliable empathy and care, to make a space for this third area of creative growth even in the face of immense suffering.

It is here that Winnicott as doctor and psychoanalyst sees a relationship between ministry and medicine, though he notes, "I do not deal with the religion of inner experience, which is not my special line, but I deal with the philosophy of our work as medical practitioners, a kind of religion of external relationship."[35] He sees a common denominator in religion and medicine pointed to by the word *cure*, believing that cure "at its roots means care," not simply the later understanding of remedy. Of the role of the doctor he says that "at the first of these two extreme positions the doctor is the social worker and is almost fishing in the pools that provide proper angling for the curate, the minister of religion. At the other extreme position the doctor is a technician, both in making a diagnosis and in treating."[36] Like his theory on infant and childhood development with the focus on the role of the mother, his understanding of cure is grounded in relationality, noting that what is required of the practitioner is a reliability which leads to trust. In listing the various qualities that such a relationship of care requires—being "non-moralistic," "dead-honest, truthful," reliable, accepting "the patient's love and hate" without provoking either, "not being cruel for the sake of being cruel"—Winnicott states that, "There is one thing especially that needs to feed back into medical practice. . . . It is that *care-cure is an extension of the concept of holding*."[37] He continues,

> I suggest that we find in the care-cure aspect of our professional work a setting for the application of principles that we learned at the beginning of our lives, when as immature persons we were given good-enough care, and cure, so to speak, in advance (the best kind of preventative medicine) by our "good-enough" mothers, and by our parents. It is always a steadying thing to find that one's work links with entirely natural phenomena, and with the universals, and with what we expect to find in the best of poetry, philosophy and religion.[38]

Although Winnicott was not explicit about the connections while speaking to an audience of medics rather than clergy, it is not unreasonable to suppose that Winnicott's understanding of the practice of care, if applied with the same principles of a holding relationship and environment that he applies to medicine and social work, can be seen to be present in the "care of souls"—that of the pastoral care. Further, when we explore the trinitarian model of care—Earth-making/ Pain-bearing/Life-giving—we will begin to see that the qualities of each are both reflected and enhanced by Winnicott's understanding of the triadic self and its formation. Winnicott's psychoanalytic thought can offer to this trinitarian model of pastoral care a deeper reflection on the human psyche, grounded in the relationality that begins with concepts from early life that show us reliable constants necessary for adult creative *living*, rather than simply *surviving* in the world.

Although always affirming a gap between psychoanalysis and religion, Ulanov also sees a parallel, or even a mirror, in relation to Winnicott's understanding of the self and its relations and the internal relations of the Triune God.

> The parallel in religious imagery to this incommunicable yet ever communicating self is the inner life of God imagined in the Trinity. There, never-ending communication flows out and back between what we might call God's inner object relations. The Father ceaselessly gives forth to the Son, who gives back again to the giver; this communication exists so intensely that its immediacy manifests itself as the living Spirit between them, stemming from both, expressing both, overflowing into the world, communicating being to us. The mysterious core of the self that we find and create in the space between us and others, in some tiny way, speaks, participates in, and mirrors the huge spaces among the three persons in one God.
>
> The excitement and inward gladness of being, the energy and freshness of instinct, the spontaneous gestures to communicate that arise from this core of ourselves in some tiny way reflect the unspeakable energy of God that only the word *love* captures. Jesus says he comes to give us abundant life, that in loving God with our whole heart, mind, and strength and our neighbor as ourselves, we will find this precious all-out living, the pearl for which we gladly sell all else, the true life for which we easily lose everything else. One's true life mirrors the "True God from True God" words used in the Nicene Creed to describe the Son's relation to the Father.[39]

In the three chapters that follow this one, we will reflect on both theology and Winnicott's psychoanalytic thought to explore the following trinitarian model of pastoral care grounded in the pastoral practice of the chaplains at Ground Zero. In doing so, we will examine those psychic and relational spaces in pastoral practice and selfhood that mirror in some tiny way the *love* of the one true God.

A Functional Model of the Economic Trinity

> Eternal Spirit,
> *Earth-maker, Pain-bearer, Life-giver,*
> Source of all that is and that shall be,
> Father and Mother of us all,
> Loving God, in whom is heaven.
>
> The hallowing of your name echo through the universe!
> The way of your justice be followed by the peoples of the world!

Your heavenly will be done by all created beings!
Your commonwealth of peace and freedom
Sustain our hope and come on earth.

With the bread we need for today, feed us.
In the hurts that we absorb from one another, forgive us.
In times of temptation and test, strengthen us.
From trials too great to endure, spare us.
From the grip of all that is evil, free us.

For you reign in the glory of the power that is love,
now and forever. Amen.[40]

This contemporary rewrite of the Lord's Prayer, by the English Anglican priest and devotional writer Jim Cotter, offers a trinitarian model that is simply descriptive, yet alludes to a deeper understanding of what love lived out may look like in all its triune possibilities. In addition to its formal and everyday liturgical and devotional use, this prayer has received acclamation in both popular and more scholarly arenas.

However, the editors of *A New Zealand Prayer Book—He Karakia Mihinare o Aotearoa*, from which it is best known, made a minor but significant rewrite to Cotter's original version. Cotter's original text uses the phrase "Life-giver, Pain-bearer, Love-maker" rather than "Earth-maker, Pain-bearer, Life-giver." Cotter himself prefers the original version, seeing it as more of "a trinitarian dance."[41] Whether or not the editors thought the term *Love-maker* was too controversial, Cotter's original version locates, as Augustine seems to, much of the time, love as a function of one hypostasis in the Trinity. The prayerbook version has a stronger explicit emphasis on creation in its description of "Earth-maker," as is appropriate for its context in a bicultural country strongly influenced by the depth of Maori spirituality, with its strong focus on creation and relationship to the earth. This reorientation makes "Life-giving," however, something that is not limited to creation but part of the ongoing dynamic of a resurrection reality. The deletion of "love" from the specifics of this trinitarian description leaves open the possibility of seeing love as reflective of the unity of God and not one part of God's being in the world.

It is this exposition of the economic Trinity, that of *Earth-maker*, *Pain-bearer*, and *Life-giver*, that we will expound in functional terms as a psycho-theological model that will be useful to the pastoral caregiver working in the face of a trauma. It is a simple and powerful model of the *economic* Trinity that addresses current concerns about the use of language and its impact, the connection to the contexts where people find themselves and choose to be, and faithfulness to trinitarian theology, while departing from ecclesiastical language.

In using a model of the economic rather than immanent Trinity for pastoral practice, we have the opportunity to move beyond the paternal relations expressed in the language of the immanent Trinity, "Father, Son," which, though true to the witness of the life of Christ in Scripture and the history of the church, has a problematic overtone of patriarchy so difficult for many women and men. In acknowledging, however, the connection between immanent and economic trinity, the use of economic language can be seen not to critique or change the traditional formulation of the immanent "Trinity, which Cotter does later in the prayer, noting God as "Father and Mother of us all," but to offer an alternative that is a complement to other models of the *economic* Trinity such as "Creator, Redeemer, Sustainer." As such, its language is not gender-inclusive but gender-neutral, which can be accessible to those that find gender-inclusive versions problematic even if they agree with the concerns about patriarchal contexualization.

This model of the Trinity also offers language that is able to be interpreted in relation to many different contexts and yet also that renders it, as trinitarian theologian David Cunningham could hope, "more intelligible, to both Christians and non-Christians (while recognizing the differences between these two audiences)."[42] The terms *Earth-making*, *Pain-bearing*, *Life-giving* are more connected to everyday language and psychological understanding than traditional renderings of the economic Trinity ("Creating, Redeeming, Sustaining"), while still retaining the religious economy of salvation. They are, if you will excuse the pun, "down to earth." Although we do not commonly speak of "earth-making," being *grounded* in something, being earthy, and speaking of "the place where you stand" are common understandings. We speak of "painful" experience more often in common parlance than the more theological "redemptive" suffering. Finally, the term *life-giving* speaks of a greater movement than "sustaining," which could be interpreted as speaking more of a return to adaptive functioning in the face of trauma than to someplace new. In recognizing the difference between "these two audiences," two further steps need to be taken.

Reinterpreting the Trinity for Pastoral Practice

Methodologically, we move from the divine Trinity to the reflection of such as the image of God in humanity as seen through the window, or "mirror," of theology. However, as we are *not* God, not the "Earth-maker, Pain-bearer, Life-giver" but only a reflection of such, then this trinitarian image needs to be reframed into active relational functions, into how we are in relationship that expresses who we are in our being and doing. As such, this reframing is a reflection of the relationship between immanent and economic Trinity. We need to reframe "Earth-maker" into the dynamic term "Earth-making," "Pain-bearer" into "Pain-bearing," "Life-giver" into "Life-giving." "Earth-making, Pain-bearing, Life-giving" can then become an active reflection of our participation in salvation history as an outworking of God's love in the world. These terms intimate relationship, even if not directly descriptive as are the terms in the immanent Trinity. Yet they preserve that sense of both inter-personal and intrapsychic that characterizes our relationships, and, as we will see, suggest a mutuality and creative engagement that is transformative.

To be able to explore how "Earth-making, Pain-bearing, Life-giving" is reflected not only in theology but in psychoanalytic theory, we must explore in depth each of these elements. What are the essential characteristics of each? How do they relate to each other? This mirrors the former reflections on *hypostasis* and *perichoresis* as regards the immanent Trinity. Such exploration lead us to a model that has a consistency, connection, and integrity that can be seen in light of essential relationship rather than an arbitrary choosing of what is either popular or personal. The next three chapters will seek to explore both the depths of each element of this interpretation of the economic Trinity, and to see how this is contributed to by the thought of Winnicott, leading us to an additional parallel model of "Holding/ Suffering/Transforming spaces." Our explorations will lead us to explore both the community or multiplicity of the elements and their unity in love.

The question arises: Is "Earth-making, Pain-bearing, Life-giving" a trinitarian description of love grounded in the realities of pastoral ministry? John Milbank, when writing on Augustine, asks a similar question: "God has been revealed as love, and, therefore, one must ask, is love itself triune?"[43] Milbank says that for Augustine the answer is yes and consists, as we have seen, "of lover, beloved, and the love that flows between them. Thus," says Milbank, "the prime analogue for the Trinity is relational, which is to say, neither psychic nor political."[44] Catherine La Cugna states the question in this way: "According to the doctrine of the Trinity, God lives as the mystery of love among persons. If we are created in the image of this God, and if our destiny is to live forever with this God and with God's beloved creatures, then what forms of life best enable us to live as Christ lived, to show forth the Spirit of God, and ultimately to be deified?"[45] But what does the mystery of love mean, which goes beyond a feeling to a way of being in the daily lives of those in ministry?

This book asserts that, as an image of the triune God, an economic trinity in the self of Earth-making/Pain-bearing/Life-giving is the way we live out the love of God in our daily lives in relation to others and that the fullness of this leads to growth and health, even in the midst of trauma. To explore this thesis we will look in depth at each of these three spaces and see how they are manifest in the pastoral care of others (and of those caregivers), through the exploration of the experience of the ministry of the 9/11 T. Mort. chaplains.

chapter 2

Earth-Making
The Holding Space

Matins
In the morgue, many men, two metal
tables, white walls, boxes of gloves, supplies, places
to record observations.
Outside the doors
Port Authority Police Officers gather
and wait for one of their own.

Two litters brought in—one bag on each
table, shapeless, black, dirt-covered vinyl
Shrouds.

Uncover. Full room of silent men
listening to prayer.

First one:
Thanksgiving again for the finding.
Litany at Time of Death . . .
From all evil, from all danger,
from all tribulation,
Good Lord deliver them.

The Lord's Prayer
said by men together
in the presence of violent death.

Accept O Lord, a sheep of thine own flock,
a sinner of thine own redeeming . . .
May their souls and the souls of all the faithful departed
through the mercy of God,
Rest in peace.

Next table.
Shorter prayer.

Thanksgiving for the finding,
gratitude for the workers,
peace for the family,
God's blessing,
Amen.

Hats back on,
gloves on,
and the first bag is opened.

Whole body:
An adult male
the stink of death is present
Wallet found
His name is:
Photo taken,
the flash brighter than the fluorescents.

Bag closed, gloves changed,
second bag opened:
Upper right arm.
Ulna.
a hand.
Almost indistinguishable from the mud
that surrounds it.

Another photo, bag closed, and
honor detail forms up, presents . . . arms:
Both bags reverently placed into a waiting ambulance
and escorted away.

The liturgy is repeated
Twice more tonight.[1]

Earth-Making: The Cycle of Creation

In Christian practice in a number of denominations, the liturgy at the time of death
is a powerful reminder of the whole cycle of not only life and death, but also cre-

ation and redemption. Like baptism, where birth and death are intimately entwined through the symbology of drowning and coming up out of the water as baptism into the death of Christ and his resurrection, in the "Litany at the Time of Death" and the Burial Office, there is reminder, not only of the resurrection, but of creation. In the Burial Office in the Episcopal *Book of Common Prayer*, the Commendation states:

> You only are immortal, the creator and maker of mankind; and we are mortal, formed of the earth, and to earth shall we return. For so did you ordain when you created me, saying, "You are dust, and to dust you shall return." All of us go down to the dust; yet even at the grave we make our song: Alleluia, alleluia, alleluia.[2]

Then is said the piece included in the "Litany at the Time of Death" that the chaplain above said in the Temporary Morgue at Ground Zero: "Into your hands, O merciful Savior, we commend your servant *N.* Acknowledge, we humbly beseech you, a sheep of your own fold, a lamb of your own flock, a sinner of your own redeeming. Receive *him* into the arms of your mercy, into the blessed rest of everlasting peace, and into the glorious company of the saints in light. Amen."[3] Here, there is a recognition that the soul which returns to God and the remains which are as the dust—like the "hand. Almost indistinguishable from the mud that surrounds it"—are that very being which was created in love by the one to whom they are returning. The phrase, "earth to earth, ashes to ashes, dust to dust," is not simply about the finality and fragility of life, but about the spirituality of physicality: the earth that we return to is the earth from which we are made. More than most places, this was apparent at the T. Mort.

> **And I just remember that one time where they brought this body in, it looked like that anyway. And it was the shell of the clothing that survived. They opened it up there was nothing in there, *just ash*. . . . the fire chief was there and a few others were there and I sort of went up to them and gave my condolences. And he turned around, and that really blew me away, he says, "You know, it's a happy day; we got one of our own back." Wow. Different way of looking at it then. So that helped me in a way, too, to look at it in a different way as well. From their side of it . . .**

What was also celebrated, however, was that this being made of ash, dust, and earth was returning to the Earth-maker, God, to whom these souls were commended.

Earth-Making: A Theological Perspective

The first movement in the trinitarian model, "Earth-making," from a theological perspective is about creation and creating. It harks *back* to the creation narratives and *forward* to an eschatological understanding of what we are created for, by references to new creation through Christ in Scripture. It also attends to the *present* holding of creation in being. Creation narratives ground us in relationship with God, with each other as humans, and in the web of creation that sets us in the context of our relationships with our planet and its inhabitants, and with the universe around us. These narratives are foundational texts that suggest a ground for issues of identity—who we are in relation to others and our world—and of purpose—what we are called to do. For one chaplain, who understood it as much as an insight of aging as in the Ground Zero experience, this was about experiencing humanity as one, being connected with all creation and grateful for the presence of Christ, the new creation.

> I think what has stayed with me most is the oneness of humanity. I think that's part of the aging process. You begin to make those connections with all of creation. But particularly with humanity as you grow older. You don't think in terms of separations culturally or educationally or racially or politically or whatever. Those things become less important. . . . I've been able to feel that sense of humanity with persons that I might not agree [with] in other ways, politically or taste-wise or interest-wise or whatever it might be. There's still that sense of humanity. And that's a nice thing to feel. I think an additional gratitude for priesthood—the privilege of it. And I took from it, again the sense of Christ, the new creation walking with us. And I like that best of all.

With the parameters of genesis and the eschaton, together with texts about the "new Adam," creation is not seen simply as a "historical" concept but about being in becoming, a relational understanding of personhood. As such, then, from the perspective of theological anthropology, Earth-making is about the creation of space: environmental, relational, and personal.

In the last chapter, brief mention was made of Augustine's reference to the first creation story in which God makes humankind "in God's own image. Male and female he created them."[4] This, for Augustine, reinforced his understanding of God as multiple rather than simply unitary, for him a trinitarian allusion. Creation of human persons in this text is seen as the pinnacle of creation, after the creation of the physical environment and its animal inhabitants. Further, it indicates an understanding of God who creates not out of *need*, but freely out of *love*, that which is different from God. Whether there is the sense of creation *ex nihilo*, out of nothing, or creation out of chaos there is the sense of a God who delights in the creation. This God delights particularly in the creation of humanity that is somehow the image and likeness of God, and yet is free to choose to live out of that relationship with God and its obligations, or not. As such, creation or creating reflects the Triune God's nature as love and it is such that brings creation into being. One chaplain described the human person as a very complicated being. Although perhaps referencing the physical, psychologically as much could be said; however, these chaplains continued to be impressed by the realization that even in the human fragments, creation and the holiness of such seemed so present to them.

> [Blessing the bodies and the body parts] kind of reminded me of the two times I was present at autopsies. And I was struck, when I viewed the autopsies, the thing that I felt—that it was a religious experience because here you have this organism that somehow came into being, we don't know exactly how it all began. But it was a wonder to me, at that time, that more things wouldn't go wrong in this terribly complicated being. And yet being absolutely clear that it was holy. And so, whatever the fragment was, I considered [it] was part of creation and holy.

Another chaplain, discussing Scripture, which became more meaningful to him during his T. Mort. chaplaincy, spoke of a particular psalm and its relation to a particular recovery of remains.

> Psalm 43: *"I've carved you on the palm of my hand."* That whole passage there came through very strong, especially when her hand was brought into the morgue. Oh, wow. That really spoke loud and clear. And maybe even sort of when the medical examiner was *looking at the hand*, even sort of seeing what was there. Even that, it was "wow." I still remember that night.

Perhaps, in other disaster-response ministry, where chaplains were not involved in the blessing of bodies and body parts, references to creation would not be so explicit; however, a theology of creation and one's theological anthropology can be implicit in the creative acts of pastoral care that are upheld by these theological perspectives.

Given the context of our conversation about the 9/11 disaster, where we see a ministry of love in the face of a trauma caused by human destructiveness, it is worth seeing how Augustine's trinitarian theology—and here its emphasis on creation and love—was taken up by a theologian who came to see the doctrine of the Trinity as the place we start our theological conversations, particularly in the midst of a context that threatened to co-opt language about God to ratify a theology based on hatred, fear, and exclusivity. Swiss theologian Karl Barth, whose neoorthodox theology was formed in the crucible of an emerging Nazi Germany, turned from the liberal Protestantism prevalent in his time to a theology that was grounded in the understanding of God as "wholly other," not something to be manipulated by culture or context, but the one who reveals Godself as "the one who loves in freedom," and thus critiques all our attempts to bind God to our own way of being. Therefore, any reflection of God's love in ourselves *cannot*, for Barth, be seen as a vestige of God whose essence is love and our possession of a little bit of that in our being that binds us to the God who created us. The image of God in the human person and God's own constitution as "the one who loves" is more complex than that. Despite this, Barth's revelational theology shows a relationality that is formative in the relation of God to humanity, that of God as love *in* Godself and *to us* as Creator, Redeemer, Reconciler.

Although Barth most often locates the function of God as Creator to the "essence" of God as Father, in his pneumatic theology it becomes clear that creation is a role shared by all persons of the Trinity, or "modes of being," to use Barth's terminology. Creating, for Barth, is a natural outcome due to God's nature as love, which constitutes the very reality of the Triune God, and yet at the same time, unlike the begetting of the Son and procession of the Spirit, is a free choice out of that love.

> By being the Father in Himself from all eternity, God brings Himself forth from eternity as the Son. . . . He is the Father of the Son in such a way, that with the Son He brings forth the Spirit, Love, and *thus He is in Himself the Spirit, Love.* Of course He had not to be the Father of the Son in order to satisfy a law of Love, because Love was the reality which even God had to obey. "The Son is the first, the Spirit the second in God," means that by being the Father of the Son, by, as Father, bringing forth the Son, He brings forth the Spirit and so the negation of existence in loneliness, the law and the reality of Love. *Love is God, the highest law and the ultimate reality, because God is Love and not vice versa.* And God is Love, Love goes forth from Him as His Love, as the Spirit which He Himself is, because he posits Himself as the Father and so posits Himself as the Son. In the Son of His Love, i.e. in the Son in and with whom He brings Himself forth as Love, He then brings forth also in the *opus ad extra*; in creation the creaturely reality distinct from Himself, and in revelation reconciliation and peace for the creature that has fallen away from Him.[5]

Because of who God is and how God is in Godself, love, for Barth, is the "highest law and ultimate reality." It is a love that is revealed to us in creation and reconciliation, which sees humanity as a creature separate and distinct from God, which has fallen away from God, but which is created out of love and for communion.

> The Love which meets us in reconciliation and, looking backwards from that, in creation, is therefore and thereby Love, the highest law and ultimate reality, because God is Love antecedently in Himself; not merely a supreme principle of the connection of separation and communion, but Love which *wills and affirms, seeks and finds in separation the other thing, the Other person in communion also, in order to will and to affirm, to seek and to find communion with it (Him) in separation also.* Because God is Love antecedently in Himself, therefore love exists and holds good as the reality of God in the work of revelation and in the work of creation.[6]

Here creation, reconciliation, and pastoral practice are intimately entwined. Here creating is inclusive of recreating and reconciling, a way of being that "wills and affirms, seeks and finds in separation the other thing, the Other person, in order to will and to affirm, to seek and to find communion with it."[7] Here the love that binds the Trinity together, and therefore constitutes the very being of the Triune God as being-in-relationship, is that which is an image for us, not only of the one who created, but the one whom through love continues creating. As such, Barth's description of the Triune God is as good a description of the pastoral task as any, where we, too, can reflect this love in our relationships as we manifest a care that "wills and affirms, seeks and finds in separation . . . the Other person, in order to will and to affirm, to seek and to find communion with [them]."[8]

Joan Dalloway gives a similar description, of the creating God who continues to seek out communion with us while respecting our separation from God, when she speaks of "The Three Pastoral Questions" as a model for pastoral care.[9] Dalloway locates her first pastoral question in the second creation narrative in Genesis, the story of Adam and Eve. Her interpretation of the story gives a lovely description of Barth's God who seeks and finds the other in separation for communion. The first pastoral question, for Dalloway, is "Where are you?"—the question of the anthropomorphic God to Adam after the fall, the disobedient act of eating from the forbidden tree.[10] Dalloway suggests that God knows the answer to all God's questions of Adam and Eve, but makes space for them, gives them the opportunity to tell their own story, to take responsibility for their own actions, before holding them to account, punishing them for their actions but also caring for their needs. Here relationship is not simply about communion and separation

Image 2.1. A New York City firefighter gazes into rubble dubbed "God's House," due to the many "crosses" found there. (Photo by Mike Rieger/FEMA News Photo.)

but about responsibility and care. It is respectful of the other, even in the face of the other's sin and destructiveness.

Dalloway suggests that pastoral care follow this question in terms of creating pastoral relationship. Here, care is shown by allowing the other to tell his or her own story even if you know part of it, by respecting the other in his or her separateness, and by walking alongside the other rather than following a "from on high" model of power in pastoral care.[11] One chaplain spoke of this in response to a photograph (fig. 2.1), "There's got to be somebody in there. One of those firefighters might have said what one said to me, and that is, 'I'm here every day because I'm looking for my father.'" When asked, "So how was it to hear comments like that knowing that the people working on the site knew people that they were looking for?," the chaplain responded, "Well, it made me just want to sit with them and let them tell their story to me and not necessary to say anything to them, because what could be said? But simply to be with them. Let them know that I wasn't afraid to hear it."

In the scriptural narrative, in the conflicted relationship between God and humanity, Dalloway's focus highlights that the creation story is seen not as finished with the creation of Adam and Eve but in the *re-creation of the relationship in the context of sin and brokenness.* Likewise for Barth, for whom a doctrine of creation *follows* the revelation of God in Christ, who redeems us through the Spirit that reconciles us to Godself, it is from this place of redemption and reconciliation that we truly know what the image of God is, both prospectively and retrospectively, rather than a chronological anthropology, as if we could interpret what the image of God is in a context without sin and suffering.

In emphasizing, however, the relationship of creation to re-creation, which means continually creating conditions for love to manifest, this should not be seen as separate from the sheer physicality of creating. Earth-making is about physical space, the physical, the earth, the humus of humanity. We see this physicality affirmed from both the psychological and theological sides. Winnicott notes that Sigmund Freud "said that the ego is essentially built up on the basis of body-functioning; the ego is essentially a body ego,"[12] which indicates that we should not think of psyche simply as mind but as a psychosomatic unity. We see a similar emphasis on physicality from biblical scholar Phyllis Trible who, in exploring the image of God from the perspective of the Genesis creation narratives, draws us back to a semantic perception of "Adam" as not being a name but a description: "earth creature."[13]

> Then Yahweh God formed the earth creature [hā-'ādām]
> dust from the earth [hā-'adāmâ]
> and breathed into its nostrils the breath of life,
> and the earth creature [hā-'ādām] became a living *nephesh*. (2:7)[14]

As presented in the first episode, with the definite article *hā-* preceding the common noun *'ādām*, this work of art is neither a particular person nor the typical person but, rather the creature from the earth (*hā-'adāmâ*)—the earth creature. . . . This sexually undifferentiated earth creature owes its existence to Yahweh God. It is not a "self-made man," a patriarchal figure, a superman, or *Übermensch*. Only two ingredients constitute its life, and both are tenuous dusty earth and divine breath.[15]

Here, being a person, an earth creature, is about the unity of the psyche, the earthly body that both houses and embodies it, and the very breath that enlivens it. As such, Earth-making is about being embodied, enfleshed, but also ensouled or enspirited, the thought that spirit is in the space between psyche and soma, and that new life is breathed into the space in that unity.

This is also experienced in the *dis*-unity of these elements. As the chaplains blessed bodies and body parts at the T. Mort., the smallest physical elements of these earth-creatures symbolized the complete sense of the person who was created in such fragility. Although the image is not of creation but of destruction, the sense of care for these elements of dust and bone reflects the respect and care of the Creator, who breathed life into these disparate elements that were created. One chaplain spoke of this in response to being asked what it was like to bless the bodies and body parts recovered at Ground Zero.

[It was] overwhelming, but not emotionally draining. Overwhelming because of you're not used to realizing that a bit of bone, a quarter of an inch, could perhaps be all that remained of a human being. That would hopefully mean eventually destined for that victim's family to be buried. And to realize that, *we're from dust and to dust we return.* And this is true because at times all we're dealing with almost is specks of dust to which people became.

Whenever I was there, there was never a full torso found, there was really just bone fragments. It gave a whole new meaning to that verse. And the realization of, even though we return to dust, there's still so much value. Because the respect—again, these hardened blue-collar workers are normally the kind of guys you expect to walk over old ladies to get a seat on the subway—they all were so moved. And that was just so overwhelming for me to see—the respect. I am trained through my religious theology, through my activities to work with human beings, to work with the deceased, to show respect to the dead. It's natural. It came logically to me. Even though I'm not used to dealing with bone fragments, it was just that extension that was easy to accept. It's a part of the human being. But to see how others, who normally seem to be a little bit more callous, in their normal kinds of professions would just become so reverent and so overwhelmingly spiritual when finding a bone fragment, to me that was the real redeeming factor of that experience.

As the chaplains engaged in blessing in the dust and destruction of Ground Zero, these fallen earth creatures who had been infused with the breath of life became paradoxically and perhaps painfully infused with the very breath of the chaplains and those that worked to recover them.

> To be able to sit there and hold someone's hand and at the same time let them cry and at the same time watch them make some kind of movement towards—I don't want to say accepting, I don't want to say healing—I just want to say getting some form of support, some surrounding of some kind of feeling that, regardless of what's happened and *who you're breathing in* . . . (That was a big thing for a while—it was not *what* so much, it was *who* you're breathing in.) . . . That they are in fact in God's hands, that we don't see them anymore. And you had to move people towards that—yes, there was a horrible disaster and there were a lot of people who died—but we need to realize that there's a bigger picture that we do need to plug into.

Those at Ground Zero had to work constantly in an environment that not only contained the dead, but indeed at times, as this chaplain noted, even *was* the dead. Some workers became conscious that the dusty air that they were breathing in may have contained not only the chemicals and toxins which many became concerned about, but also the ashes of those who had been incinerated by the explosion of the jet fuel and pulverized by the collapse of the World Trade Center. The very earth of Ground Zero contained those that Trible describes as "earth creatures," a fact workers both respected and perhaps needed to dissociate from, simply to carry on with the job of recovery. A chaplain described the difficulty of this:

> What I found most difficult was that sort of hearing the number of people who have died, what they thought had died and a few they were finding. I found that very difficult to deal with. Yes, the people were respectful down there—all the workers, the ironworkers, and all of that—very respectful. . . . But you know that they'd be walking on *somebody* or whatever, flicking out their cigarettes on someone, on the remains of people. I wasn't blaming anybody. It wasn't that, but just trying to figure out, How many are still there? And whatever for?

Such concerns of the chaplains' experience of the dusty breath and earth of Ground Zero underline Trible's exegesis of the second Genesis creation narrative, which reinforces the "earthiness" of creation of the human being. However, in Scripture this Earth-making is not seen as simply physical but that the human person, the earth creature, is seen also in its relation both to God and to the earth, as one with a responsibility to "serve" the earth, from which it was formed. As such, the creation is about both identity *and role* in the context of an interdependent relationship between humanity and God (but not vice versa), and humanity and the space on the earth in which God places us.

From being a totally passive object, the earth creature becomes an object who must work. Thus, its life develops further through the responsibility that Yahweh God has planned for it. . . . First, the earth creature is assigned the job of tilling a particular space, the garden of Eden, but not of tilling the whole earth (cf. 3:23). Life expands within boundaries. Second, a new infinitive joins the tilling: *to keep it.* . . . The two infinitives, *to till* and *to keep,* connote not plunder and rape but care and attention.[16]

Again, the paradox of work in the "particular space" of Ground Zero was that those who were literally tilling the earth with "care and attention," were doing so due to destruction rather than creation. However, their doing so exemplified the kind of care and responsibility called for in the creation narratives. Three chaplains described this earthy work in response to the experience exemplified in the following photograph:

Image 2.2. Raking for remains. (Photo by Larry Lerner/FEMA News Photo.)

Ah, the digging. That certainly brings back memories. I remember one day thinking, feeling kind of useless because everybody was digging and I was just standing there. And so the Fire Chief said, "Well, grab a rake." And I said, "What am I looking for exactly?" And he said, "Something sharp, something soft, or something stinky." And that stuck with me. Because the bone shards are like little sharp pieces and the flesh was really soft and when you hit the smell, you knew it. So I thought that was an apt description. And ever since then and it was pretty early on, they just said, "Grab a rake and help." So I did. But they went through every single inch. Not right here, but when they loaded stuff into trucks and took it over to Staten Island, they went through it again. They found lots of stuff again. . . . But the work that these people did day in and day out on their hands and knees.

It always amazed me the number of guys that actually said that they wanted to keep their rakes. And I don't know how many hours they actually did that. But the looking, looking, and looking. The determination to go through every single scrap, just in case they might find another body, they might find another body part or some other artifact. But the part when they would do that was when they thought there was somebody in an area or something. There was just, there was just a different mood at that time, well, obviously. It was just the determination to always, always fulfill that mission was so important.

Another chaplain also reinforced that sense of mission,

They just did it [the recovery effort], they did it well. And there were some that stand out that brought humor. And phrases, I remember phrases that one EMS worker would use, he'd say, "Well, got to go get dirty." That meant pick up a rake and look for remains. And they had a mantra which was, "We need to bring them all home. Everybody needs to come home." That was their guiding principle. And everybody agreed with that, we're going to bring them all home. And I think they must be so frustrated now that about a thousand they can't even find.

Beyond the mission, identity, and earthy physicality suggested both in Trible's readings and the Ground Zero experience, Trible also suggests that there is a human relationality in the creation story that is played out in the creation of man and woman. Trible's reading liberates the Genesis creation narratives from the traditional readings that assert a hierarchical supremacy of chronology presuming a priority to the male over the female, that see a male "Adam" created before the subsequently dependent female "Eve." In Trible's exegesis of the passage, "Adam" cannot be seen to become a name for a male person until the separation—woman being taken from the side of *hā-'ādām*.

> And *hā-'ādām* said,
> This, finally, bone of my bones
> and flesh of my flesh.
> This shall be called woman [*'iššâ*]
> Because from man [*'îš*] was taken this.[17]

But no ambiguity clouds the words *'iššâ* and *'îš*. One is female, the other male. Their creation is simultaneous, not sequential. One does not precede the other, even though the timeline of the story introduces the woman first (2:22). Moreover, one is not the opposite of the other. In the very act of distinguishing female from male, the earth creature describes her as "bone of my bones and flesh of my flesh" (2:23). These last words speak unity, solidarity, mutuality, and equality. Accordingly, in this poem the man does not depict himself as either prior to or superior to the woman. His sexual identity depends upon her even as hers depends upon him. For both of them sexuality originates in the one flesh of humanity.[18]

Hā-'ādām previous to this is the "earth-creature" that is made by God from the dusty earth and the divine breath. Here the humus, the earth, is the very stuff of humanity and connects us with all other creation. Here also is the divine breath, enspiriting or ensouling us, breathing into us the very life that sustains the body and the psychic life that makes it more than a creature but a person in relationship with Creator and the created. Both the relationship between God and the earth-creature and the relationship between the finally sexually differentiated humans speak of a relationality that is about both separation and communion, about unity, and about particularity. This creation story, as it continues through the disobedience of the humans who are dependent on their relationship with the God whom they image, ends in a place of suffering. Trible concludes:

> Life has lost to Death, harmony to hostility, unity and fulfillment to fragmentation and dispersion. The divine, human, animal, and plant worlds are all adversely affected. Indeed, the image of God male and female has participated in a tragedy of disobedience. Estranged from each other, the man and woman are banished from the garden and barred forever from the tree of life. Truly, a love story gone awry.[19]

Whether the second creation story in Genesis is seen as a metaphor for the evolutionary beginnings of humanity or a mytho-history of the first origins, a feminist reading of such a passage is both profoundly humbling, as we connect with the very earthiness of what it is to be human, and a critique to patriarchal interpretations that read a hierarchical relationship that flows from God to "man," and on to the relationship with "woman." Rather, we are called to see relationships with the other from a basis of continually re-creating that which speaks of "unity, solidarity, mutuality, and equality," even in a world where hostility, fragmentation, and dispersion are consequent on our freedom and loss of it.

One may think that such critiques of patriarchy in referencing a creation narrative have little application to pastoral care. Many of the chaplains, however, were highly aware that the firefighters who comprised a majority of the workers at Ground Zero came from an organization that many see as highly patriarchal and that a large majority of these come from the Roman Catholic denomination, which does not allow the ordination of women. Yet their experience was most often one of "unity, solidarity, mutuality, and equality." One male chaplain shared this story:

> Three or four of them got together (this is the day that [*a female chaplain*] and I were on together and she'd gone somewhere) and they said, they came over and said, "We've got to talk to you because . . . We call you 'Father,' right? Now what do we call her? 'Mother'?!?" And it was so delightful. Because they were in the military structure they want to have the right term. And they're really saying, "We value her priesthood, and how do we? What's the right way? We don't want to offend her, we don't dare ask. Because we're just suppose to know." It was just kind of fabulous. I thought, "Four hundred years from now you'll be ordaining women too." So I told them that, in New York, "Mother" was not uncommon and that they should ask her. And they said, "We'll call her 'Mother.'"

Whether it was their commitment and respect inherent in what this chaplain describes as a "military structure," the commitment to the task of recovery, or the experience of the chaplains' pastoral care, the women chaplains predominantly experienced being treated with equality and respect, as were their male colleagues, working with those who accepted the ministry of blessing on behalf of their brothers and sisters, sons and fathers, represented by the fragile remains recovered in the dust and mud.

The fragility and ambiguity about the "human condition" is implicit in the creation narratives. It is of note that the phrase in the Genesis narratives, "and God saw that it was good," said of each part of the creation, is *not* said of the creation of the earth creature, the human. "And God saw that it was *very* good" (Gen. 1:31) is said on the day of the human creation, but only of creation as a whole. One can read both eschatological forebodings into this, along with the prefiguring of redemption even in the act of creation, for to create another in freedom leaves the opportunity for such disobedience and the suffering that results from such acts.

One T. Mort. chaplain was most angered by the Christian church's inability to articulate the destruction of the World Trade Center by Islamic Salafi Jihadists as "sin," and to engage in dialogue with moderate Islamic communities about this, not from a perspective of judgment but to foster the voice of moderate Islam. For him it was not enough to act out of love but to create opportunities and relationships to articulate together what love is and what it is not. He felt that the church's role is not to defend moderate Islam but to empower its voice by engaging it in dialogue about the nature of sin and its example in the 9/11 terrorist acts.

> If you deal with it from the standpoint of dialogue, you'll be wonderfully blessed. Because it's in the dialogue. I think we made terrible errors in the

whole business. And by this I'm not saying engaging Bin Laden and the perpetrators in dialogue, because that's not going to happen. But we haven't engaged Islam in dialogue. We tried to defend it. "Oh, that's not what Islam is like." We don't know what Islam is like at all. I mean, I've been in Riddah when I've seen them trample a woman to death. What's Islam like? It's like many things. I have fantastic hope because Christianity was once there. I mean, if Christianity was once there . . .

And we need to do everything we can to engage the voice of moderate Islam because it's there but it's not heard. And they don't dare speak up. And there is a prevailing sin in Islam and that's basically, "I will not criticize a fellow Muslim." But bishops do the same thing, "We're all one, we speak with one voice." So I think the church has done nothing to engage the voice of moderate Islam. I am not a defender of Islam. I will be in dialogue with them, but I can only write a Christian apologetic. Only a Muslim can write an Islamic apologetic. And we've done a very poor job on that. Every bishop has done a very poor job on that. Every pastor has done a poor job on that. Why? Because it just hasn't seemed important. We had an opportunity to speak out, but it was too close to September 11th. What country wanted to maintenance all the ports? Dubai. And we could have said, "Yes, by all means. Help foster a voice of moderate Islam." But Senator Schumer had to become political on this and refer to September 11th and security. And where was the church? Silent. They should have spoken up. We have done nothing to influence the voice of moderate Islam.

In the environment of Ground Zero, which for many seemed closer to hell than to the Eden of the earth creatures, the disobedience and suffering that characterized the fall was as present a reality in the sin and brokenness exemplified by the destruction of the lives of those in the WTC and other sites. Such a context demands, at least for this chaplain, a response that is not simply about rescue and recovery but about a solidarity, even in sin, from a faith perspective that recognizes *not* "There but for the grace of God, go I," but "There in the name of God, have been I." Like Barth, who sees the created image of God having to be read from redemption, and Trible, who sees the creation story as encompassing the fall, this chaplain saw the need to speak out from this difficult place of sin and brokenness.

In the context of Ground Zero, the creation narratives ground us in an understanding of Earth-making that is about self in the context of environment—wonderfully created but also sinful and broken—and, through the role assigned to humanity as stewards, environment in the context of self. It is about the self that *can* reflect the creative and redemptively re-creative relationality of the creating God, the Earthmaker. Again, it is also about space, the space of the created world—our environment and its boundaries, and the very physicality of our beings. It is about that inner space formed by the breath of the divine one. And it is about that relational space between self and Other, whom we seek in separation and communion, in which we can act or act out of our vocations to be who we are called to be even in the context of the kind of suffering experienced at Ground Zero. In this way, the fragile earth creatures that we are can express the love of the God that created us and calls us home, and the hope of creation—which can be seen as an eschatological promise: "and God saw that it was very good."

> I think to be able to function in a needed way as a priest was life giving and affirming. Getting to know the workers in a camaraderie way was life giving. The fact that they were involved in a task that hopefully we will get through together was life affirming because we were at work at it. I think the fact that *all of creation*, particularly in this case humankind, *are in God's hands* and we don't have to worry about that is life affirming. And, from what I understand, God's kind of hope for *wholeness for the whole creation* is life affirming and when you're involved with something that is trying to work out of a bad situation to a better situation that is life affirming.

One can see from the readings of Barth, Dalloway, and Trible the relationship between immanent and economic Trinity, and even in the pastoral narratives, the importance of an understanding of *perichoresis*, mutual indwelling, as not only applicable to each person of the immanent Trinity, but to the economy of God, lived out in the context of this fragile earth and its creatures. Although one can codify pieces of the chaplains' narratives as being particularly about Earth-making, Pain-bearing, or Life-giving, you can see strands of the other within the dialogue. Each is related to the other in these awful and awe-filled stories of Ground Zero.

Earth-Making/Holding in Winnicott's Thought

Whereas the creation and ongoing creating we see in the scriptural narratives is formed by the I-Thou relationship between God and the world, God and humanity, Winnicott's description of the creation of the human person through relationship, as noted before, is initially primarily with the mother figure. Yet the I-Thou of the mother-infant dyad shows a similar attention to environment and personal relationship where the created one is given respect and "allowed" to tell his or her own story. At a preverbal level the telling of this story of selfhood is through bodily motility and psychic experience, and a listening to that as an accurate attunement to the story of who the infant is as it forms in relationship.

The primary task of the mother figure is to provide a hypostatic union of environment and person where the child may be held in its becoming, in the "complex psychological field"[20] of relationship. Winnicott describes this creative relational process as "Holding," and it is this shorthand for this dynamic yet complex function that I believe we see reflecting the creating that is described by the term *Earth-making*. Such holding enables the infant then to develop relationships, a "living with"[21] others both individually and as community or group. This formation of the individual Winnicott sees as the "clue to social and group psychology."[22]

This holding is both a physical thing, "which is a form of loving"[23]—the kind of holding and handling required to feed, clothe, bathe, and otherwise care for an infant—and also the psychic holding and handling of the relationship that gives the infant not only the physical, but the relational and psychic space to develop into a person. This kind of holding is achieved through such *empathic attunement* that the infant's inner world becomes enfleshed through the mother's response and what is initially experienced as inner phantasy[24] becomes experienced as external reality. An infant desires to be fed, the breast or bottle appears, and its inner world is mirrored to itself in the experience of care. Of course, the "appearing" of that which meets the infant's needs is not a magical event but a relational one, one where the mother is attuned enough to know whether the cry is one of hunger, pain, tiredness, discomfort, or fear. As such, the creation is not simply the creation of the self of the child, but the creation also of the "mother," as she or he too learns what it is to attune to another. The "good-enough mother,"[25] Winnicott tells us, will get it right *consistently enough* to meet both the infant's physical needs as well as the need of the forming self whose inner reality is validated through outer response and who begins to relate to others not simply through "omnipotent phantasy" but comes gradually to see them as an-other object, person, a part of an external world of which they, too, are a part.

One can see the connections between the chaplain's empathic presence and the holding empathic relationship in the parental care through one chaplain's description of the essence of 9/11 disaster-response ministry:

> The phrase that was being used for awhile was comfort in the midst of chaos. That was the gift that the church brought was [in] that chaos. There's some big plan that the construction people have on this whole recovery effort, but to the naked eye it's not going to be obvious. But then in the moment the planes hit and the people coming out on September 11 on the way through— I really think it was comfort. Hope maybe came from that eventually, but I would say comfort was huge, because we were so violated. And like I said before, our joy was taken from us. There had to be comfort. Which I think comes from us so early on when our parents comfort us. How a kid can pretty much hold it together until he sees his mom and then the skinned knee and everything brings out the tears and all that. I saw that. When you get the comfort from your mother, she didn't heal it, she just makes you feel better about it. And that's what the presence of ministry here was.

The empathic presence of the chaplains in the Ground Zero disaster response and T. Mort. did not heal the suffering, but somehow their handling and representing of the bodies and all that they signified in prayer and their holding relationships helped those who were working the disaster site hold it together (and also let it go and be held by the other), and provided for some a comforting presence, both in community and in being alone together.

In Winnicott's understanding of development, to hold this space also means to *afford* the developing self space, not to impinge on it. Like Barth's description of seeking communion with the other in their separation, here the mother is both environmental as well as personal. The mother does not, for Winnicott, make the child who she or he is but facilitates an environment that allows the unfolding of maturational processes that enable the formation of a true self, not one that is wholly compliant to what the mother wants, not one that is an extension of the parents, but is a creative and unique person in her or his own self. Winnicott gives the name "false self" to that compliant, adaptive structure in the psyche that protects the true self. It is easy to read this term pejoratively; however, Winnicott sees this function in health much more like an inner reflection of the holding relationship between mother and infant. He writes, "In the favorable case the false self develops a fixed maternal attitude toward the true self, and is permanently in a state of *holding the true* self as a mother holds a baby at the very beginning of differentiation and of emergence from primary identification."[26] Hence, "holding" can, paradoxically, be seen as its opposite—giving the infant space to be alone (together)—not to abandon but to afford space for the infant and child's own spontaneous gestures and personal ideas, which develop into a creativity and experience of feeling real and alive in relation to the world, rather than annihilated by it.

To do this holding, however, the mother needs to be able to hold her own "stuff," her reactions to the infant's expressions of instinctual drives and relational demands. Like Augustine's conception of the human love of God that can contain hate and alienation, so, too, the mother needs to contain herself as she responds to an infant which expresses both love and aggression—at times an aggressive, excited loving—that even as it expresses the infant's desire for her, also can appear to seek to destroy her in its ruthlessness. In her holding herself, she can learn as mother to care for herself enough, most often through the experience of others caring for her, to care for her child enough to suffer the love that forms the self in relationship. In this we see the relational matrix of care also, in that the mother's *self-care* is in the context of her own caring environment, where "good-enough care can be enabled to do better by being cared for themselves in a way that acknowledges the essential nature of their task."[27] The term *self-care*, both in parenting and in professional fields, is, therefore, something of a misnomer—perhaps the cumbersome but more accurate term would be "communal and personal self-care." This can be seen in the vignette from one chaplain getting off a difficult shift:

> Once, I don't know what it was, but I was really traumatized coming off of a night [shift]. And there was these two big black women and they were dressed

like they were going to church and I didn't know why, I didn't even know what day it was. But I was in my collar and my hard hat and the whole thing. And they said, "Well, how's it going?" And I just started to cry. And the two of them just started hugging me and giving me tissues and that was exactly what I needed. And I just felt very cared for. I just felt angels had come to see me. Once there was a transit worker where I wasn't even on duty, it was the day after I was on duty, and there was no place to grab hold of on the train to hold on, it was that crowded. And she just looked at me and said, *"Don't worry dear, just hold on to me, I won't let you fall."* And that was, she had no idea what that related to, but for me it was a message, "Just hold on, I won't let you fall." But things like that happened all the time. So if anything, it was a life-affirming experience.

Like the eschatological focus of the theological understanding of the creation of humanity, it is worth reemphasizing that Winnicott sees the creation of the self not as a given but as a potentiality that matures through the facilitation of its environment where the mother holds and handles her infant, physically and psychically, with accurate attunement rather than intrusion or abandonment, which translates to the inner capacity of the child and later the adult to hold her- or himself without fragmenting. In this we see creation not simply in terms of the physicality of birth, and the body which is our own personal earth, but the creation of a holding environment in which the human psyche may develop and grow. Although Winnicott is always speaking psychologically rather than theologically, I think in his radical developmentalism we see most clearly the theological principle of loving as we have been loved, in that we learn to love by being loved. In the T. Mort. chaplaincy this can be seen to be about the chaplains who were providing that holding relationship for others and who were doing so in the context of being held in relationship with others, which many interpreted as being held by God: "Just hold on, I won't let you fall."

Like the "space-holding" and "space-affording" mother, the pastoral caregiver provides that relational space where the person's true self has a chance of being revealed, rather than that which complies with internal and external expectations. Pastoral caregivers work to hold the relationship through their empathic presence, through the use of accurate empathy, to hold their own countertransference, and attend to their own needs for holding, particularly as they are engaging in difficult ministry, such as disaster response and/or encounter with deep trauma.

Earth-Making/Holding as Pastoral Method

Earth-making and Holding together form part of pastoral matrix, where each mirrors creation and re-creation from theological and psychological perspectives in the experience of pastoral care. Even as the psychological reflects the theological, it also is earthed in the experience of the pastoral relationship, even in the midst of a disaster.

The Earth-making/Holding part of pastoral method is about building the pastoral frame and alliance, without which the relationship falls apart. It is as simple as the physical environment, the space of the pastor's or pastoral psychotherapist's office and person; as the frame of psychotherapy with its boundaries of time and money; as the pastoral conversation in pew or at the beside; as the beginning of a conversation with someone in a collar or chaplain's disaster response vest. It is as complex as the relational field—the space created by two subjectivities coming together to engage in a process that transcends the sum of the two elements—and as the difficult space in which a disaster is situated, as for the chaplains at Ground Zero after the 9/11 disaster, with all its physical earthiness and the earthiness of those who worked the disaster.

Unlike most pastoral ministry, however, disaster-response ministry with those who are continuing to work in rescue and recovery is about "holding it together." One cannot and should not look for the same kind of cathartic expression and working through as may happen in pastoral psychotherapy or even in the clergyperson's office. For those actively working a disaster site, holding may be as symbolic and environmental as it is about personal engagement. Yet even in the environmental holding, a powerful sense of community may arise. A chaplain describes it this way:

> It was that we really could connect. That I really felt that if people could look at me and see and get some hope or *something to hold onto*, if I could make them at least be able to reach some peace for a second, then all my years of study were worth it. I think a lot of people there, their faith was increased instead of diminished. Just a feeling that we're all connected and that we can all help each other.

The earthy reality of Ground Zero ministry was experienced in different ways by the chaplains. Some experienced recovery workers continually seeking them out to talk with; others described the complexity and care in what can seem like incidental encounters but highlight the need for chaplains always to be aware of what a pastoral presence means and how it can lead to more personal encounters.

> It was pretty rare that someone would say, "I want to come and talk to you." But it was pretty common if you were leaning over the fence just watching the construction that someone would come and lean over the fence and watch with you. There would be a couple of minutes of conversation about nothing and then there would be, "My buddy was found down there yesterday." I have this whole theory that people will say things when they're not looking you in the eye that they would never [say otherwise].

Although there were some women who worked the recovery site, this chaplain thought that this kind of ministry was typical of ministry (of men) with men, reinforced both by the culture of the uniformed services and the construction workers and part of the reality of the Ground Zero environment.

> **They are macho kind of men. But it's not unlike parish ministry in that the result is you wind up giving them permission to seek counseling. I mean, that's an hour's encounter. "I really feel better; I think I will look into counseling." It's hard. You know it well. I remember some resistance at one point, the fire department had mandated some kind of debriefing counseling, and they were not pleased about that. But I'm guessing that, because they spend so much time together, they do a lot more of that looking-over-the-fence or cleaning-the-truck kind of unintentional processing—mostly men, as you know, and mostly, "This needs to done, we'll worry about our emotions later," typical stuff.**

The reality of working a disaster site is indeed the demand of the task and the need to hold one's emotions together enough to be able to do it—"This needs to be done, we'll worry about our emotions later." Another chaplain described the need to hold one's emotions together as keeping on one's "game face." This is not a disparagement but recognition of the demands of the task and the depersonalization required to hold onto it. Likewise, the chaplain recognized that need in himself, so as not to burden those he was working with.

> **Number one, I think a concern was bracing myself to see the mangled bodies, you know, Would this be too grotesque to be able to handle? More than anything, I want to be effective as a priest. I did not want to wind up getting sick or getting emotional in front of everybody. It's like I have a role here, I want to make sure I can do my role. That, and also very concerned about how's everybody else. How's everybody else doing, kind of emotionally, spiritually, handling this? Because it was nothing any of us had ever experienced before. Walking around, periodically I would have some pretty intense conversations with people and recognizing on the one hand, letting them talk, but at the same time recognizing that they have work to do there. And they have careers and you don't want them to kind of risk, in particular, I think getting too emotional or whatever. People needed to keep their game face.**

Despite the need to minister in such a way that the disaster-response workers can continue to do their task, the pastoral purpose and power of such holding should not be underestimated, even though it may be present only in a single encounter and not entail the kind of working through that is prevalent in other pastoral ministry.

Spiritually, it may reflect the *apophatic* way, the way more characterized by "not knowing," by silence, by seeming emptiness. Yet, in reality, like that spiritual path the sense of communion is as present as the way characterized by knowledge, words, and a seeming fullness of encounter. Again, one should recall Barth's comment of the creating God, who "wills and affirms, seeks and finds in separation the other thing, the Other person in communion also, in order to will and to affirm, to seek and to find communion with it (Him) in separation also,"[28] as one reflects the "space-affording" side of the holding relationship. One chaplain's encounter with a contractor at Ground Zero shows well this paradoxical fullness of communion even in the midst of a largely silent encounter.

> I was one day in the Pit and I was watching one of these really big construction guys handling one of the really big cranes. You had to look up to see the top of the tire, much less where he was. And every time they would whistle for a break, he would climb down from his cab and walk around the other side of the machine away from all of us and then it whistled again and he would walk back, climb up and go to work. So one day I decided to find out what he was doing. I climbed up on the rig when he climbed down and walked around. He was sitting on the far side of the rig looking down on the ground and sobbing. This huge guy! So I sat down next to him and he saw me and I kind of patted him on the shoulder and I just sat there with him and he cried and mumbled and talked to himself and cried for a while. And I just sat there keeping him company. And the whistle blew and he blew his nose and he got up and he looked down and said thanks and he went up. The next time I was there, and I saw him and he comes over to me and he says, "Chaplain, I can't thank you for everything you said. I feel so much better." I hadn't said one word. I just sat there with him. He says, "I can't thank you enough for everything you said." He said, "It really helped me."

This encounter reflects so well the power of pastoral presence with a deeply empathic connection and the care, respect, and willingness to seek out the other shown in the creation narratives. In one way the chaplain created a space that the contractor felt contained what he needed to hear; in another way, the chaplain courageously and respectfully entered the space of the other.

Again, we can see how Winnicott's theory of space holding and space affording, the capacity to be together and the capacity to be alone, functions in the pastoral relationship in a similar example of another of the Ground Zero chaplains.

> One night when I was on duty at the morgue, we were going through a quiet spell, so I walked out to one of the "safe" areas. I was watching the firefighters combing through piles of debris, searching for human remains. They, together with the NYPD and the Port Authority Police, gave of themselves completely

in this task. The firefighter group took a break. A group of them were together, resting, having a drink of water or coffee, which the Salvation Army volunteers were bringing round. I noticed one firefighter sitting all alone on an upturned bucket. I picked my way over there, asking how he was doing and wanting to talk with him. He didn't want to talk to me. So, I found a bucket and turned it upside down and sat with him. Not a word was said between us. After a good, long time he got up, turned to me and said "Thank you, Father," and left.

Another difficult moment was when I was called down in to the Pit on another occasion when they had found the remains of a couple of firefighters. I had to wait for the rescue workers to bring them out and place them on a rescue board. I looked around the group standing there and made eye contact with one of the firefighters. He was the one I had sat beside on the bucket a few months earlier. He looked no better that morning than he did that night we sat together. We nodded acknowledgment across the rubble, and eventually when I got back home sometime that morning, I crawled into bed for a few hours with a deep ache in my heart and tears flowing down my cheeks.[29]

The chaplain in this encounter shows, I think, the delicate and exquisite ability to be in relationship with the firefighter without intruding on his aloneness. His empathic doubling of the firefighter provided a physical alliance, showed respect for his not wanting to talk, a willingness to be in pastoral relationship on the firefighter's own terms through joining with him in his silence, which displays an environmental holding that is not often discussed in pastoral care. In such a situation it would have been very easy to either intrude upon the firefighter or simply leave him alone. The expressed wish of the firefighter was not to talk with the chaplain, which he respected, yet it seems clear in the former's expression of gratitude and later acknowledgment across the rubble, that an empathic relationship was created all the same and that the chaplain's presence was not experienced as an impingement but that the two could be alone together.

Winnicott notes "the basis for the capacity to be alone is a paradox; it is the experience of being alone while someone else is present."[30] He goes on to describe this holding while not impinging as "ego-relatedness," which "refers to the relationship between two people, one of whom at any rate is alone; perhaps both are alone, yet the presence of each is important to the other."[31] Winnicott muses that such ego-relatedness may be the very basis of the transference relationship of the adult patient to their therapist. One can posit a similar theory about the ego-relatedness arising in this pastoral encounter where the chaplain supports the firefighter with his silence and bodily presence, perhaps enabling him to do whatever he needed to do alone. Without projecting anything onto the firefighter's psychic state, it is important to note what Winnicott thought happens to the infants when allowed to be alone in the presence of another.

When alone in the sense that I am using the term, and only when alone, the infant is able to do the equivalent of what in the adult world would be called relaxing. The infant is able to become unintegrated, to flounder, to be in a state where there is no orientation, to be able to exist for a time without being either a reactor to an external impingement or an active person with a direction of interest or movement. The stage is set for an id-experience. In this setting the sensation or impulse will feel real and be truly a personal experience.

It will now be seen why it is important that there is someone available, someone present, although present without making demands; the impulse having arrived, the id experience can be fruitful, and the object can be part or the whole of the attendant person, namely the mother. It is only under these conditions that the infant can have an experience which feels real.[32]

It is perhaps in time of disaster that we get closest to this infantile experience, the feeling of being unintegrated, floundering, without direction and shut down to externals, rather than what, in a nondisaster environment, would feel like "relaxing." And yet Winnicott indicates, at least for the infant, this is all part of the process of fruitfully experiencing life from a place of feeling real rather than dissociated. What is needed, however, is a container for the experience, either in the establishment of an "internal environment" that has been built up through experiences of care, or through caring relationships with someone we either know we can trust, such as a friend or colleague, or unconsciously assume we can trust, through a transferential relationship, such as a chaplain whom we may not know but who gives us the space to be alone together. This example shows the care of the pastoral relationship that is so much more than words, a holding of space, a "being with" others in a way that allows them to be with themselves rather than takes them away from themselves.

The need to be alone and *not* impinged upon is powerfully described by Lieutenant William Keegan, the Port Authority Police Department officer in charge of the night shift of the PAPD WTC Late Tour Rescue/Recovery Unit at Ground Zero.

Help is a dangerous weapon in the wrong hands. The CISM [Critical Incident Stress Management] people had their hearts in the right place trying to deal with the mental and emotional health of the workers, but they were just too eager and intrusive. They seemed to assume that if someone refused help, he was screwed up for not knowing he needed it. On the other hand, accepting help meant he was definitely screwed up. Somehow the *help* got lost. It was not unusual for someone to wander off alone for a while to rest, think, or pull himself back together. *Private communion was important to an individual's balance.* The CISM workers didn't understand that. Being alone meant you had a problem.

If they saw someone alone, they descended like locusts with questions: "Are you okay?" "What's the matter?" "Would you like to talk?" "Want to discuss it?" Their demand to be allowed to help was just one more pressure.

> At one point there were so many CISM people trying to find someone to cure, we couldn't take a leak without running into one. Their approach was always the same. "*You okay? Something the matter?*" asked the CISM member. "Nothing's the matter," the worker insisted. "*But you're over here alone, and you have your head down.*" That made the worker angry. "Listen, Jack. Take a look at what we've been doing these last six hours. I *feel* like being alone and putting my head down." "*Being alone can be a sign of*— Of being alone. Go away, please?"[33]

As noted earlier, most often when describing the essence of their chaplaincy at Ground Zero, clergy named it as "ministry of presence," a being present to others without necessarily "doing" anything such as praying, blessing, actively listening, or speaking—something that is missing in Keegan's description of the well-intentioned help of the CISM member above. Chaplain Emile Frische described it in this way, when reflecting upon his experience of ministry to the spouses of those from Cantor Fitzgerald who died in the World Trade Center on September 11.

> "Ministry of presence" would be the best way to describe this. Words were not needed. Making sure they had water, tea, coffee, and tissues—all a very necessary part of my ministry to them. One of these women asked where God was at that time and why did He allow all this to happen. Those two questions were always there. "Where was God right now?" she asked. I looked around at the hotel workers and pointed to them. Then she came out with a statement that just blew me away: "What I need right now is a *God with skin on.*" Isn't this what I am called to be every day of my life—Jesus alive in the world today—"God with skin on" for others?[34]

This ministry of presence is both a symbolic function and it is a relational way of being that reflects in some sense the presence of God with us, even when we don't feel it. Symbolically, a pastoral caregiver represents something that has little to do with them personally, a trust and positive transference in the role of clergy, particularly for those with a religious affiliation. The signs of the pastoral caregiver's identity as a person of God enables others to experience them at times, as this woman so aptly described, in an incarnational sense, a "God with skin on," connecting to their own God images and desires. In the following narrative, the chaplain describes a situation where her symbolic presence takes on a "Moses holding the staff up for the people to see" flavor.

> One day I couldn't get into the site. This was when T. Mort. was at Trinity Place, and I was doing rounds at the site and this one new guy just wouldn't let us in to the site. And then this ironworker comes over after that guy walks away. I was with [*a partner chaplain*] and we were just going to walk around another side or something. . . . And this other guy looked over and he says, "Come

Image 2.3. Flag on top of "the Pile" affixed to the antenna formerly atop the WTC. (Photo by Mike Rieger/FEMA News Photo.)

here" and he took us underground through the subway tunnels and he said, *"I'll show you where you need to be."* And we're just following him and going, "Where on earth are we going?" And we ended up climbing up and ending at the top of the pile where the flag was planted. This guy knew his way in and then he said, "This is good. You'll be up here and then you can see when we find something and then we can see you. *It's good that we can see you and know that you're there."* And then he leaves, and [*my partner chaplain*] and I are going, "I don't think we're supposed to up here, but . . ."

And then this fire chief comes over and we're thinking, "Okay, he's going to kick us out." And he just said, "I'm so glad you're here." And he goes, and he said the same thing as the ironworker, "We can see you and you can see us and we know where to find you, whatever. So just stay here." And so eventually about an hour later they did find remains and we went down and then the ironworker comes back. He had cut out two crosses from a beam. I still have it. I keep it in a drawer next to my bed.

Sometimes a pastoral caregiver's sheer bodily presence may be enough for these deep symbolic connections; at other times a more active role is required. Often, in a disaster, given the rawness of emotion and the level of vulnerability, the identification of the chaplain with those images may be all it takes. In some areas of pastoral ministry, pastoral caregivers need to earn their right to be there. That may not be so in the disaster-response field; however, chaplains can as easily *lose* their right to be there. One chaplain described this reality:

I ran into some [*denominational*] minister who was complaining that they wanted him to bless things [which was not a part of his tradition], and when he left, boy, did they complain about him. They were not happy with that. The sense I had from the firefighters in particular is that they work in a very clearly defined team. And if you're the hose guy you don't deal with the ladder, because lives depend on that. So they had a sense of what the chap-

lain was supposed to do. They might have, because they're mostly Roman Catholic, referred to it as "blessing," but they didn't really care if you were an imam and you came and said your prayer for the dead, that was perfectly fine. But if you said, "No, we don't bless," that wasn't, that's not the right answer.

Maintaining the sense of presence can be a delicate act, which is why it has more to do with creation than application, as much with art as with skill.

This method of creating space, this ministry of presence, is both about the space we hold between us and the other as pastoral persons, and within ourselves. It is a space that needs to be negotiated both internally and externally with those that may be very different from ourselves in culture (racial, ethnic, religious, sexual orientation, and socioeconomic classification), gender, personal characteristics, and professional development.[35] The pastoral caregiver needs to engage in some careful introspection to examine the effect of these elements in their own pastoral and personal formation to enable an openness and facility to work with diverse others who may be more or less conscious of these forces in themselves. Russell Haber notes that "Culture unconsciously and intuitively shapes our definition, experience, projection, and expectation of day to day living."[36] Such a comment reminds us that the pastoral space, even though it may be negotiated very quickly, is never a given but is generally earned. Some professional cultures or clinical venues are more defined subcultures in themselves. A chaplain working in a psychiatric hospital may find it a very different culture than in a general hospital. Many chaplains working on disaster sites find themselves paradoxically treated with deference by the uniformed services and also excluded if they do not fit the culture of what chaplaincy means in such context.

At Ground Zero chaplains had to negotiate pastoral relationships in a multiplicity of cultures and power structures. From the FDNY (Fire Department of the City of New York) with its distinctly different subcultures of firefighters, EMTs, and paramedics, to the PAPD (Port Authority Police Department), whose responsibility included the World Trade Center, to the NYPD (New York Police Department), to the medical examiners, those from the FBI, OEM (New York City Mayor's Office of Emergency Management), the ironworkers, and other involved parties. Each culture is very different and the way one builds rapport and a pastoral alliance may be very different indeed from one to another.

Here one is reminded of Winnicott's theory of the "True Self" with its ability to act creatively and spontaneously, both qualities needed in pastoral care with such diverse cultures. Winnicott states in terms of the early formation of the True Self, "The spontaneous gesture is the True Self in action. Only the True Self can be creative and only the True Self can feel real."[37] Later the True Self becomes more of an inner reality rather than a seemingly separate organization in the psyche, but it is from this place that a continued sense of being real and creative is drawn. One chaplain reflected on a similar theme in discussing the essence of ministry, saying it was about "being real with people. Letting them tell their stories if they want to tell them. If not, letting them be. Inviting them to participate, but not insisting upon it. Mostly being real with them. . . . Not pretending that you have the answers or anything like that."

The external holding in relationship was often reflected in an internal holding. One chaplain described this as "holding the space" and "witnessing."

> I'd make [going to St. Paul's Chapel] as part of my rounds. I'd walk in, get some coffee, get some food, whatever time it was there was always hot food being made—whether it was midnight or two o'clock in the afternoon there was always food going on. Because I always knew I had to take care of myself, so I always made sure I ate and drank. And everybody else I found who I saw that wasn't, I'd remind them. And so I'd stop in and I'd see people that we knew from face to face out in the areas and I'd just sit down with somebody and just talk. That was our whole job, was talking to people. And praying and the blessing and all of that was our duty. But our job was to talk to people or to just be with people. *Just to sit and hold a space.*
>
> Some people wouldn't talk to us at all, they were in too much anger. We represented God and God wasn't who they wanted to talk to right now. And we learned to just be in the space without being in their personal space to see who around them [needed care], but just by being there. I think everybody had a turn-around after a while. I think everybody got over that anger and began to allow God back into the equation, just because we were there. Not that we wanted anybody to become religious, but we were *trying to hold the space for them* to come back to. A place of not hating, of not denying that spirit still lived. That there was spirit in all of us that still lived. That within each of us there's a spark of the divine and we can go on. And so we were caretakers and that's what chaplains do.

This chaplain describes a "holding of space" that is bounded on one side by the divine, represented by the chaplain, and on the other side the divine whose "spark" (or image) is in those to whom the chaplain is ministering. Here, the process of care not only can be interpreted in a trinitarian way, but also the relationship between God, the chaplain, and the workers.

In many pastoral situations sensitively holding that space may be enough of a pastoral intervention. In pastoral work we may find that often all that is needed is to allow the other to tell their story and to receive it, empathically hold it without interpretation or transformation. By sharing their story, those we care for may experience transformation in simple revelation, where in the space between two persons one's experience of being known and accepted, being held in relationship, is in itself a gift.

At other times more verbal and seemingly active care or interventions are required. Sometimes it is as simple as asking the right question in the right way. Other times it requires the use of what Gerald Egan terms "advanced empathy," and another time it may require the chaplain to be present and companion the person physically, not just verbally. The former is shown in this pastoral encounter.

> I was sitting in [*a firehouse*] one day with a couple of fire [officers] who were in charge of the phones, waiting for calls. And there was one of the shift captains sitting at a desk, and [*another chaplain*] was there, and we were talking about what it had been like on the very first [day]. And [the other chaplain] just turned to him and said to him. "So where were you on the day that it happened?" And he began to talk. And he told us how he'd been in [*another part of the city*]. And he had left the shift September tenth, the night shift at [*his firehouse*] and driven back home to [*his borough*] and was just getting there when it all happened. And of course the bridges were all closed and he couldn't get in and all. He struggled to get back here. And getting back here and starting on the cleanup of the rubble and realizing how many men of his own company were gone and he was alive and he talked for an hour and fifteen minutes straight. And then he said, "Well, that's probably about it." And he put his helmet on and he put his jacket on and he walked out. The lieutenant turned to us and said, "He hasn't said to us word one about his whole experience here since 9/11. Not one word."

Again, we can see that the skills needed to hold are as basic as building a pastoral alliance, using careful attending and listening skills, and the ability to engage in basic empathic attunement and reflection (where we "reflect the person's experience, feelings and behavior, identify core messages, and listen to the context"[38]). And they are as difficult as a more advanced empathy (which makes the implied explicit, identifies themes, builds bridges between feelings, experience, and behaviors, and enables the person to both trust themselves and the carer enough to share more fully[39]) and the process of holding our own countertransference reactions.

Although Egan accurately describes the skills of advanced empathy, the challenge it presents is that to attune empathically to the other is not simply a cognitive process of "demonstrating empathy," but an affective one, where one *feels with* the other. One chaplain described the in-the-moment experience of this empathic attunement:

> Now part of the task is "being present." So, if a fireman's there and he's crying, I'm crying. I'm not crying because he's crying so that I can *demonstrate empathy*. We're both reacting together equally in that sense. But would I upon occasion, during a shift, go around the corner and weep? No. So part

of what *authenticity* is in a case like this is being fully present. Part of the way one could logically but inaccurately take from what I'm saying is that emotions would somehow be withheld or avoided or renounced or hidden. Quite the contrary, quite the contrary.

Another chaplain describes almost a need for the opposite, simply to hold to the task of blessing the remains down in the Pit.

My big thing was I never wanted to cry. I just was like, while everybody's saluting and doing alright, and the one thing the chaplain cannot do as they put the radio to his mouth, he can not choke up. Just say something. I would really have to go into a place of *being present but also removing myself*, and after I spoke coming back to be fully present. Because for me to be fully present and to speak and to really take people in and look them in the eye and everything else, I think I would have really lost my shit, so to speak, on a fairly regular basis. And I probably would have been asked never to come back. But, you know, I would do it again.

The empathic challenge of being present leads to the kind of building of relationship that can hold even the most difficult of material, not simply our grief and trauma, but the ways that can transform into the worst of who we are and what we can do to ourselves and others. In such pastoral care, the chaplain needs to be aware of the possibilities of suicidal and homicidal ideation.

And I remember one day; it was in March. It was about two o'clock in the morning and I was walking around the Pit and I encountered, just outside that mobile fire station on the east side, a guy fully dressed in [fire] gear perfectly clean. And I stopped to talk to him. And he started telling me his story that on "the day of" he went in with nine men and he was the only one that came out. And that was the first day that he had been able to go back and he had never been able to go down into the Pit. And we sat and talked for a couple of hours. He told me how his life was falling apart. How he had no relationship with his wife or his children anymore. And how he really didn't know what he was going to do. So I asked him if he'd like to pray with me. And by then he knew I was a rabbi and he was a nice Irish Catholic fireman. He said, "I don't know? What are we going to pray?" I says, "Well, how about we start with 'Our Father Who Art In . . .' He says, "You know that prayer?" I said, "Yeah." And we prayed and we talked some more and I said, "I'll tell you what? How about if I go with you and we go down into the Pit?" He looked at me and said, "Well, maybe we could do that." And that roadway bridge was finally complete, so we walked down that. And we walked from area to area where people were working and we spoke to some of the people in the Pit and I guess about five in the morning he says, "Well, you know, I think I have to get home." And he thanked me and we talked a little bit more and then he left. And a day later when I got home there was a message on my phone from him. And he said, "I want to tell you that I came down there that day looking to say goodbye to the world and *planning to commit suicide*. And thank you for what you did. I think I have the strength to find my way back."

The chaplain who companioned this suicidal firefighter gave both time and person to this care. He notes that he spent two hours talking with the firefighter. Also of note is that he attuned both to the firefighter's own religious tradition, in the offer to prayer the Lord's Prayer that was not from his tradition, and to the perhaps unexpressed desire to go down into the Pit. In this way, it appears that the chaplain spiritually and pastorally, as well as physically, went down into the Pit with the firefighter. Although the latter's suicidal ideation was not expressed during the pastoral encounter and consequently the chaplain did not explore intent, plans, and means to commit suicide, he did realize that this was someone that needed the kind of care that meant that he would walk with him in the empty places. It seems that the emotional and spiritual holding, which Winnicott would call "ego-support" or "ego-relatedness," enabled the firefighter to work past his desire for physical annihilation, perhaps in identification with the nine men of his company that were annihilated in the towers.

One chaplain related another scenario early in his ministry after 9/11. In it he described a literal "holding" of the "bad object."

> I was hanging out at Seaman's Institute [one of the early informal respite centers] and I was sitting there pretty much like this and this guy walked over to me and said, "Here, *hold this*." It was his gun belt, weapon included. And then he sat down opposite me and started talking. And it blew my mind because cops didn't do that. It's called "surrendering your weapon." I mean, that's the way it's phrased. You *don't* "surrender your weapon." First, my initial impression was he was suicidal, but he wasn't, *he was homicidal*. He wanted to shoot his boss. So I talked to him for forty-five minutes or so and handed it back over to him. . . . It's one of the other things, healthy things, that chaplains provide, that priests provide, the collar, whatever, and that sanctuary. You want people to feel safe. And they very often do. Not always, but very often they do. And that happened pretty often. At the respite center at the T. Mort., at St. Paul's, wherever—that medieval sense of sanctuary.[40]

Often clergy are trained to look for suicidal ideation, but they don't necessarily hear the threat of homicidal inclination. In this case the police officer certainly had the means to commit homicide, and certainly a fantasy directed at a particular individual, if not a plan. In his conscious and deliberate handing over of his weapon, however, and the chaplain's respectful realization of the magnitude of that gesture, the intent to commit the act appears to have been mitigated. In this case it seems that what we may call institutional transference, what the chaplain termed as "sanctuary," symbolized by the clerical collar and office, provided the safety in the relationship that the police officer could not just hand over his weapon but also had to give his story to the chaplain to hold. Despite hesitations in hindsight that we the readers may have, the chaplain discerned that there was no immediate threat to either the officer's boss or himself and handed the weapon back.

Such symbols of the pastoral office became important for those who did not normally have them in a way that made them immediately identifiable. This was both about role and representation. One chaplain discussed this in terms of the ministry:

> I'm suppose to be a symbol of "the presence of God." To be a mouthpiece for His word and to be one to give the assurance of His grace. But, [*another chaplain*] recognized to be a symbol of God's presence he had to be recognizable so he bought a black [clerical] shirt. Not that the black shirt does a thing. . . . But it's the assurance of God's presence, the church's presence at least.

Another chaplain shared,

> When I was blessing the remains I always prayed for the families, whoever's family it was, husband, wife, daughter, son, uncle, aunt, and all of them. It was a peaceful time for me, really. Apart from the first couple of days. But for me to pray over the remains, even the smallest, smallest part. Sometimes it would be a couple of little pieces of bone they would have there and that was amazing, too. To be invited to pray over the remains of that person and that's all you saw. So you know *this* was a person. And just the marvel of that nothing. . . . For me to see how some of the medical examiners handled the smallest part of the remains, too, was really, really great, the respect and the dignity in there. So my prayer sort of piggy-backed on, off, and on the way that I saw them handling the remains, too. But for me it was a prayer of hope. In a way grateful that the families were not there to see that. I think it gave a deeper freedom in a way you could pray. Maybe it's not right but it's what I felt at that time. . . . To pray that wherever they thought their heaven was they'd be there, whatever name they gave to it, no more suffering, no more pain for them. And just praying whatever name they gave to God, *that this God would be holding them safe in his arms* and that was usually the prayer somewhere. That would be the main part of my prayer for them.

Such situations show that "Holding," although it can sound like an easy catch-all phrase, is no simple task. Holding the story, holding the person, holding the object, holding to the task, all require immense emotional and spiritual resources for the pastoral caregiver to hold their own reactions and countertransference. To do this the chaplains needed to be held themselves. Remembering Winnicott's description of maternal care as both environmental and personal, it is helpful to see what were the holding places, processes, and relationships that enabled the chaplains to continue this ministry over nine months.

Holding of the Pastoral Caregiver

The "friendship and support" of others had a large impact on the chaplaincy at Ground Zero. It is to be remembered that "A significant issue involved with compassion fatigue is isolation."[41] It was important for the chaplains, therefore, to maintain both a sense of community with those within the recovery effort as well as, for many, to be able to talk to those outside of it that could be trusted to hold the confidence.

Although, after mid-November, when the chaplaincy came under the auspices of the American Red Cross (ARC), the chaplains worked singly on each shift, some of them built or continued relationship with each other that provided a degree of self-care and what has popularly been called "debriefing."[42] One chaplain noted that he and another chaplain "debriefed quite a bit over martinis over this, but we kind of [talked about] the things we've noticed." Another chaplain shared his concern in saying that the part of his experience that bothered him most was that

> . . . there was no organized support for the chaplains. I mean, there wasn't for the ironworkers either, but the police and the fire department had more recourse. And we were volunteers, so we weren't on staff doing this, so we had no medical or coverage for what we were doing. And there was no debriefing for us, [so] we kind of debriefed each other. I had two other minister friends, we had a buddy system between the three of us, because we were all working either with the families or here [at Ground Zero] and we could call each other 24/7 with whatever it was.

This connecting with other chaplains was done primarily outside the shifts. A couple of the chaplains highlighted the fact that "defusing," the ten- to twenty-minute postshift conversation that happened at the Family Assistance Centers, did not happen at the T. Mort. This was perhaps in large part due to the small number of chaplains, whereas at the Family Assistance Centers, at least in the early stages, a SAIR (ARC Spiritual Care Aviation Incident Response) team member was assigned to oversee the shift and defuse the chaplains. At the T. Mort. there was no such oversight and the chaplains coming on for the next shift prepared themselves for their own experience. Approximately 55 percent of the chaplains who completed the questionnaire said they never participated in a defusing. Most who did participate in defusing, when asked how often, responded with "occasionally," "not often," or a number from once to two or three times. Only one chaplain said, "Almost every shift." Another chaplain noted that they had participated in defusing "Always, until at T. Mort." One chaplain, in speaking about the ministry to the workers at Ground Zero, went on to speak about the chaplains:

> People's emotions were sort of on edge. . . . You could tell they [the EMTs] were anxious or, I wouldn't say depressed, they were kind of steeled. That was like they weren't allowing themselves to feel anything. Including the chaplains. The chaplains had steeled themselves to come on duty. They were not ready to really debrief you. [Those coming in for the next shift] were kind of "Okay, I'm going to do this. I volunteered to do this. I'm going to do this." And so I tried a couple of times. I felt there was a big resistance to that. And that's fine and so I just backed off. I said, "They're just like me, just trying to get in and out and do the shift to cope with whatever came up."

Later, when sharing about debriefing, this chaplain went on to say, "And of course it was never really done for us until the end, after it was over. . . . Nobody debriefed us, never." When asked about defusing the chaplain noted that the chaplains would

> . . . chat a little, but mostly, they'd seen it, they'd been there, and they didn't really need. . . . They didn't really feel they were there to be your defuser. And there were no mental health people there. We'd go down and find mental health people at the end when they had the bubble [Salvation Army tent, also know as the 'Taj Mahal']. But they were not trained to be the debriefers. So there was nobody, really. You just had to work it out on your own.

Another of the chaplains, however, shared that it may have had to do with the process for defusing or debriefing that was set up and did not work with the chaplains. One chaplain, in commenting in their questionnaire on defusing, said, "This was a joke." This may have been partly due to having to go off-site for "debriefing" rather than it being available on-site. However, that may have simply underlined the clash of cultures, where the debriefers needed to be peers rather than people seemingly disconnected from the disaster.

> I remember, it must have been two or three weeks after I was working down here at Ground Zero, the Red Cross got themselves organized and said we're going to have debriefing teams so when you come off a shift, you have to come back up to the [Red Cross] building and come to debriefing. So the first shift after that dictum came down, I came off my shift and I came back up and went up to the debriefing. And here were these three people, a man in a suit and tie and women, well dressed and well coiffed and I'm walking in just off my shift

and somebody said to me, "How do you feel?" I said, "You guys got to be kidding. *This is what debriefing is? "How do I feel?"*[43] Do you have any idea what's going on?" I think they were embarrassed. I said to them, "What you need to do is go down there, experience what it looks like, smells like, feels like, and then come back here and I'll help you." And I left and never went back.

We formed our own groups. We would, on every shift, all get together at one point and when nobody was calling for us, we'd take some time off and go together. Whoever was on shift at the time: chaplains, sometimes, we'd do it with, depending on the M[edical] E[xaminer]. Some of the MEs were very armored, really held themselves separate, and I guess they're doing that every day, they have to. I guess they can't get terribly involved with what's going on. But with the chaplains and sometimes with some of the police we were working, crime-scene people, who had to photograph everything, they had to see everything. And we'd talk about our experiences and how we were feeling and what we were feeling and what would help us and what wouldn't help us. We talked to some of the general workers, some of the FEMA workers who were kind of in an upper level and were in the organizational level of FEMA. And we'd talk to them about how they were feeling about doing what they were doing. And afterwards, some of us would get together either in person or on the phone and we'd talk about how we felt, what happened.

And it's remarkable, I think—I don't know if you're going to find it with everybody—but all the ones I spoke with, for those of us that had the ability to stay, I hate to use this word, but we were easily able to unload daily stuff and take a deep breath and do whatever we had to do for the next day or two before we came back and not come back with the baggage from the time before. The people that I talked and counseled with who had the most difficulty were overwhelmed with it and couldn't come back and needed to really work through stuff.

It is notable that the discussion of how one was feeling was acceptable with peers. Here, there was a sense of community and connection that transformed such topics with an air of solidarity and collegiality.

Two other chaplains, however, were more receptive when the American Red Cross sent someone to St. Paul's Chapel, to do debriefing, intentionally taking advantage of the opportunities when they felt it was right for them.

They had a, I guess a psychologist, come by at St. Paul's Chapel at one point and she said, "Would you like to talk about your experience with me?" And I said, "No, thanks. Maybe later." I saw her later and I did. And she just listened and asked questions and brought some things out and I found it helpful to talk about it with her guidance, her compassion.

> There was a Red Cross person at St. Paul's, a woman, who was there to debrief volunteers. And she asked what I was doing. And I don't know how she found out—well, I did have my collar on, that's why, had my hat with the cross on it—and she realized, and she came over and she talked with me for about ten or fifteen minutes or something like that. A very professionally done way of letting me unload just a bit . . . asking me how it was going, how I felt. If I felt that it was a kind of a nurturing thing, if it was something that was viable and important for me to do. I think that was [what she was] trying to bring to it. And I was able to talk through a little bit of that with her. And I found it very helpful.

The approach of coming to the chaplain, accepting no for an answer but also leading in with "How's it going?" rather than "How are you feeling?" mirrored the chaplain's own ministry: respectful, appropriate to the site, mission oriented but empathic, as this chaplain says, "nurturing."

Others had friends that they relied upon outside the chaplaincy and Ground Zero communities. This seemed vital for maintaining a sense of the connection of both "worlds" and the integration of functioning between the True Self and that compliant, adaptive self structure which is also necessary. A chaplain shared,

> I'm eternally grateful to my friend [name], who at the time lived near me, and when I would come home from working a shift, would call her up and we would go out and eat. And to just sit over maybe two beers or so and in part it helped, because one of the things I needed to do was to get the smell out of my nostrils, you know, it would last with me through the evening. And so it was just really great to just sit with somebody who really understood, kind of like I didn't have to stay alone and whatever I said was what I said and that's it. I think I unloaded whatever I needed to unload at the time, while at the same time to just kind of, with her help, being pulled back into the reality of life. And here we are, life is going on and what have you. I mean it, I think that really helped.

A number of chaplains found their existing resources of such holding relationships with their psychotherapists and spiritual directors immensely helpful during their chaplaincy. Others sought out professionals such as clinical psychologists, psychotherapists, and psychiatrists during or after the chaplaincy. Almost 40 percent of the responding chaplains reported an increase in emotional care such as counseling, psychotherapy, psychoanalysis, or another associated therapy. This could be an increase in the amount of sessions or a beginning of therapy in some way. Another 15 percent reported no change in one or another of the modalities.

As the chaplaincy at Ground Zero finished, many of the chaplains who had continued to work through the nine months were offered the opportunity to have what some termed as a "debriefing," and others as "an exit interview." The language around the term *debriefing* has become problematic. There are both popular uses of the term and more specific clinical uses. Many have simply focused on the former, which has come to mean a post-event conversation with a trained debriefer or mental health professional, often on a one-to-one basis rather than ICISF's (International Critical Incident Stress Foundation) seven-stage, two- to three-hour, structured group process, which generally has three to four debriefers and up to twenty or so participants. Debriefing itself is part of a whole array of interventions that includes one-to-one conversations, but the term *debriefing* is reserved for the group process. Forty-two percent of the responding chaplains said that they had participated in one or more debriefings over a period from the last day of shift to sixteen months after Ground Zero closed. These show the confusion of terminology as these debriefings ranged from the exit interview to a group gathering without any facilitators to trainings. The diversity in many ways met the differing needs of some of the chaplains, as can be seen in the following two reflections.

> Then there were intentional debriefings later. We had a meeting at St. James that was led by people that had dealt with catastrophe. And it was debriefing for us, but it was also training in traumatology. So we all sat around this table and we shared our experiences. And I mean there were a lot of tears. I wasn't particularly crying, but *I was feeling people's pain and I told my story and it was painful*. But everybody in that room knew what I was talking about. And I knew what they were talking about. I could feel with them as well as think with them. But that was good to be able to share. To have a whole day devoted to us, to our needs.

> I organized, executed, and participated in a retreat for T. Mort. chaplains, which was kind of a unique thing. Only time that happened specifically for that. And I got LDRNY [Lutheran Disaster Response—New York] and the Lutheran Center to provide some money for T. Mort. chaplains to get together with [other] T. Mort. chaplains. This, and it only happened once, it was distressing to [some people] that T. Mort. chaplains could get together and work with each other and be healthy, without having someone [like an external facilitator] there . . . to help.

In the questionnaire, chaplains were given the space of three paragraphs and given the incomplete sentence, "Three things I would like to tell new disaster-response chaplains are . . ." One chaplain simply wrote, "I. Debrief. II. Debrief. III. Debrief." When asked about it during the interview when he was sharing his dismay at the lack of defusing and debriefing during the chaplaincy he said, "Yes, that's right! That's right! I mean it was a wonderful thing when you could finally tell your story."

Research on "Compassion Fatigue among Chaplains, Clergy and Other Respondents after September 11th"[44] indicates that the chaplains who worked solely with the Red Cross showed fewer symptoms of compassion fatigue and burn-out than those who worked at multiple sites. Stephen Roberts, Kevin Ellers, and John Wilson suggest that "Clergy who participated in defusing sessions, which low-ered clergy isolation, on a regular basis when working after a disaster were at lower risk for compassion fatigue than those who did not participate."[45] We can see that as far as the chaplains at the T. Mort. are concerned, this was not necessarily the case for them. However, I suggest that one contributing factor, rather than defusing sessions, may be the holding and boundary setting provided by having both a fixed beginning and end to a shift, and also a schedule, that became a once-per-week deployment for the T. Mort. chaplains, which enabled a continuity sustainable over the months. One can see the contrast in one T. Mort. chaplain's encounters with what became known as one of "the Pit chaplains," early on in the recovery process:

> And I remember there was a kid down there from the Salvation Army, from [*another country*]. He had been down there since Friday and he hadn't slept. He was a chaplain, African American gentleman. And they just left him down there. He had been there, he hadn't slept or anything. I got down there on Monday or Tuesday and they said, "Well, we're having a hard time bringing up this recovery." And I said, "I'll just walk down the ramp," which nobody is really allowed to do. I'm just going to walk down the ramp and check it out. And he was down there at the bottom with the fireman and his eyes are like saucers. And I could tell he was gone, he was totally frazzled . . . like immo-bilized. And I sort of chatted with him and got him back down to reality a little bit. And I said, "Why don't you walk up with me and we'll just sort of lead the [body out]? They need us to lead them out," because the firemen seemed to be grieving, too. So I said, "Let's you and I walk up here," and so they gave us a microphone and I said the Lord's Prayer. And I hear the Lord's Prayer echo-ing through everybody's radio in the entire place. Oh, my goodness. And he said some prayers and then we got it out. But I could see there was no care given for a lot of the Salvation Army chaplains. They were just totally left on their own. So I'll give Red Cross credit that we had fixed times, definite shifts, and you were expected not to go beyond that.

The importance of realistically time-limited shifts enabled the chaplains to be able to give their all when present, as contrasted with the young Salvation Army chaplain that seemed to be in a state of sheer exhaustion, physically, emotionally, and spiritually. One chaplain described the efficacy of the holding of a shift for himself:

> Part of what can *hold me together* while I'm going through it is also *holding in my head* the notion that some time later today or tonight, before you go to sleep tonight if no time sooner, at the point of doing that you're going to be

able to breathe the air and you will be separated from this. This is not mine, this is somebody else's. And that's what helps me. It sounds crazy, it's almost like *I hold it out to myself* as that will be the treat later on. Of just, you will eventually be able to do that. And because of that, it enables me to stay longer and be present without feeling I've got to get out or I can't handle this. It *holds me in check*, of being able to realize, you can do this for somebody else because eventually you're going to leave. And that also makes me as best as I can, to *hold on to remembering* it's not about me.

In an earlier description of empathy, one chaplain spoke about "reacting together equally" with the workers at Ground Zero. This equality was two-way. One transformative factor for the chaplains was the sense of community with those they were ministering to and alongside. In this they were both held to the task and cared for in the task by the workers around them. This communal holding is exemplified in one chaplain's experience with the firefighters he worked alongside.

I don't know if you have the [media] picture of the last day when they were taking out the last piece of steel? When they were ready to do that and they were organizing who was going to stand where and who was going to do what. And I was at 10/10 [Firehouse] at the time and the chief came in and said, "Uniformed service personnel are going to line up over here." And somebody said, *"Well, what about the chaplain?"* And he said, "No, no, no this is only for uniformed service personnel, not chaplains." And all the firemen there said, "Well, fine, if he doesn't go, we're not going." So I went. We got the important appreciation from the people we worked with.

Like the sense of sanctuary described for the police officer that handed over his weapon, that sense of sanctuary persisted for the chaplain, too, in the respite centers. One chaplain noted that "It's like life revolved around the respite centers." One chaplain after another in the interviews, however, consistently and favorably mentioned one such center—St. Paul's Chapel, the small Episcopal church that is a chapel of Trinity, Wall Street, immediately adjacent to Ground Zero, which had survived the destruction. This became a place of haven for both rescue workers and chaplains alike. A chaplain enthused, "The ministry that was done at St. Paul's was phenomenal. The fact is it was the worst comfort in terms of a respite center. The food was not as good as the rest. But it was the most popular, because it was a church." In a similar vein, another chaplain shared,

St. Paul's [was] where they'd come in and cry, they'd come in and fall asleep. It was where you didn't have to be strong. You were allowed to not be the strong one there and nobody was going to put you down. And you could do it alone. You could do it together. It was where you could be and nobody was going to bother you and you had all the help around you that if you wanted it. St. Paul's really truly was a haven. It was filthy. It was a haven.

Another chaplain described, "It's your meaning of sanctuary. It was a sanctuary. But [it is] just circumstance that St. Paul's is sitting there."

This sense of respite and self-care was more complex for the chaplains as they often considered themselves still on duty for the workers at the respite centers rather than having respite themselves.

> The transformational moments were really in the St. Paul's processing of the event coming back. Sitting in the back row, sitting next to someone who's crying and someone else on the other side who's eating a sandwich and having the music play . . . it wasn't exactly a normalizing experience but it's somehow that sense that we're going to get through this together. It was very transformative. Maybe that's another part of how I survived, I don't know.

> St. Paul's was just such a very special place. It was nice to go there and be able to have a couple of moments, like these people were. . . . Sometimes you'd end up being the chaplain. But there were people there who took care of people so well. You can just see on the faces, the people, where it's one thing to do the work, but when you think about it how it all comes, it impacts you when you just have a moment to let your brain actually start to get around it.

Like most sites, many continued their pastoral task but it also gave the chaplains an opportunity to be cared for themselves. As noted earlier, as well as ministry as a respite center, one of the strands of early Ground Zero ministry functioned from this location. Therefore, many Episcopal clergy who were chaplains at the T. Mort. felt strongly connected to St. Paul's Chapel both through denominational affiliation and site of ministry. However, both rabbis and other Christian clergy at Ground Zero attested to the breadth of the ministry at St. Paul's.

> As sad as the whole event is, I don't remember a time that I felt . . . well, maybe because we could go to St. Paul's. You know, if you thought, if it was getting a little too much. Just go and have a cup of coffee and someone would be playing the piano or there would be that strange little Eucharist going on while people have their sandwiches and that seemed comforting somehow.

> All the people in St. Paul's, they were never in the Pit, but they were with everybody all the time, they heard all the stories. So we could sit and talk. And when somebody from St. Paul's or somebody from the different chaplain's offices who were down there, when somebody like that said to you, "How are you?," you could actually tell them. To everybody else we knew it was polite and we all said, "We're fine, thank you."

And its uniqueness was, of course, it was open up to people of all faiths. But it became the setting, became the time for people to reflect more than you could in any other place. . . . Where they could have an opportunity, being a quiet space, to reflect. And a house of God I think was just more impactive.

This shows that the care and hospitality provided at St. Paul's Chapel both to recovery workers and to the chaplains themselves was seen not simply as a physical or even an emotional activity but spiritually, as a house of God, caring for the whole person. One Christian chaplain said, "That was a place where I really felt like that's what church is all about and that's the body of Christ fully working as an organism where everything was for the greater good and, I would say, for the glory of God what everything everybody did. You know, the musicians playing, the people serving the food, the people providing physical help and aide. It was all just wonderful."

Away from the disaster site, other things held the chaplains. Among these were the ministries they exercised in pastoral fields other than disaster-response ministry. For those that had spouses or partners to go home to, the holding was sometimes both emotional and physical. Several chaplains commended the incredible care they got from their partners who were there to care for them after they returned from caring for others, and who bore the challenge of their exhaustion and frustration. One noted, "And she was willing to listen to everything that I had to say, so if I needed to talk about something that happened that night, she was okay to listen to it. And that, I think probably was the best debriefing of all, because *she would hold me.* . . . sometimes when I was just saddened while she was holding me I could cry and get it out."

For many it was their daily prayer life that held them. A number of the chaplains interviewed described the daily office or other forms of formal prayer as being very important for them during the time of their ministry at the T. Mort. Others described a renewed sense of personal prayer and meditation. A few described the desire to pray in calm, peace-filled places, such as in nature, by the ocean, or in front of "a meaningful stained-glass window of Christ at the Cathedral of St. John the Divine." Others described intercessory prayer during the evening news or over the newspaper's pictures of the 9/11 dead. Twenty-one percent of the responding chaplains noted an increase in their practice of daily liturgy, as well as of journaling begun or increased in frequency. For 48 percent, the same was true for meditation; 39 percent increased the use of a spiritual director; 75 percent increased the practice of prayer, while 24 percent reported no change. Three people reported a decrease in daily liturgy, journaling, or meditation. Other increases noted had to do with Bible reading, contemplating nature, listening to music, and "serious talks with God."

Eighteen percent reported no change in any of their spiritual practices during their chaplaincy. These ranged from those that spent two days at the T. Mort., to those that spent twenty-four days, from a Greek Orthodox priest to a Franciscan brother. However, these numerical results need to be interpreted in light of subjective reporting. Compare two chaplains' reports of "No change" in any of their spiritual practices to their later comments:

> I found most helpful the regular round of praying the daily office and daily Eucharist and spending an hour each day in personal prayer, which is my normal pattern. I did not see my spiritual director any more often but the dynamic of the sessions was intensified because she, too, worked at Ground Zero as a chaplain (but not at T. Mort.).

> I have never felt so proud being a priest as during those months of work at Ground Zero. I was proud to be a priest, to help in an area which was new for me—and to try and be in some small and insignificant way the presence of Christ and the church to tired and hurt people. I still have my clothes that I wore down there—hat, shirt, etc., unwashed and in a box.

Religious attitudes reported may give a clearer picture. Seventy-nine percent of the reporting chaplains found "personal prayer" was more meaningful. Forty-eight percent found congregational life more meaningful during their chaplaincy, the same for their usual ministry. Fifty-eight percent wrote that preaching seemed more meaningful, and 42 percent found the same for Scripture. Of the reporting chaplains, 67 percent found that liturgy was more meaningful, with only two chaplains finding it less so. A number of the chaplains shared that their use of the daily office, often individual liturgical prayer of the church, had decreased but their extemporaneous and spontaneous prayer to God had increased. Returning to the idea of holding, one can see the impact on the prayer life in the example from the following chaplain:

> I kept up the daily routine, the morning and evening prayer, and mass. But by the other times of prayer, my style of prayer isn't so much in discussion, in the form of asking God to do certain things as much as it is thinking about Him just *holding up certain people in prayer*. I know that there's someone with God in mind, they're friends of God and mine and just holding them up and God knows what they need. If I had been having a conversation with someone, during my prayer time I would picture that person in my mind and *hold them in the presence of God*. Sometimes it was one of the fire chiefs who was talking with somebody and told him to go home and the person didn't want to go home and there was an argument and the fire chief finally insisted that he leave and go. And I remember *holding up that incident in prayer*. Not knowing the other person's name or anything else, not seeing the face because I was seeing it from the back and hearing the voices. But it was holding up the incident as if it was. I would be holding things up in prayer in that sort of general sense. Because very often my prayer is holding up particular people and events, just in silent meditation and that was the thing that was impacting me then.

A number of chaplains described a change in their form of prayer or ability to pray. One chaplain noted that his prayer used to be "more intercessory, now it is more to do with extolling the glory of God." Another chaplain felt a greater intensity and meaningfulness to the words of prayer: "I just think of words like 'Deliver us from evil.' All of a sudden I got an understanding of that as opposed to, I can't think of anything in my life where I would say, 'That's what Jesus was talking about, that's why you pray that line.'" Others described the sense of a greater authenticity, deepening, and sincerity in their prayers, such as the following chaplain:

> Much more sincere, much more sincere. Because it gave the meaning, the Jewish prayer ritual has communal prayer at least said privately three times a day. And *the first three blessings* have their own key points. The *second blessing deals with death, deals with the resurrection, deals with the value of life*, and I don't think I ever, you know. . . . Other activities have occurred, private losses and friends who passed away. So 9/11 was not the only time I recognized in a personal sense the impact of what someone's life may have had upon me. Throughout life I've had those experiences. But as a collective activity, surely prayer, especially praying at Ground Zero, especially that first year when you still had the rescue workers, and the Hanukkah and Passover, High Holy Day program we had that first year, sure, it took a special meaning.

One chaplain noted that the fatigue level meant that they couldn't pray in the same way as they would keep falling asleep, so they began "praying in snippets," and found this profound particularly at Ground Zero. Several chaplains found their ability to engage in the daily office destroyed, yet found a sense of transformation through the process of connecting both with God and others in a new way. One chaplain who struggled deeply with God, theodicy, and anger about the terrorist attacks ended up saying, "I think because of all of that, too, my whole relationship with Him has deepened. I can say that honestly, not in a pious way but in a real way."

As intimated by the anecdotes surrounding the Oklahoma City disaster response, it seemed like the chaplaincy at Ground Zero had a deep spiritual impact, which made people assess their daily lives, ministries, relationships with others and with God. Unlike those anecdotes, however, none of the chaplains who filled in a questionnaire left the ministry, only one in his mid-sixties retired, a couple picked up different ministries, and two returned either to chaplaincy or parish ministry as a response to their experience at Ground Zero.

Finally, one chaplain's reflections on the changes to his prayer life show the kind of theology that can emerge out of disaster-response ministry, such as that after September 11th at Ground Zero.

> The interesting thing, this is now would be four and half years later, last spring. . . . Just the week before he died I was talking to [*my spiritual director*] and I

said, "I've basically stopped praying the daily office." And he made great fun of that, he said, "Well, you don't pray, you don't, you know." But that kind of personal devotion in a strict form has just not been useful to me, less and less so. I used to be regular every day, morning and evening prayer. Well, you probably are still required to. And I found that more and more I need to do things like sit and meditate. And I find informal times to pray, so that *my prayer life has turned around totally*. Over the course of years, but . . . Yeah, I can't do morning and evening prayer unless someone else is there and if I got down to just reading the lessons at some point, and then I just stopped doing it all together. I'm happier to sit for ten minutes and just say, "Okay, just be quiet." Am I crazy to say this? I think that, so much of what we do is agnosticism, a sort of reading to God. And my sense is that God knows all this stuff. We say this intellectually. *But then you have an event like this and you come to know part of the horrors that God already knows*. And you think, Why am I needing to say, "Have mercy on your servants"? Why don't I wait and see what God has to say to me?

This idea of coming to understand that in a disaster, and the more traumatic spaces of any pastoral relationship, a pastoral caregiver comes to know part of the horrors God already knows, to represent God in the midst of those horrors, and to discover the presence of God in the spaces where that horror takes place, is reminiscent of Augustine's description of the image of God in the human person as involving memory, understanding, and will, and through these all the love of God that we are called to live out. In and through the experience of creatively ministering in the environment and to the people of Ground Zero, the chaplains exercised the kind of holding, reflective of the God who holds us in being, even as we witness the horrors we inflict on one another. Yet, in and through the holding, the presence of suffering was the palpable breath of Ground Zero, a breath that was often painful to take, as we shall see in the stories that follow in the next chapter.

chapter 3

Pain-Bearing
The Suffering Space

Sext
Sitting next to a bride,
a bride and wife for twenty five years,
half a union of two people.

All her life's hopes, fears, dreams, her security
to have and to hold has come to this:
a chair on a pier in a white curtained booth
a blue rug, a table, a computer, the face of a lawyer
concerned, patient, waiting—

Her trembling hand as she picks up a pen fumbles
with it, puts it back down—
Oh my darling, my darling, O God, he's gone, isn't he—
He's really gone. Oh my darling. My sweet, sweet love.

Her breath on my throat. Her tears
on my cheek. And we're quiet
in a moment of hush.

Then she gathers herself to sign the affidavit
and, as a blow to her body, admit for ever
that her husband is dead.[1]

Pain-bearing is painful. Yet it is part and parcel of the context of pastoral care. Most of the chaplains found the empathic connections with the suffering of others deeply touching and at times incredibly sad, sometimes not only a "body blow" to the other but to themselves. But, as one chaplain said when asked whether he experienced sadness or a sense of his own suffering, "I wasn't aware other than the horror of the situation and that aspect of it and what people were going through; it didn't touch me individually, I didn't lose a family member, I didn't know anyone who had been lost."

In such a pastoral reflection, why would we use the word *pain*? As a pastoral psychotherapist I would generally not use the word *pain*, to discourage somatization—a feeling with your body instead of your emotions—or to encourage people not to distance themselves by generalizing but to be specific about what it was that was "painful," to get closer to the sadness, the anger, the fear. Here, paradoxically, for the same reasons I choose to use the word *pain*—because it is all-encompassing but does not prescribe. It acknowledges that at times we do hold things in our body that we do not have the time, space, or resources to hold in our minds, and it declinicalizes and humanizes what we will explore under the terms *trauma* and *stress*. It locates pain in the space of affect and of meaning in the subjective experience of the human person. One can see all that is spoken of under these terms simply in the natural language of some of the chaplains. As we will explore, finding the language is a part of the task of coming to terms with the reality of suffering that we face as humans, as this chaplain graphically described:

> Probably the people who helped us the most at the very beginning of being in the Pit were the volunteers who had been chaplains at Oklahoma City who came here. And we were kind of overwhelmed, like "My God, what do you do?" They were the ones who told us, "Find your center. Do one thing at a time. Figure out where you're going to go next. Take one step at a time. Don't look at the whole thing because you'll get crazy." They had the experience of working through that and so that kind of was the process.
>
> If something was really sticking, if something was really awful . . . I mean, *the painful thing* was when they recovered enough of human remains that you could actually see the face. And some of the faces were in awful grimaces, really the horror of death, the horror of knowing they were dying in that moment. Or maybe they had more than a few minutes of being buried alive in that rubble before they died. It was like everything you ever saw in horror movies or horror comics and that would stick in the gut in the heart.
>
> And so we could sit down with somebody, [like this] wonderful woman, [*name*], and she had the most irreverent attitude to everything. But you could sit and talk to her and she would sit and listen and wait until she knew that each of us was beyond *the hurt point* because we had now got it out. Because it was almost literally like reaching in and grabbing a hold of *this shaft of pain* and pulling it out of our bodies and literally having it gone. And then she'd make some very funny statement or something and having us laughing hysterically and it was gone. It was over it was finished. It was a wonderful process.

The Pain of Ministering to Those in Pain

Those chaplains that worked with multiple populations frequently carried a personalization of the T. Mort. chaplaincy that was often hard to bear. For many of the chaplains this was necessarily the case, as chaplains were not immediately assigned by the American Red Cross to the T. Mort. Many worked at the Family Assistance Centers first, ministering to those searching for loved ones or, as in the case of the woman referred to in *Sext* at the beginning of the chapter, coming to terms with the reality of the death of a loved one, to later working alongside those that may have been recovering that person's body in the space of Ground Zero. Others had worked at St. Paul's Chapel or other venues where families congregated outside or worked with companies that had "lost" colleagues in the collapse of the WTC. When asked when he experienced being most sad, one of the chaplains replied, "When I'd be back home laying on my bed trying to sleep, that was the hardest time." When asked what it was that he carried with him at that time (i.e., What was he "holding"? What was he "bearing"?), he responded:

> Basically *the pain of the families*, what the families, the friends, the relatives were going through. Especially in the beginning, there were a lot of them saying, "They haven't found my son yet. They haven't found . . ." Thinking they were still alive at that stage, and it's been over two to three weeks. That's what they were thinking. [And having shifted from working with the families to the working at the morgue with the bodies] *making that connection there that these [bodies] could be some of the people whose families I was talking to*, and working with them. Nighttime was hard. Well, whatever nighttime was for me.

The American Red Cross had a guideline that once a chaplain began working at one of the mortuaries, the Disaster Mortuary at the Medical Examiner's office or the T. Mort. at Ground Zero, they could *not* cross back to working with families. In other disasters this guideline would provide a containing frame that would insulate the chaplain from a tendency to personalize that might be overwhelming. At Ground Zero, however, both in recovery and ritual there was no way of avoiding this reality, as often those working on recovery were police or fire department members searching for their own colleagues, their brothers and sisters in the service, and in some cases their literal family members. Both in the searching and in the finding, there was a lot of pain that had to be borne. To some of the chaplains this was apparent, without any pastoral enagagment at all. One chaplain, in sharing his initial impressions of the recovery site, said:

> What I remember being struck by was the heat and the smell. You could smell it from far away. But then the other thing was just the heat. . . . The thing that

I kept marveling at during the time there was the skill of the heavy-equipment operators. It was amazing watching that heavy equipment and the way they were doing things. I was in awe of that. And also there was a pain on people's faces—*the pain on people's faces was remarkable*. There was some conflicting things. There was the awe of the operators and *a sense of sharing in people's pain*. Sometimes there was a bit of anger over the way some of the other chaplains were addressing the situation, they seemed to be compounding people's pain rather than *being with them in the pain*.

This "sense of sharing in people's pain . . . being with them in the pain" was to all intents a "bearing" of the pain with them. In most cases on a recovery site, one cannot and should not make any attempt to work through the pain as the workers have to keep on working. This issue was highlighted by the DMORT (federally activated

Image 3.1. Spray-painted dedication in the midst of Ground Zero (New York, September 23, 2001). (Photo by Andrea Booher/FEMA News Photo.)

Disaster Mortuary Team), who "worked" the Hurricane Katrina disaster and accepted the "embedding" of chaplains into their team (several of which had responded to the WTC disaster). Board-certified chaplain Tim Serban writes:

The DMORT teams initially feared the chaplains would tap too hard on the exterior of their teammates' defenses and potentially unravel them in the midst of a difficult recovery operation. In such situations, when a recovery worker in the field begins to talk about the emotional fallout of their experience, chaplains must be effective in applying what I call *spiritual duct tape*. The chaplain must effectively use his or her skills to help keep the recovery worker contained and focused on the task at hand until they are safely disengaged from the active disaster area. The chaplains' role is to help protect the DMORT recovery workers engaged in the active process of body retrieval. If a chaplain begins to tap too deeply into the defenses of the recovery worker in the field, the team could potentially lose the member in the most critical part of their work.[2]

In the case of the WTC recovery effort, however, defenses would naturally unravel of their own accord, when the recovery workers would find "one of their own." Additionally, when the body or body part of a service member was identifiably found, the ritual of blessing took on the ceremonial character of that service. There would generally be a blessing by a chaplain both at the site of recovery and an honor guard would form as the body or body part/s were removed. At a waiting ambulance there would be another blessing or commendation and the ambulance would generally be escorted directly, flanked by motorcycle police escort, to the Disaster Mortuary rather than to the T. Mort. trailer. This ritual of blessing, removal, and procession would often be timed to allow the members of one's own company, precinct, team, division, or their family to be present. Out of respect for "the fallen member," sometimes the recovery team could wait for long hours for those coming from off the site to assemble for this "ceremony."

> The ceremony has such seriousness to it and dignity. And you couldn't help but feel sorry for people, the amount of grieving and mourning and trying to live with all of this is hard. And with it the traditions really weren't designed for this level of loss—to have traditions of people from your own house should be the ones to carry you out. So you'd have these situations, like upon finding somebody, do you call the house to tell them to come? And it's like given the amount of this, it's not a situation where it's just one person. And the possibility of calling people over and over again. It really pushed the feasibility of these traditions to their limit. And God bless them, people tried to live up to them as best they could, I have great respect for them. These were always emotional.

One of the chaplains related being witness to a moment when the situation of finding one's own became overwhelming.

> Later on, [*name*] was there, he was the chief of one of the fire department units . . . and we had worked together a couple of times on different things. And that day, it was way down, the Pit was way down already below the pipes that kept the water out. . . . And they found three bodies, three firefighter bodies. And he was furious. . . . He was kicking them [the gurneys] and he was kicking them and kicking them and he was going "Why now? Why now? Why now?" And I just held onto his shoulder and his hand.

Like those working on body recovery, it was also the chaplains that had to find a container for their own emotional pain in response to the suffering of others so they, too, could continue their work. Sometimes this was impossible:

There were some days when there were a lot of remains uncovered. A lot. And Ladder [x] had a large contingent in the Pit that night. And they just happened to find a lot of their guys. They'd been coming in all afternoon. And I was down there a lot and out a lot and down and back and down and back and down and back. . . . And I think when [this fire company] was there, there would be just processions going on and multiple remains being brought up and bag after bag after bag just being uncovered, checked out by the M.E., covered up again, tagged, stuck in the corner ready to go in the ambulance up to Bellevue.

And there was this guy there that I got talking to, he was one of the drivers, firefighter. And he was standing there, he and his guys. . . . I talked to him for awhile on and off . . . and just to see those guys, their reaction. And this is like months later. This was probably in January or February, it was a winter month. There was just something about it that was so tragic. I don't know whether it was getting to me for the first time or what, I don't know. But I was overwhelmed with the tragedy of it. Not by the dead but because of the living.

Image 3.2. An FDNY fire truck is dwarfed by a mountain of rubble at Ground Zero (New York, September 27, 2001). (Photo by Bri Rodriguez/FEMA News Photo.)

The dead, they're taken care of, they're done. But the people that they leave behind. And these guys were just kind of, they didn't know what to say to one another almost. It's just the way they were standing, you know?

And finally they brought one of the big trucks up to escort the ambulance up, because the ambulance was filled with remains. And [the firefighter] drove and as he went by, I was just standing, I helped escort the remains into the ambulance. And when he went back and got in the truck and he drove, as he went by he just gave me this little up hand wave out the window. And that, like, killed me. It just freaking killed me at the time. I didn't know what to do. And fifteen minutes later, I was off shift and I walked up to the end of Liberty and I just went totally to pieces. I mean, just like completely out of nowhere, I just went completely to pieces and I just hugged [my wife whom I was meeting] and hugged her, it was insane.

Pain-bearing *is* painful. It entails something beyond the Earth-making/Holding of the previous chapter. Working with the pain of others means we open ourselves to our own suffering. This may be because of empathically sharing, or bearing, others' pain, or it may be that it opens up that which has been or continues to be painful in our own lives. Yet it is often the case that in pastoral care, be it at a disaster site, or in the daily sufferings of what the world and we inflict on each other as humans, that we are called to suffer, to bear the pain of others and in that bear our own.

Pain-Bearing: A Theological Perspective

Pain-bearing is both anthropologically and theologically grounded in the tension between the best and worst of humanity. As animals, we have evolved on a social, technological, and neurological level, far beyond other mammalian life. Animals are *not generally* capable of the sort of altruism that humanity is, to go beyond the affiliations of familial group, society, and procreative drives to care for the other.[3] However, nor are animals capable of the radical destructiveness that is shown in both individual violence and genocidal destruction wrought by humans that is not determined by physical defense, protection, or sustenance. What disturbingly distinguishes humans is both their ability to love and their ability to hate. To be human is to be able to be both creative and destructive, in a way inconceivable in animal life. A chaplain reflecting on 9/11 shared, "The only sense to it is, is 'the human condition' and just the way we are. We see it *as the culmination of the worst thing* and it certainly is the worst thing that we can remember having. But it's got a long history in ways."

Theological anthropology will not let us view the recourse to violence and destruction in humanity simply as signs of illness or aberration, but encourages an engagement in the pastoral field that recognizes human responsibility, grounded in a moral and ethical worldview that equates harm to others under the theological category of "sin." However, in a trinitarian theology this consciousness of sin and the contradiction in humanity that we can both love and hate in a way that no other can has to be seen in the light of the Triune God who created us, redeems us, and calls us to new life. For Christian theologian Jürgen Moltmann, to explore who this God is, we must begin not with the history of humanity in creation, but the history of God at the point it intersects the history of humanity, at the point of this greatest contradiction, at the cross.

> God is unconditional love, because he takes on himself grief at the contradiction in men and does not angrily suppress this contradiction. God allows himself to be forced out. God suffers, God allows himself to be crucified and is crucified, and in this consummates his unconditional love that is so full of hope. But that means that in the cross he becomes himself in the condition of this love. The loving Father has a parallel in the loving Son and in the spirit creates similar patterns of love in man in revolt. The fact of this love can be contradicted. It can be crucified, but in crucifixion it finds fulfillment and becomes love of the enemy. *Thus its suffering proves to be stronger than hate. . . .* If one conceives of the Trinity as an event of love in the suffering and death of Jesus—and that is something faith must do—then the Trinity is no self-contained group in heaven, but an eschatological process open for men on earth which stems from the cross of Christ. By the secular cross on Golgotha, understood as open vulnerability and as the love of God for loveless and unloved, dehumanized men, God's being and God's life is open to true man.[4]

Moltmann grounds the being of God at the point of its greatest philosophical contradiction also but, like Barth, proceeds from the revelation of God in the person of Jesus as that which defines the nature of God, before and beyond philosophical tenants. This shows a God that loves, that suffers, and that takes suffering into Godself through the suffering of the Incarnate One, the second person of the Trinity. This does not answer the questions of theodicy, of why God allows such suffering, but takes us beyond to the notion that God allows such suffering even in Godself. Unlike many theologians who would see suffering as solely related to the incarnation, Moltmann sees it intimately related to the Trinity, where it is not only the second person of the Trinity who suffers, but that the Son suffers the abandonment unto death, the Father suffers death of the Son, and the Spirit unites us, as sinful humanity in this suffering of love, where

> All human history, however much it may be determined by guilt and death, is taken up into this 'history of God', i.e. into the Trinity, and integrated into the future of the 'history of God'. There is no suffering which in this history of God is not God's suffering;

no death which has not been God's death in the history on Golgotha. Therefore there is no life, no fortune and no joy which has not been integrated by his history into eternal life, the eternal joy of God. . . . To think of 'history in God' however, first means to understand humanity in the suffering and dying of Christ, and that means all humanity, with its dilemmas and despairs.[5]

In some sense the action of the chaplains can be seen to flow from this trinitarian space. Although many had thoughts about the terrorists, which varied from seeing them as enemies to seeing them as fellow sinful humans, the chaplains' focus was not so much on the questions of sin and guilt, but on the suffering of others, and how they could participate in a loving response to that suffering, which for some was yet another example in the history of suffering. Moltmann notes that an understanding of God as one who can suffer in love and still retain God's freedom grew out of "an understanding of the meaning of the suffering of love from the history of the passion of Israel and of Christ." Paradoxically, for the chaplains, it was both suffering in the history of humanity and the history of God that made this a little more bearable. When asked what it was that enabled him to hold and contain the enormity of the experience of his chaplaincy at Ground Zero and cope with it on a day-to-day level, one rabbi said:

Well, even now that's an easy question to answer but I think you ask as though it's overwhelming. I would say *Jewish history*. We just commemorated a couple of weeks ago *the saddest day* in the Jewish calendar, which marked a day that both holy temples were destroyed to Judaism. Destruction that's, in its own magnitude, greater than 9/11 from a historical perspective. That day of Tisha B'Av, the ninth day of Av, is not just the day of when the first Temple was destroyed, but the second holy Temple was destroyed. The day the Spanish inquisition began. 1492. I think a committed Jew has learned to live with all that their life presents, good or bad, as a ride. I remember Myron Cohen, the Jewish comedian, used to joke how it seems to always be that Jews answer a question with a question. I remember once giving a sermon, "To me that's not a joke, it's a philosophy." Because you go through life, you go through history, there's so many questions. And if you ever fall apart at every question we'd have never survived as a people. So I think for me it's the Judean historical experience.

And *this* is part of it because the fanatics, who were the cause of 9/11, probably opposed Israel and Judaism even more strongly than they did the United States. So that, if anything, I see in this but another perspective of those forces of antisemitism. Throughout history you could avoid evil. In this case it was the evil that affected a much broader set of people. So that's why I never saw 9/11 as the overwhelming experience incomparable to anything else that happened.

From this chaplain's focus on the suffering of the Jewish people, to the following chaplain's focus on the suffering of God in response to the same question, the answers show that a theology of suffering is one thing that can assist us in facing suffering. I would proffer, however, that it has to be a theology that is integrated with both the rest of one's theology and the reality of the world where we suffer.

> God helped me, assisted me, still does. He's always there, the helper, the Spirit. And *the fact that God had suffered in Christ helped, too*. To know that God would endure suffering and even death and understood that. To believe that God walks that walk with us. Going through terrible times like this we're not comfortless, I mean, there is comfort at least. And to read that, "I will not leave you comfortless," "I will send the comforter to you." To read that in the Bible is one thing, and to pray about it and study about it but to experience it in this setting, to feel it, to feel the comfort. It just brings it alive.

In a sense these Jewish and Christian chaplains together reflect Moltmann's intra-trinitarian theology, which sees not only the suffering of the Son, but the abandonment of the Father in relation to the cross. The rabbi continued on to say,

> No different when we asked, "Where was God in Auschwitz?," that the Katrina victims asked, or the tsunami victims asked. . . . We live from the Jewish perspective since the destruction of the Second Temple and the exile of the Jewish people, from a Jewish perspective in which God's world presence is hidden. And that's part of *the sense of loss of the divine presence which we suffer*. We may have shown, I may have shown, a ministry of presence. . . . Somehow, from a Judean point of view, since the destruction of the Second Temple, the world has experienced *the ministry of divine absence*. Not absence of not being there, the absence in terms of not being there *actively*. There's active listening and there's active absence. I'm there, but I'm hidden. A sense of hiddenness becomes a part of our own theological perspective. Hopefully a time will come when God's revelation will be much more pronounced and much more positive in terms of its impact.

Here, the God who hides Godself in relation to our suffering can be seen in Moltmann's thought regarding God the Father who not only suffers the grief of the suffering of the Son, but abandons him to it, and the Son in a sense becomes godforsaken and "the Father also forsakes himself."[6] Moltmann emphasizes this seemingly to hold together a trinitarian theology that is not simply a sophisticated form of monotheism, but in doing so he risks reflecting a theodicy which theologian Dorothee Soelle names as "theological sadism."

Any attempt to look upon suffering as caused directly or indirectly by God stands in danger of regarding him as sadistic. Therefore it also seems to me problematic to ask, "What is the cause of the suffering of the God who suffers with imprisoned, persecuted and murdered Israel," or whether Christ suffered merely because of "human injustice and human wickedness." Jürgen Moltmann has repeated the attempt to show that Jesus suffers "at God's hands," that God causes suffering and crucifies—at least in the case of this one person. On the one hand, Moltmann carved out the figure of the "crucified God," the "suffering, poor, defenseless Christ," and criticized the ancient ideal of an apathetic God by portraying God as the "God of the poor, peasants and slaves," who suffers "in us, where love suffers." But this intention, this passion for suffering, is weakened and softened through the theological system which transmits it. God is not understood only or even primarily as the loving and suffering Christ. He is simultaneously supposed to occupy the position of the ruling omnipotent Father. Moltmann attempts to develop a "theology of the cross" from the perspective of the one who originates and causes suffering. This correlates with an understanding of suffering as a process within the Trinity, whereby "one of the persons of the Trinity" underwent suffering which another person of the Trinity was the very one who caused it.[7]

This highlights the complexities and challenges of trinitarian theology, which can appear to split up the Trinity in such a way as to make it sound tritheistic rather than triune. Soelle goes on to say,

> When you look at human suffering concretely you destroy all innocence, all neutrality, every attempt to say, "It wasn't I; there was nothing I could do; I didn't know." In the face of suffering you are either with the victim or the executioner—there is no other option. Therefore that explanation of suffering that looks away from the victim and identifies itself with a righteousness that is supposed to stand behind the suffering has already taken a step in the direction of theological sadism, which wants to understand God as the torturer.[8]

A theology of the Trinity has to take into account suffering but cannot do so by splitting off the sufferer and the cause of the suffering. Yet perhaps neither can we solely, as Soelle would do, ally oneself only with the victim of suffering, but see in the suffering of Christ, and the empathic suffering of the Father, the God who is willing to suffer our worst to show us that God does not require suffering of us, but will be with us even as we cause each other to suffer.

It [blessing bodies and body parts] was just a profound honor. Whether it was a bone from someone's finger, it ran from that extreme to whole bodies, to members of service. It was why, in a way, I was ordained. Why I went into the ministry. It was to be engaged in the work of bringing the holy into human life on a regular basis. And so whether it was the ministry of presence

of just standing as the workers were working or leading the procession out from the site and then up to the morgue and then the final honor guard as the motorcycles assembled and everybody left the morgue in the convoy. It was to represent that God had not abandoned humanity. No matter how bad it looked, *God had not abandoned us.* That we didn't have any answers for why. That God was still with us.

Paradoxically, unlike Soelle, who seeks to ally herself with Christ the victim, at least in one of the Gospel stories, it is Jesus the victim who allies himself with his own executioners—"Father, forgive them. They know not what they are doing" (Luke 23:34). This is an expression of the trinitarian God, who knows, understands, and loves. One of the chaplains commented that it was important for him to realize that even the remains of the terrorists, had any survived, would also have been blessed by the chaplains. In fact, the Medical Examiner's office indicates that terrorists' remains were indeed found.[9] There cannot be a more potent example of Christ's words to "Love your enemies and pray for those who persecute you" (Matt. 5:44; cf. Luke 6:27, 35). Another chaplain stated,

There were several times when we actually knew the person's name because that's why the firefighters [from offsite] came. At first, they were unrecognizable. So you didn't even always know if it was a man or a woman. You kind of had a general idea. So that when the medical examiner would open the bag, and do their initial assessment, you always knew that this was a person, somebody's father, this was somebody's daughter, this person comes from somewhere. And somebody would ask me, "Well, yeah, but sometimes, it could have been one of the terrorists or whatever?" And I said, "Yeah, but they're still somebody's brother or father." When talking with some of the workers and stuff, we all kind of admitted that we pretty much figured that they were incinerated. And more of a human moment, more of a noncleric role moment, and I said that there's a certain part of me (that my heart doesn't like, that that person was destroyed that way), I said, "It's part of what helps me, [to] realize that most of the people that we're hopefully blessing are those that were victims, that were not perpetrators, but were those that were innocent at the time." Because the numbers outweigh the number of people that were killed, [those] that were victims far outnumbered the terrorists to the point where the odds were in our favor that we're dealing with people who were innocent at the time.

If Soelle suggests we are often abandoned to theological consolations that in essence indicate a position that almost seems to commend suffering or, alternatively, a secularist apathy, what she seeks to break is a theology of suffering that leads to either this "Christian masochism"—an image of a sadistic God who causes or allows suffering for some greater meaning—or "post-Christian apathy" in relation to suffering, by attending to the suffering itself. She indicates that the problem of suffering cannot be *solved* but it can be *met* with a voluntary fellow-suffering of love.

> Where would I take the pain? In some ways I kind of feel like the pain never really left there. Especially because some of the guys were bigger than I was at the time, it was such a very tactile community, that the pain was diminished by embraces, by holding hands to pray the Lord's Prayer, by human contact. The pain was diminished. I didn't feel as if I had much support at all from my church body, they had another agenda. And that's where some of my sadness and anger goes. But the pain was more left there.

This voluntary fellow-suffering was what the chaplains represented but also what they experienced in the mutuality of the experience of community that cared for them in their suffering even as they cared for the community.

> But I remember I also went blank on prayers. I don't know, it was something about the site and the Christmas tree and the truck and the legs and I forgot the Lord's Prayer. I don't know how many times, thousands of times, I have said the Lord's Prayer and I just, in the middle of it, blanked. Which freaked

Image 3.3. Chaplain assists workers at the World Trade Center. (Photo by Andrea Booher/FEMA News Photo.)

me out a little bit but I made up something else. It's odd how you can say something so many times and all of a sudden your memory just goes blank. . . . It's just gone, it's gone. "Our Father, who art in heaven, hallowed be thy Name. Thy kingdom come, thy will be done on earth as it is in heaven. Give us our daily bread and, and, and . . ." And it's gone. I was so embarrassed. But the guys were actually comforted by that. I said, "I'm sorry." And they felt actually good that I forgot, that I was human. I came back the next day but I had written it down. I was so paranoid that I had to write it down.

What Soelle does is ask, as we have, why some suffering enables us to grow and some just leaves us mute, breathless, and devastated, as described by one chaplain:

It's just, for me, I began to be sad when I first saw the images to some degree. But the wave happened when I came down. It just was overwhelming. I was really sort of taken out by the whole thing. Just emotionally and I don't understand why this particular thing devastated me. Whether what the series of circumstances were but I got devastated at a deep, deep level inside.

Soelle argues that Christ's solidarity with us in the incarnation and crucifixion leads us *not* to simply be present to others in the suffering but to act in ways that are *transformative* of the structures which cause it, a conquest of powerlessness. She says that the first step toward overcoming suffering is to find a language that leads out of the muteness. Like the chaplains who could simply but profoundly provide a holding space in silence in the last chapter, Soelle writes,

Respect for those who suffer *in extremis* imposes silence. Thus theological reflection begins not with extreme suffering but with less radical stages. Unbearable suffering excludes change and learning. Unbearable pain produces only blind and short-lived actions. But when is pain unbearable? When we are struck by disaster our first reaction is that it cannot be endured. Later on we are amazed at how much a person can stand, much more, in any case, than we expect at the initial moment of horror. This initial phase of pain, which we experience again and again (Phase One), leaves us dumb and mute. The weight of unbearable suffering makes us feel totally helpless; we are stripped of the autonomy to think, to speak, and to act. . . .[10]

The first step toward overcoming suffering is, then, to find a language that leads out of the uncomprehended suffering that makes one mute, a language of lament, of crying, of pain, a language that at least says what the situation is.[11]

Soelle sees the language of suffering as encompassing three phases: muteness (phase one); lamentation (phase two), which expresses communication; and finally, changing (phase three). One chaplain put it this way: "Anything we can do to put our life experience within the realm of God's presence and authority, and if we take it out of that, which we do all the time, what we have is the church, nothing to say about it, just cry with everybody else, if that makes sense. I don't think we should just cry with everybody else but to have something to say about it, and that's not 'Pollyanna's say' but *something* to say about it—that the wages of sin is death and that's not the end of the story." Soelle indicates that from the point of communication, there can develop a sense of solidarity and an ability to change the structures. This solidarity expresses the perspective of God's presence with us as we are present in solidarity with others. We can see reflections of this in the experience of several chaplains.

> On New Year's Eve one of the men had brought in a body that they found. Not just a body part, a body. One of the men who brought it in was the natural brother of the person whose body he had brought in. And I was with him. I had to go in to be with the Medical Examiner, you know, and then I came out and he was still there and we were having just a little bit of a conversation and while we were having the conversation, radios were bursting, you know, everybody was wishing each other a "Happy New Year" over the walkie-talkies. And it was a real test of sadness. This was how the New Year was starting for this man, you know, with the discovery of his brother's body. And being there, I think that was probably, the [low] of the overwhelming experience of sadness there. Sadness, I don't think was the main thing that I was feeling there, though. My remembrance is, most of the time I was there, I was experiencing the sense of *the presence of God in that place.*

Despite Soelle's clear movement from muteness, to lamentation, to solidarity, Winnicott's thought and the experience of the chaplains have shown us, however, that there can be a solidarity, even in the mute phase of suffering, which negates the isolation that Soelle speaks of, but is an expression of being alone together. What is unbearable alone may become "bearing the unbearable" in a sensitive, empathic pastoral relationship. Presence, therefore, is not to be negated, even if it appears inactive. What Soelle highlights for us, however, is that we cannot also get stuck in the suffering but need to move toward a place of transforming the structures, thereby conquering the powerlessness induced by suffering. Like the mutual indwelling in relation to the Trinity, we can see in the example of the blessings at Ground Zero, the coming together of the finding of language, the solidarity, and the movement for change, expressed in Soelle's work.

> I was here on Christmas Day. I said I wanted to be down here because some of us had all said, "Let's work it, let's do it." So I walked over to Vesey [Street], where the officers worked, and [an officer] motioned, he said, "Come over. I need for you, if you could, to talk to this guy." Well, he had come because his wife had been killed in the towers and he had asked if he could. He hadn't

been down, he hadn't been to any of the things with the other families or anything. But because his parents live somewhere out west, his in-laws lived out west and everything, he ended up being alone on Christmas because he wanted to be. And that he wanted to come down and that was the day he wanted to visit the site. So, he said, he wanted to know if I'd take him over. And I said, "Well, really, I can't, but if an officer does, we can all go over." It was weird, because I always carried [a prayer book], just in case, because you never know when you'll need the standard prayers and stuff. We got another officer and the three of us walked over to the edge of the Pit and he wanted to do a committal. So Christmas Day, we did a committal for his wife. Because he said where the floor she was on and everything, that the chance of ever finding any remains for her were probably pretty much nonexistent. So that was huge, out of all the committals I've done that was probably, well, it always will be the most memorable because of its uniqueness and because he trusted the people at the site enough to come down and ask. And you know, it's one of those things that you say is a "God thing."

Given what I have briefly recounted of Soelle, perhaps it is a surprise that where she comes to is to the acknowledgment of the solidarity of God with us in our suffering, through the incarnation, through the image of God in us, and through our living out redemption actively.

That "God is always with the one who is suffering" entails not only consolation but also strengthening: a rejection of every ideology of punishment, which was so useful for the cementing of privileges and for oppression. There is a mystical defiance that rebels against everything ordained and regulated from on high and holds fast to the truth it has discovered. "Not God himself, not angels, nor any kind of creature is able to separate God from the soul who is in the image of God." That is the extension of Paul's thought: Nothing "can separate us from the love of God" (Rom. 8:39).[12]

Redemption does not come to people from outside or above. God wants us to use people in order to work *on the completion of his creation*. Precisely for this reason God must also suffer with the creation.[13]

God is not in heaven: he is hanging on the cross. Love is not an otherworldly, intruding, self-asserting power—and to meditate on the cross can mean to take leave of that dream. Precisely those who in suffering experience the strength of the weak, who incorporate the suffering into their own lives, for whom coming through free of suffering is no longer the highest goal, precisely they are there for others who, with no choice in the matter, are crucified in lives of senseless suffering. A different salvation, as the language of metaphysics could promise it, is no longer possible. The God who causes suffering is not to be justified even by the lifting of suffering later. No heaven can rectify Auschwitz. But the God who is not a greater Pharaoh has justified himself: in sharing the suffering, in sharing the death on the Cross.[14]

It is this solidarity of the God of the cross, who says "I and the Father are one" (John 10:30), which can lead to a living out of love, even in the midst of suffering, an active responsive place, where even when one is devastated can lead one to communication, community, and communion with the one in whose image we are made. Connections between the one who suffered for us and is with us in our suffering can be seen in the reflections of one chaplain, who understandably was consciously present on the memorable Christian "high and holy days" at Ground Zero.

> . . . on Christmas Eve or early, right *after midnight on Christmas Day*, taking communion to the police and National Guard who were on the perimeter. And I started walking until somebody that I knew from Ground Zero gave me a ride in a garbage truck from checkpoint to checkpoint. And you know, *how appropriate on Christmas for the body of Christ to be coming in a garbage truck*. . . . *Good Friday morning* when a member of the bomb squad's body was found. And he had the jacket on so it was a fairly quick and certain identification. And they brought in the whole bomb squad as *the body was going to be taken from the shed up to the ambulance*, up the ramp to the ambulance. There were bagpipers and, and everything else, you know, it was like two or three o'clock in the morning on Good Friday. And it was just sort of, *This is what Good Friday's about*.
>
> And I was there on *Easter morning*, too. At mass at the foot of the cross and somebody from Hawaii gave thousands of orchid leis to all the workers there and enjoying the irony that people were decked with orchids on Easter Day at Ground Zero. . . . There was on Easter Day a very simple chorus that was sung during the mass. And it's a chorus that has stayed with me and from time to time I find myself singing the chorus, which I had never heard before that particular time. "Listen, listen, listen to my heart song. . . . I'll never forget you, I'll never forsake you. . . . Listen, listen, listen to my heart song." The only time I ever heard that was that Easter Sunday. And as I say, that's the one that stays with me.

"Never forgetting, never forsaking," it is this position in relation to suffering that was the model for many of the chaplains, who sought not to forget or forsake those they were working with, even if at times they failed.

Judith Herman, in her book *Trauma and Recovery*, says that recovery from trauma also unfolds in three stages. "The central task of the first stage is the establishment of safety. The central task of the second stage is remembrance and mourning. The central task of the third stage is reconnection with ordinary life."[15] Herman acknowledges a variety of models of recovery and configurations for them and notes that "in the course of a successful recovery, it should be possible to recognize a gradual shift from unpredictable danger to reliable safety, from dissociated trauma to acknowledged memory, and from stigmatized isolation to restored social connection."[16] This focus on remembrance in the second phase of recovery was symbolically and literally paralleled in the recovery task at Ground Zero, from those that were working to "re-member" the bodies, to remembering the families, to remembering those working on the recovery, to remembering who we are in an eternal sense. "The prayer that I use would often times have in it, Eternal God our Father, as our lives are experienced in bits and pieces and apart, so we see *these bits and pieces* as you have already made them whole in your kingdom, so make our lives *whole* and reconstruct and give them new meaning." From re-membering, to remembering:

> **Well, "pain" would be the wrong word. The "grief." I think grief you deal with by promise and prayer and remembering. Not by forgetting. I deal with grief anyhow by remembering. My remembering and having some sense of remembering that whole sense of relationships that happened down there. I didn't know any of the people whose body parts were there so, kind of remembering in that sense and so it's really remembering God's promise that this will pass away.**

At Ground Zero there was for many chaplains the paradoxical sense of the remembrance of the whole, and the remembrance of the Holy God, in the dismembered bodies. One clergyperson, who very early in the disaster recovery went down to the first T. Mort., preached about seeing a sign one of the recovery workers had scrawled upon a piece of cardboard and propped on one of the tables that was receiving bags of body parts. The sign read "The Body of Christ." Like our former reflection on creation, this sense of the fullness of creation even in the destruction of the creature, the re-membrance of the whole in the part, and, for the following chaplain, in the mind of God, is reminiscent also of Augustine's understanding of Trinity in the human person as the relation of memory, understanding, and will.

> **I saw that within every part, whether it be a body part or a whole body, you really have the fullness of God's creation in any one part. The cell structure and the wonder of that wholeness and *to remind the people there that our wholeness will, on this Earth, will only be kept in the mind of God*. Because eventually we will all be dust or parts or particles. And so I think theological awareness always made me stand with a sense of awe and mystery and wonder of God's creativity and God's promise and capacity for restoration.**

This reminder could be helpful in the face of the inevitable failures to remember, even for the chaplains, as they sought to cope with what they were facing. It was sometimes these failures, and the failure of those around them to remember them, that was most painful.

> Looking back, I just think if I could repeat a moment or going forward to file away so as to do better, I always remember one time where it turned out that there were two bodies that they had found, one pinned on top of the other. And it took them like five hours to get them extricated from the rubble and the debris. And when they got them, they wanted the chaplain. And I went down and prayed, blessed them, what have you, and it wasn't until I left and it all happened so fast that I thought afterwards, I thought I should have spoken directly to the people who just spent five hours recovering. I mean, I doubt they walked away going, "Jeez, get a load of him, you know, he didn't even"—I mean I kind of said, "Hello," to everybody. Like afterwards I thought, "God, I wish I had acknowledged to them what tremendous work they just did." And I thought, they were standing, and I don't think they were standing up looking for me to speak. I don't want to turn this into a moment where I needed to be the star. But later that day, I thought, "God, I wish I had just said something and not kept them there forever, just to say, I just want to tell you on behalf of families, you know I don't even see the people, but kind of in this chain, I want to give a word of thanks back to you." Or just bless them or something. And I just thought, 'I'll never let that happen again.' But that was a little something that I kind of thought, "God, I forgot, it felt like I forgot they were there." You know, caught up in this moment of what they, we had here.

One can see in this chaplain the capacity for concern that is tinged with guilt that leads to the conscious thought "I'll never let that happen again." Here, we can see something of the early development of empathy for the other, that leads us out of an isolated state to focus on the other, initially, in the thought of Winnicott, the one from whom we learn empathy in relationship. It is this development that allows us to empathize with others on a deep emotional level, rather than simply *apply* pastoral skills of reflective listening and attunement that can look the same but do not touch the real self.

Pain-Bearing/Suffering in Winnicott's Thought

Donald Winnicott was strongly influenced by the two psychoanalytic theorists, Sigmund Freud, whose theory gave birth to psychoanalysis, and Melanie Klein, whose work with children gave rise to a theory of internalized objects and formation of the self in relationship at an earlier chronological age than that on which Freud generally focused. Winnicott's work reflects both an identification with them and a departure from their ideas. Although accepting Freud's concept of the structure of the psyche, with id, ego, and superego, Winnicott's ideas otherwise reflect a relational structural model that shows how adult responses are structured in the relational templates of infancy. Klein's work gives a picture of formation from infancy as a rich inner life initially populated by parts of objective relationships and persons that only gradually are integrated into a relationship with a whole person that one recognizes as the one who both nurtures and frustrates, is both good and bad, and can survive both our love and hate. Klein's focus often seems to be primarily on the fantasy life of the child in response to the primary caregiver, whereas Winnicott's formulations place greater emphasis on the primary caregiver's response to the child and the relationship between them. Perhaps, however, it is Klein's thought in her 1937 paper "Love, Guilt and Reparation" that Winnicott comes closest to, even as he reframes the guilt into a "capacity for concern" and empathic response. Klein writes:

> My psychoanalytic work has convinced me that when in the baby's mind the conflicts between love and hate arise, and fears of losing the loved one become active, a very important step is made in development. These feelings of guilt and distress now enter as a new element into the emotion of love. They become an inherent part of love, and influence it profoundly both in quantity and quality. . . . Side by side with the destructive impulses in the unconscious mind both of the child and of the adult, there exists a profound urge to make sacrifices, in order to help and put right loved people who in phantasy have been harmed or destroyed. In the depths of the mind, the urge to make people happy is linked up with a strong feeling of responsibility and concern for them, which manifests itself in genuine sympathy with other people and in the ability to understand them, as they are and as they feel.[17]

This process happens through identification with the other and with the love and care for the other. In the case of the chaplains this is both identification with the ones who have died and with those who are grieving their loss. But it also entails an identification, at some level, with those who have caused the destructiveness. Whether this is simply an identification with our own infantile destructiveness, as Klein would indicate, an identification with humanity in its destructiveness, or a more conscious identification with the destruction of the terrorists, in response to our own destructiveness, Klein asserts, "making reparation is, in my view, a fundamental element in love and in all human relationships . . ."[18] This desire for reparation, in some sense, is a desire to repair that which has been the object of destruction, which is not simply the external objects, those literally destroyed and the relationships lost, but the destruction of our own sense of self and worldview, which may manifest as feeling overwhelmed by guilt, grief, or anger. As noted earlier, this enables one to move from a place of passive helplessness to a place of active and even creative response, which many integrate into a sense of ongoing vocation. Winnicott writes,

> I have sketched some aspects of *the origins of concern* in the early stages. . . . But this balance has to be achieved over and over again. Take the obvious case of adolescence,

or the equally obvious case of the psychiatric patient, for whom occupational therapy is often a start on the road towards a constructive relation to society. Or consider a doctor, and his needs. Deprive him of his work, and where is he? He needs his patients, and the opportunity to use his skills, as others do.[19]

The difference that Winnicott develops from Klein's views relates to external reality. In the developing infantile capacity for concern, the loved object must "survive the excited states" and "hold the situation in time," and there must be an "opportunity to contribute."[20] In the context of the holding relationship, the child begins not only to receive the empathic care from the mother or other primary caregiver, but to develop empathy for the mother who is the object of its aggressive loving and destructive impulses, through "concern" for her survival. The child then seeks to contribute to the well-being of the mother whose continued presence makes this possible. As we can see, Winnicott sees this desire to respond, to contribute in the face of destructive impulses, as not only applicable in early life but something we seek to achieve "over and over again" in life situations as disparate as a psychiatric patient and the doctor who may treat him or her.

Likewise, those clergy in New York who were not able to contribute through participating in chaplaincy were perhaps left in a more difficult space than those who worked as chaplains—despite the potentially traumatizing elements of that work—as demonstrated by the research that indicated that those clergy who worked for the American Red Cross alone were actually less traumatized than those who did not work as chaplains anywhere. You can see how this urge to respond, in relation to what could feel like overwhelming affect, functioned in one chaplain's narrative.

> **Well, the first time I went down, when I came back up and I walked into St. Paul's, I just broke down. And I don't think I've stopped being sad. I mean, that's later, that's now. Go back to then. . . . I think I felt sad whenever I thought about it. It was sad to me and *I think the sadness and grief drove me to do something because I couldn't live with just not doing something*. So I kept coming, I brought parish groups down to volunteer at St. Paul's, that kind of thing. The sadness of others affected me. I'd talk to people who'd lost somebody. It was like scuba diving in a lake of sadness. Am I the scuba diver? It's like just swimming in a lake of it, I would say.**

Through the opportunity to contribute, the sadness becomes transformed in reparative function; however, it does not negate the suffering itself. Like Klein's affirmation of ambivalence, which is the sign of the developmental achievement of what she called the "depressive position," and what Winnicott calls the "capacity for concern," a chaplain's reflection shows the various levels of identification and the sense of a maturation in relation to a world where such suffering can and does happen.

Most sad? I guess every time they recovered and I saw a recognizable body or part, something that you just knew was a human being at one point. There was an infinite sadness. I had no attachment to the Trade Centers themselves. I didn't feel bad that the buildings were gone. I didn't have any feeling about that. But every time there was a recognizable body or body part, there was an infinite sadness. A sadness for *everybody who had been lost*. A sadness for *all the people who had been affected by it* and had been left behind. And sadness for *what this whole thing signaled*. Life as we know it was changed forever and we were going to have to live a different life in a different way and it was never going to be the same again. That's when I was feeling the most sad. That the carefreeness of childhood, which is what America felt like up until that point, was gone. We all had to suddenly grow up and be adults.

Although Winnicott describes the development of empathy in the child as due to the ability of the mother to mirror back to the child its own emerging self, developmentally, to "grow up and be adult" the child also needs the primary caregiver gradually to fail at this task. We need to introject that sense of care without having it provided externally, that which Winnicott names as the "good object imago."[21] This delicate process is also reflected in the separation of the child from its caregiver, at carefully graduated steps, so the child can learn to hold themselves without the other's presence. This is balanced, of course, by the caregiver's continuous reliable return.

However, there are times when this inner holding does not sustain, nor does the outer reality match the need. This, for Winnicott, is that which constitutes trauma, an interruption in the very sense of "being" that can feel annihilating. One would expect, as the self matures, that these needs become less so, yet in adult situations of potential trauma, the outer holding is as important. We can see this in the act of self-care by one chaplain who was leading a small team early on in the disaster:

I guess that was when the most traumatic things happened. You could cite random things but I remember there were four of us and they found, I don't know what you call it, a void. And there was just this tremendous amount of remains in there and they were bringing out bags. And at that point, there was just not the Pile; they were moving down in to the lower levels and I could remember the drivers of the little Gators were in tears, they were just sobbing. It was just very emotional, I just felt this aura of sadness. And they brought bag after bag, forty-some bags at one time. Just red bags everywhere. So I thought, "Okay, I better get [my little team] out of here," because they hadn't been down, they hadn't seen a lot of stuff I had seen, been down to the bottom and all this stuff. So I thought I'd better get them out of here. Actually, just get them up to one of the respite centers. So I just felt there's some times where you get too much trauma you just can't recover from it. And it was really pretty traumatic with people crying and the EMS people and the ladies crying and everybody was very upset and they were sitting there with a screen, shaking the screen to find what wouldn't fall through the screen. So it was just like everything was just like, "Wow," stimulus overload. So I got them, after that I said, "You know, I think we ought to just move, retreat here, and take the sign. And just sit over here and have food, just eat and don't worry about going back today." So I guess that was a very poignant time.

This chaplain acted to contain the amount of trauma his team was exposed to, even if it meant temporarily ceasing to function pastorally. It is a wise and difficult decision not to come back one day, so one can return later. To do that one has to hold what may be experienced as guilt, in the face of need that can be overwhelming, and spill over into other times.

[I] kept working and working and working but then you knew somebody else was there. That sort of urgency. Similar to that. I had to be here for that in case they found someone. That sort of a guilty feeling of being away even on your day off. Couldn't maybe enjoy it. It was somewhere in the back [of my mind], saying, "You know somebody else is down there probably suffering just as much as I am from lack of sleep, etc., etc." And here I am supposed to be having a day off, I found that difficult.

Winnicott, however, takes this sense of guilt and looks to a developmental stage beyond this where one can use this sense of guilt, not by reactively splitting, where one becomes in a sense a "bad object" that fails to live up to the idealized "good object" that one should be but to use that sense to feel a realistic responsibility "that is at the back of all constructive play and work."[22]

The word "concern" is used to cover in a positive way a phenomenon that is covered in a negative way by the word "guilt". A sense of guilt is anxiety linked with the concept of ambivalence, and implies a degree of integration in the individual ego that allows for the retention of good object-imago along with the idea of the destruction of it. Concern implies further integration, and further growth, and relates in a positive way to the individual's sense of responsibility, especially in respect of relationships into which the individual has entered. Concern refers to the facts that the individual *cares*, or *minds*, and both feels and accepts responsibility.[23]

If "concern" or empathy is the development of an internalized relationship of care, a desire to contribute to the "repair" of some loved person that has been damaged, that then gets externalized in other relationships of care, how does this function in the face of potentially traumatizing circumstances, where the destruction can seem absolute? Let us then explore trauma and how Winnicott's thought contributes to an understanding of Pain-bearing/Suffering in the face of trauma as it relates to the chaplains at the T. Mort. What is it, therefore, that is traumatic and what might Winnicott's theory have to say about this in a helpful way?

Post-Traumatic Stress

Post-traumatic Stress Disorder (PTSD) has two core components: "The person has been exposed to a traumatic event in which both of the following were present: (1) the person experienced, witnessed, or was confronted with an event or events that involved actual or threatened death or serious injury, or a threat to the physical integrity of self or others. (2) The person's response involved intense fear, helplessness, or horror,[24] which causes significant distress and impairment of functioning. Therefore, in assessing what is traumatic for others we need look to both the event and the sense of helpless, fear, or perception of horror—that which is horrific or horrible *to them.*

> That's when the horror set in. The fact that this is something out of hell. This was not real, it couldn't have happened. It's not, nothing can be like this and life can still go on. That was the first feelings when I saw this kind of thing. Yeah, I can remember about where this was taken from and looking down. And thinking, "God help us." Maybe we'll find somebody alive in that mess,

Image 3.4. Early days of rescue period turn to long months of recovery at Ground Zero. (Photo by Bri Rodriguez/FEMA News Photo.)

but how is it possible? How is it possible? How can there ever be enough people and enough things to clean it up? It seemed to be impossible.

The T. Mort. chaplains' prime task was to be there to bless the bodies and body parts of the 19,916 human remains that were recovered from the site. These statistics denote what can be objectively described as "the horror" of Ground Zero—the recovery of approximately seven body parts for each person killed, in the context of ministering to first responders recovering parts of people they may well have known. Diane Myers and David Wee note the stress of such work:

> A particular, unique stressor in disaster is exposure to dead bodies, especially when the condition of the bodies reflects the violence of the disaster. Bolin (1986) uses the term *horror* to describe the witnessing of death in disasters, including the accidental discovery of bodies, the unsightly physical condition of corpses, and the nature of the cause of death. He concludes that horror is a significant generator of mental health problems. . . . Usano and McCarroll (1994) provide an in-depth discussion of exposure to traumatic death for workers involved in body recovery, identification, transport, and burial. . . . Factors involved in the traumatic impact of dealing with bodies included the stress of anticipation of the experience; inexperience with handling the dead; nature of the stress of exposure to traumatic death; sensory stimuli; novelty, surprise, and shock; identification and emotional involvement with the deceased; unique combat stresses; and coping strategies before, during, and after exposure to the dead.[25]

What Myers and Wee describe as horror can be seen in one T. Mort. chaplain's reflections. His description captures the "traumatic impact" of the first day of ministry at Ground Zero.

I had been with friends from England all over this lower Manhattan and up in the Trade Center two weeks before in August. And the memories were very, very, very, real. Very, very fresh, of just having walked around or just having stood in the lobbies. . . . So I was deeply connected to the site and I think just *overwhelming devastation and horror.* **You know, "The Heart of Darkness," Kurtz says,** *"the horror, the horror,"* **and it was like the heart of darkness, if you will. Contrast, that was the site. That was the loss of life that was the shift in reality which we didn't even have a clue how extensive it was going to be for this country and for the world. I mean a huge shift in my opinion. But it was on that one hand that devastation, on the other hand actually being able to do ministry.**

Although the chaplains at the T. Mort. expected to be in close proximity to dead bodies, there may have initially been varying expectations of whether they would see only body bags or the bodies and body parts themselves.[26] Past experience, preparation by others, and projection of expectations may have mitigated the impact of witnessing dead bodies and their varying states in which they were found over the months. From the chaplains' accounts, however, the objective reality of body parts that the chaplains either weren't expecting to see or found very intimate was particularly tough.

> Yeah, when you thought everything was just going to be scraps and pieces, suddenly you have a whole person, with the legs over there and the body over there, clearly something had happened to separate the leg from the body and probably related to their death, but that was sort of *when your guard was sort of being let down at that point*. And suddenly you have an entire person recovered there. That was a poignant thing. Well, I mean the body's been there since September, its odor's like overwhelming. So it's like all your senses are involved with that sort of thing. And I'm sitting there with the Medical Examiner trying to identify the person. It has a little gold cross here.

The two following accounts exemplify some of the most difficult of the objective side of being involved in body recovery when one is not experienced. Consequently, some readers may choose to skip over these accounts.

> Well, one day they brought that red bag in and it looked like a rubbery piece of something, a balloon or something. And it was shredded and it was maybe, I don't know, twelve inches long. And the M[edical] E[xaminer] looked at it, and he would look at things and he would smell them, because there was a certain odor to death or something. He would identify it as human by that. . . . One time they found chicken bones from a restaurant that was in it and they knew it wasn't human by smelling it and also the tactile thing. This he identified as someone's esophagus. And that gave me great pause, to be seeing somebody's esophagus. This is all that's left of this person—an esophagus. It's so deep within the body and everything else is shredded and gone, its dust. Here's an esophagus. It's got all kinds of holes in it, but that's what it was. And I thought, "Oh my God." Ridiculous, it was pretty vivid in seeing somebody's insides like that. And I think about that. And I think today, I don't want to see anybody's, especially members of my family, I don't want to see anybody's esophagus or innards like that again. And that was one of those moments. What was the word you used? Upsetting? Worst? Well, that was about as "worst" as it got.

> The things that were upsetting, that were disgusting, that sometimes didn't come up for months afterwards, because, like I said, I'm really good at "I'll deal with this afterwards." We found an absolutely gorgeous hand. It was a

woman's hand. It was just one of the most beautiful hands I've ever seen in my entire life. And you sit there and you wondered did those long fingers play the piano, things like that. There was a woman who was found, it was just a skeleton and she was pregnant and the fetus was inside, that one still brings tears to my eyes. Even though I wasn't here when it happened, I know what a body sounds like when it hits the ground and it pops. I would hear that sometimes.

As you can see from this last account, some of what was traumatic was, according to DSM-IV criteria, "experienced or witnessed," and some was what the chaplains were "confronted with" through the stories of others. This will be discussed more fully below in our discussion of Secondary Traumatic Stress; however, the last account highlights that the chaplain did not have to experience falling bodies directly to suffer the "intrusive" auditory hallucination of hearing the bodies hit the ground.

Although you can begin to see the subjective interpretations in relation to the objective reality in these accounts, this is not to downplay the impact of the objective reality. The following account exemplifies both the "horror" of the objective reality and the pain of the empathic relationships with those who were working to recover the bodies. In recognizing the importance of subjective interpretation, the former needs to be held in tension. That being said, I think this next account shows the reality of both. The narrative that follows comes in response to a question about when the chaplain experienced sadness. Some may wish to skip this account.

I don't know if it's most sad or most traumatized, but there was one night, it was cold. It was like forty degrees and drizzly, it was just another of those middle-of-the-night shifts. The word came down that they found [a particular person] from the police because [of his equipment]. And they were digging and digging and we were out there with them. And I couldn't figure out what part of this guy's body they were looking at, because there was just this hump and it took the ironworkers to get in there. And they figured out that he was sort of hunched over, like in kneeling, and when they turned him over, he was entirely like mummified, but his face was frozen in a scream. And all of us were just like [*gasps*]. And then, they knew who he was, so they called in and it was a police officer, not FDNY, and the assistant commissioner was having dinner and all the men stood there on guard in a line for over an hour in the rain waiting for him to finish his dinner and I was almost as traumatized by that. That he wouldn't let them take the body to the morgue until he got there and yet he was out to dinner with friends. And so I didn't show anything there, but I went to pieces after that, for them.

What the DSM-IV describes as an objective "traumatic event" includes terrorist attacks that are experienced directly and "witnessed events" that include unexpectedly seeing a dead body or body parts. The DSM-IV notes that "The severity, duration and proximity of an individual's exposure to the traumatic event are the most important factors affecting the likelihood of developing this disorder."[27] The chaplains at Ground Zero were in a potentially traumatizing space. There were the physical aspects of danger and destruction all around, something that caused Occupational Safety and Health time and again to institute regulations about who would be allowed on the Pile or down in the Pit. There was the reality of blessing bodies and body parts in a variety of states, and what those bodies represented: the loss of a human life and the grief of family, friends, and colleagues. And there was the potential sense of helplessness in the face of enormous grief of those working the Pile who were friends and colleagues, "brothers" and "sisters" of the dead, grief that could not be attended to as the workers needed to continue working but could only be held and borne with the hope that each recovery would facilitate in some sense the grief of the families, companies, and friends who had lost someone in the disaster.

When asked about their first thoughts, impressions, and feelings going down to the T. Mort., one chaplain painted a picture that captures all three of the aspects cited in PTSD criteria—fear, horror, helplessness.

> **Feelings? Scared? Yeah, I was. Scared of what I would see. Scared of how I would react to what I would see. That would have been the strongest feeling— scared. The other side of it, wanting to be useful, not to get in the way. Sort of wanting to do something for the families of the remains they brought in without really knowing them. Which was that important to me, I didn't have to know them, but was for me, they were people. . . . So that side was different. Sort of actually praying over the remains, the fear that had gone. You know it [the fear and being overpowered by the smell of the bodies] was especially after the first one, after the first time. It was that time as well. I needed fresh air quick. Oh, yeah. But after a while . . . I can't say I ever got used to it, I could never say that I got used to it, not even in May at that time. You learn how to deal with it. I think that was something you suppressed. I think, it was what I did.**

Even though the chaplains felt fear and encountered that which may have induced horror, in many ways their roles on the site mitigated against the sense of helplessness. They were helpless to change the situation but they could transform it through presence and prayer, through pastoral relationship with those that were searching and through their relationship with the God whom they felt called them to be in that place. Many of the chaplains felt a sense of gratitude. Paradoxically, they felt like the "lucky" ones, as they were able to make a response. Their training, preparation, and commitment put them in a situation where they could minister, and therefore they were not helpless in the face of such a disaster. They could respond and they did. This is what researchers on Secondary Traumatic Stress call "compassion satisfaction." There is often, however, a cost to such caring.

Secondary Traumatic Stress

Charles Figley, a pioneering theorist in the field of trauma, notes in his book *Secondary Traumatic Stress* that

> being a helper, however, also brings risks: Caring people sometime experience pain as a direct result of their exposure to other's traumatic material. Unintentionally and inadvertently, this secondary exposure to trauma may cause helpers to inflict additional pain on the originally traumatized. This situation—call it Compassion Fatigue, Compassion Stress, or Secondary Traumatic Stress—is the natural, predictable, treatable, and preventable unwanted consequence of working with suffering people.[28]

Seeing the consequent symptoms as being akin to those of PTSD, Figley has emphasized the little-attended-to phrase in the DSM-IV definition, noting that not just experiencing trauma oneself but witnessing others' experience can in itself be traumatic. A description of the impact and effect of hearing of other's trauma can be seen clearly in this chaplain's reflection:

> I realized how [much] I'd sort of been through in a way because I'd been through the people telling me their stories of the very first day. And how they couldn't breathe and they'd tell me five or six times that they were going to die and one part of the brain says, "I'm dead," the other part of their brain says, "No, I'm alive," and they'd sit there and try and keep telling the stories until they could convince themselves they were alive. They were basically schizophrenic. . . . There was a lot of it. And that was traumatic to me because I have never dealt with anybody with that kind of severe trauma to their bodies. I am not trained to do that, I hadn't done that before.

Figley argues that PTSD perhaps should be known as *"Primary* Traumatic Stress Disorder," rather than Post-Traumatic Stress Disorder, since every stress reaction is "post" by definition.[29] Secondary Traumatic Stress (STS) would then be more clearly seen as the affect on a secondary person occasioned by the caring relationship with those who had primarily experienced a traumatizing event. Such an understanding acknowledges that as humans we are interdependent and interconnected, that suffering ripples out into the social system, and that what hurts you pains me also. Such is the cost of caring. Figley even argues that this ripple includes supervisors and other supporters of those who are themselves supporting the traumatized, coining the term "tertiary stress disorder."[30]

B. Hudnall Stamm of the National Center for PTSD says, "The great controversy about helping-induced trauma is not 'Can it happen?' but 'What shall we call it?' . . . It is apparent that there is no routinely used term to designate exposure to another's traumatic material by virtue of one's role as a helper. Four terms are most common: 'compassion fatigue' (CF); 'countertransference' (CT); 'secondary traumatic stress'; and 'vicarious traumatization' (VT)."[31] One can see the "vicarious" nature in the following description, which comes from another chaplain:

> A lot of people telling me, "I thought I was going to die." This kind of thing, it was just amazing. . . . I worked a long time as an illustrator and as a storyteller, that was my thing. So I'm kind of sensitive about action in stories and I'm kind of drawn into this, you're kind of feeling it with them in a way. And *as they're telling the story, you're reliving the experience*. And so you come out of that shift that you pulled, going home and this stuff is just kind of going through your head. You're just processing and processing and processing, over and over and over again. There were a lot of like things that happened along those lines where you found yourself just totally drawn in.

Stamm cites Figley's use of the phrase "compassion fatigue" to describe the secondary stress that may be a consequence of working with the traumatized in helping relationships. Figley continues to prefer the terms *compassion stress* or *compassion fatigue* as a "the most friendly term for this phenomenon."[32] Stephen Roberts, Kevin Ellers, and John Wilson, in picking up Figley's term, say that "In simple to understand language, compassion fatigue is the 'cost of caring' of working with victims of trauma or catastrophic events that shows itself as spiritual, physical, and/ or emotional fatigue and exhaustion."[33]

At the heart of Figley's work on compassion fatigue are the two strands of environment and relationship due to empathy and exposure. Clergy, psychotherapists, and other mental health professionals are regularly exposed to the traumatic stories of others, which make them especially vulnerable both through intensity and the cumulative effects. Figley cites four additional reasons that increase this vulnerability:

1. Empathy is a major resource for Trauma Workers to help the Traumatized.
2. Many Trauma Workers have experienced some type of traumatic event in their lives.
3. Unresolved trauma of the Worker will be activated by reports of similar trauma in clients.
4. Children's traumata are also provocative for caregivers. Police, fire fighters, EMTs, and other emergency workers report that they are most vulnerable to compassion fatigue when dealing with the pain of children.

Figley sees the importance of warning those engaged in trauma work, such as disaster-response chaplaincy, of the risks of compassion fatigue but sees also that it can be preventable. For clergy the primary way to mitigate the effects of compassion fatigue is to practice self-care that includes (a) supervision; (b) maintaining a sense of "connectedness" with peers, with denominational bodies, with those outside their sphere of ministry, with their families, friends, and children; and (c) having a reflective "self-focus."[35] We will see that this is not simply about taking care of "oneself," but one's "self."

Attention to risk factors of previous and cumulative trauma in those working with trauma is important. Such trauma should not necessarily rule out those persons for this type of work, but increased pastoral supervision, communal care, and "self-focus," as Figley describes, may be necessary to prevent an overwhelming increase in STS. A couple of the chaplains noted the effect of trauma in their own lives and how this contributed to the traumatic effect of the ministry at Ground Zero as we can see from the following account.

> I think it was just a lot of things coming together at once, basically. I think there was something to do with my brother; my brother had died the March before, not even a year before. And I think one of the reasons I wanted to come down here was on account of him. I don't know why. He was like seven years younger than me and just suddenly BOOM, gone, just down, he was gone. And we were very, very, very close.
>
> So I think some of my coming here had to do with my immersing myself into something that was a distraction in a way almost. Or to dissolve, or to *immerse myself into somebody else's pain.* I don't know, I never talked to anybody about it at any length, but, because I function pretty well on a self-analysis basis. And what I was doing also, I processed everything that happened here, always, by writing it down, for my eyes only, that kind of thing. I did write some things down and I would sit home the next day, the next morning, and just try to put in as great detail everything that happened, everything that went on. And it was a really big help, because once that was done, it was behind me. I pretty much did, as far as just overall trauma or being emotionally affected in any kind of way or physically affected, nothing.

Using Stamm's expanded version of Figley's Compassion Fatigue Test, which assesses Compassion Satisfaction and Burnout as well as Fatigue, research on clergy in 2004 suggested that a small but significant percentage of clergy (9.1 percent) are at an extremely high risk for PTSD even without the advent of a disaster.[36] This includes clergy in everyday pastoral care work with those who are suffering in some way. Therefore, in an environment of disaster, when people are going back to or seeking out churches, synagogues, mosques, and other faith communities to cope with a changing world and worldview, clergy are more prone to the traumatic effects of helping others.

When one takes into account that the chaplains who lived in New York and the surrounding regions had secondarily suffered the disaster themselves, and were exposed to potentially horrific sights and smells, in intense empathic relationship with those who are grieving the loss of those they are seeking to recover, we can see what a potent mix that might be for trauma. How does one work with the traumatized when one may be somewhat traumatized oneself? The answers are both in the work and in the relationships within it and around it.

Along with the risks and the measures to mitigate against them, Figley stresses that "we have a need to emphasize that this work is most rewarding: one can see the immediate transformation from sadness, depression, and desperation of people suffering the shock of highly stressful events to hope, joy, and a renewed sense of purpose and meaning of life."[37]

Although not currently categorized in the DSM, like PTSD, according to Figley and other researchers, the symptoms of STS are similarly clustered: arousal, avoidance, and intrusion. You can see these all in some of the chaplains' responses, such as:

> Still, there are occasional moments when the subway is unexplainably delayed, or you hear an unexplained loud sound, that you think, "Is this it again?" [*arousal*]

> I developed a certain sort of fear of another attack, I mean, just kind of this anxiety . . . I just remember looking up at the ceiling and I just was overwhelmed by some anxiety. I was sort of like "Okay, shut down, don't pay attention to this." But just that sense of, of collapsing and stuff collapsing. [*intrusion*]

> There's stuff that happens. I still duck every time there's a low-flying airplane over Manhattan. I mean literally duck. And loud explosive noises make me really jump. Not lightning and thunder, but crashes on the street, things like that make me duck for cover and I feel the whole process beginning again. Seeing video again or pictures again of . . . I mean, I'm not going to go see this movie, "9/11." No way I'm going to go. [*arousal, avoidance*]

A few of the chaplains could see a significant ongoing impact in their lives five years after the 9/11 disaster.

> Post-traumatic stress disease. Yeah, I'm suffering from it because there are things that set me off in terms of sadness or I'll have that feeling of horror and it'll come and go. Or I'll just feel, you know there's been so much with this "9/11" movie and a couple other things just keep on showing up on television and you're not ready for it. Something else, pop.

> Well, I'd have to say that I can't get over it. That I'm not over it. It brings tears to my eyes, I'm just not over it. It's so affecting, so deep, so whatever, I'm just not over it. For whatever reason, it's like a magnet, that brings all the other

loss and it's like the summary of loss or disaster or so that all of the others of my life collapse and it just becomes sort of this image or this icon for all those other losses.

PTSD, STS, and compassion fatigue are not simply characterized by their symptoms, but by the number of symptoms, their duration, and impact on life activities such as work, study, and relationships. For a clinical diagnosis, one needs to experience at least one symptom of intrusive reexperiencing, two of arousal, and three symptoms of avoidance. Despite the former chaplain's comment, none of the chaplains seemed to be experiencing symptoms that were significantly affecting their ability to carry on their ministry; however, the impact of 9/11 continues to persist, especially at trigger events, such as the release of a 9/11 film, or the advent of an anniversary. Another chaplain summed up a feeling common to many, "Well, you know, it's underneath the surface for all of us," before he went on to describe how, after a small plane accident into an Upper East Side high-rise apartment building in Manhattan, he became conscious that he had then been expecting something else about fifteen minutes later, as had happened on 9/11.

However, a number of the interviewed chaplains reported experiencing the following psychological and spiritual symptoms *during* their chaplaincy: intrusive thoughts or sensate experiences; hypervigilance and hyperarousal; nightmares; "falling to pieces"; anger with family, with parish; distancing, sense of isolation, and alienation with those at work, with family; depressed mood or sad all the time; prayer life decreasing; social life decreasing; sense of emptiness; and guilt.

Although a couple of the chaplains said that anger was a pattern before their chaplaincy at the T. Mort., a number of them noted how this was not characteristic of their normal way of functioning, sharing comments such as,

> But I do recall anger at times that was very inappropriate outside of the event. I definitely remember that. Somebody would say something and I was like flash and I go, "What am I doing here?" Even in my church, you know, a couple times. That was definitely not normal for me.

> I guess, what some people would say as well would rub me up the wrong way, because I would see it as not important. You know, sort of their own little cubbyhole of their own work. Not connected to people but administration that would really get me going. I'm normally not like that.

> I'd be irritable and on a short fuse at times, particularly with my wife. But I didn't recognize it. I mean, I knew I was tired, I come home and go to sleep, try to recover and get up the next day and go to work. She described me: I was goofy. . . . It wasn't normal. It wasn't *my* normal way. It was odd.

A number of the chaplains shared an immense sense of gratitude toward their spouses, partners, and families for "bearing with them" during the time of their chaplaincy. One chaplain shared how such a ministry can contribute to a sense of community at the site of ministry and a distancing and isolation at home:

> I felt a lot of bond with the folks that were doing the recovery work because, how do you go home and talk about this? What do you say? I mean, you had images and experiences, I had weeks' worth of images and experiences in one night. How do you explain that?

One can see the risks in such ministry, not only for the chaplain but also for those that were in relationship with them. A few reported relationships that did not survive the ministry. For some this was a positive choice, their 9/11 experience highlighting what was important and how they would choose to do things differently.

A number of the chaplains, when asked, commented on their dream life during their chaplaincy. A little over 20 percent mentioned vivid dreams or nightmares of such things as planes crashing into buildings, traumatic body recoveries, and experiences of helplessness. One chaplain described the intrusiveness of such an effect:

> Initially it was all the nightmares, to have no night when I slept peacefully . . . for a month and thinking, I'm going to lose my mind. To wake up in the middle of the night and have these horrible visions, some of them were just replays of what we saw. Or it would be yet another event and stuff like that. . . . And it was just such, one of those where you wake up and you can't quit dreaming, you're still dreaming, and dreaming, and dreaming. It's just a horrible thing, that I would say, those kinds of things where *you feel almost invaded by it*.

One of the chaplains dreamed about his friend who had been on one of the hijacked planes with his young son. Another chaplain's dream life showed the cumulative nature of trauma.

> . . . a lot of sleep disturbance, a lot of heart palpitations. What I realized from what I was reading, because none of us were prepared for working with trauma at this level. And there's this great book, [by] Dr. Judith Herman, *Trauma and Recovery*, and part through when I'm reading, I realize I had the symptoms and one of them was that it will, big trauma like this, will trigger past trauma. So I was having nightmares about [a traumatic situation] in my twenties, and every night. So I went back into therapy. It's like, "I can't handle this." And I had to go into therapy to deal with that. It took about three months to settle that. But that was a big one.

One of the chaplains, however, reported symptoms that were exactly the opposite.

> Well, I rarely remember dreams, but the whole time from beginning to end until we were finally done in June, I did not remember a single dream, not one. I don't know what was going on in there, but I was not remembering any dreams at all. And I my wife would tell me, "Boy, you must have been dreaming last night, you were restless, you were 'this,' you were 'that.'" Not one. I would even go to sleep saying, "Remember your dream." And that used to work. Nothing. So I'm not sure what was going on in that process. But it was kept from my consciousness.

Some of the chaplains also reported physical symptoms of stress, including sleeplessness, poor eating, losing or gaining weight, fatigue, breathing problems, digestive problems, bowel problems, constant state of physical tension, heart palpitations, overactive adrenals, and high blood pressure. One chaplain who said that he had no signs or symptoms of stress during the chaplaincy went on to say:

> Having said that, the last shift I did was early June. August, I'm at three hundred pounds, prediabetic, hypertensive, borderline congestive heart failure. Coincidence? . . . I find it causal. Now, did I start work at the morgue at a hundred and sixty pounds? No. But, yeah, a whole variety of that. One of the things, there was a bar, a New York bar, you know, good restaurant, good bar, you got the restaurant in the back, the bar in the front. Well, it turns out the woman that ran the restaurant part of it, her husband was a retired firefighter. Upon occasion I would call my wife when I would come and she'd meet me there at the restaurant and I would come in and the proprietress would take one look at me and upon occasion have a pitcher of beer if it were a hard day. I mean at one point, when they had the ramp in, I walked that ramp seven times. The least number of litters, body bags behind me was three. The highest was five. Had I had to do that one more time, they would have carried me out. . . . How could one not be affected?

One can see the complex relationship between stress, self-care, and the short-term coping that can lead to further stress. The chaplain above went on to say that now he was generally eighty to one hundred pounds lighter, and of "sufficient health for his age and height."

Like many of the recovery workers that spent days on site at Ground Zero, one of the chaplains developed extensive breathing problems and a form of lung cancer. She had surgery to remove two "lumps," part of her bronchi, lymph nodes, and an adenocarcinoma—a malignant tumor that was six centimeters in diameter. She shared that she had smoked as a teenager but had not smoked in a long time and was considered a nonsmoker medically. Following the surgery she undertook preventative chemotherapy. When asked whether she wore a mask when at Ground Zero, she commented that it was just "a paper mask for the longest time and . . . they'd clog up and then you couldn't breathe with them. So I would say it was probably January before I got a decent mask." Other chaplains commented on the wearing of masks:

> Hardly anybody wore those masks. . . . One time I went down there, they had found numerous remains, an OSHA guy said, "Where's your mask?" I said, "It's back there." He said, "You better go get it." But, generally speaking, they weren't worn as much as they should have been. One of the reasons was, especially for a chaplain, you need to communicate. You can't communicate with a mask. It was ridiculous. So you wear it around your neck. But in the photos, you'll see maybe 10 or 20 percent of the people wearing masks and the rest aren't. In fact, it was determined about two months before they closed that the masks really weren't proper, the filters were kind of general filters and there might be materials in there that could go through the filters. It took them a long time to figure that out. And then they were fitting for new masks over on that end over there. I think OSHA was over there and you had to be fitted with another mask, but I never got one.

The description of how many people were wearing masks again shows some of the challenges of working with a variety of different cultures and in the difficult conditions. It may be one question about whether a recovery worker digging for remains wears a mask; it may be another for a chaplain that is seeking to be pastorally available to speak to others. Or it may be the chaplain makes decisions that reflect the majority of the culture, as this chaplain described. ". . . some of the stuff I already knew, because I have a clue. For instance, if everyone else in the room in the morgue has a mask on because of the odor, so do I. If no one else in the room has a mask on, I do not."

When chaplains were called onto the Pile or down into the Pit, however, their main role was to communicate through prayer and blessing and in the times waiting around, with those standing alongside them. Some chose to wear masks between the blessings; many did not. In hindsight, this can seem like an unwise decision but one that was understandable for a long time as can be seen in one chaplain's reflections:

> That as a rubble site, it was unbelievable in the amount of rubble. But in the site of the two buildings, where did they go? Where did all the stuff that was the buildings go? We know now it went into the air and into the stuff that everybody was breathing. Thank you, Christy Whitman, for telling us that the air was good to breathe.

As you can see, the stresses at Ground Zero were multifaceted.

Chaplaincy and Compassion Fatigue

A 2005 study, "Secondary Traumatic Stress Among Disaster Mental Health Workers Responding to the September 11 Attacks," found that "higher STS was associated with therapist variables of heavier prior trauma caseload, less professional experience, youth, and therapist's discussion of his or her own trauma or trauma work in his or her own therapy."[38] They found no correlation between STS and gender or personal trauma history. They affirmed that STS has not been found to be due to therapist incompetence but "seen as a normal reaction to empathic relationship with trauma survivors."[39] Two things were of note in this latter study as they relate to the experience of the chaplains at the T. Mort. in contrast to those that worked at other sites. There was a significant relationship between higher STS and those who (1) worked with firefighters, or (2) worked with clients who "discussed morbid material (e.g. encountering body parts in the rubble)."[40] For the chaplains at the T. Mort. who were the ones blessing those body parts in the rubble and working alongside those firefighters, the risk of STS could be seen to be significantly high.

These aspects also stand out in the narratives of the chaplains: first, the "morbid" nature of the material and the reality of the persons they represented; second, the pain of being alongside those who were grieving for those who were being recovered. One chaplain, when asked what she found most difficult, describes this reality:

> What I found most difficult was praying over the remains. A young man from [*a financial firm*], found in December, almost completely whole torso, wallet in trouser pocket, photo ID—young, good looking; lived in [*town*], probably had young family. One good thing: family would receive news soon that he'd been found; so much DNA evidence. Also the night a firefighter's son was found, had met father and brother two weeks after 9/11 on the Pile; was on in December when he was found. Very moving, very sacred. Powerful honor guard late at night in the darkness and bright lights of the site.

Some chaplains described the difficulty of the nature of the body parts, the dismemberment, the stage of decomposition or mummification but in a way that was easier to depersonalize. Like the chaplain above, it was when they were able to personalize the part that it became most difficult.

> And at times, you started to stop seeing that because everything was so charred that it didn't necessarily look human. But there were days, and I'm sure you know this, that I know we would come to an elevator shaft or something and there would be five bodies. Full bodies that you recognized with faces and wallets and you'd see what their children looked like and that was hard. Once there was someone who was completely charred, but their hand

wasn't and it had a ring on it, a woman's hand, and it was beautifully mani-
cured and everybody just broke down. So as soon as I got a break I would
run over to St. Paul's and cry. And empty so that I could go back in. So it was
overwhelming and yet, it was so full of all different emotions.

Sometimes what you're seeing was just, it was, it's like beautiful. Do you
know what I mean? I guess you can say such a thing, I don't know. But it's
also a lesson in how frail a human being is. How small people are, really. How
small a hand is. How tiny a hand and a forearm is. There was one amazing
thing, a complete spinal column came in one time. Like just complete, not
broken, only that, no ribs. I mean how did that happen? I think one of the
most poignant and touching things was when somebody was physically identified. Because in all that, that hell that took place, you'd come in with. . . . In
all that time I was there, I never saw a full person. There was never a complete person.

As you can see, the beauty of the human body is as painful as the opposite.
The challenge of engaging intimately in prayer and then disengaging from the person was constant. If remains were found with wallets, the Medical Examiner could
make a preliminary identification. Often wallets, when opened, would hold family
pictures also. Many of the chaplains found it helpful when the person was identified as they could pray for them by name and for their family. However, this was a
two-edged sword as can be seen in this chaplain's account. A few of the chaplains
mentioned doing something similar.

There was one time where it was almost a full body recovery and the bag is
opened, the Medical Examiner starts working with it and what initially looked
like kind of rumpled laundry. All of a sudden started with a little manipulation
or what have you, it became recognizable as a suit. And with that, all of a
sudden acknowledging here's the head and in extreme decay. We're talking
and the Medical Examiner sticking his hand into the pocket of the suit and
pulling out this guy's ID from [*a particular company*] and seeing his picture
of, you know this young guy, you know probably like mid- to late twenties.
And seeing that picture where here's this guy full of life and then seeing this.
Now that, that's memorable. That's memorable. Of just feeling like, "My God,
what . . . ? That brought it home much more about what a loss of life. Versus
parts and small little fragments and things as one in the midst of this, I think
I was able to divorce myself more from the reality. That brought the reality
smack into my face, I just felt, how terribly sad. Sad.

And the other thing was I knew his name. And when I went home, I Googled
his name. And his family had some kind of a memorial Web site. And I just
remember sitting in my apartment and thinking, these people, I presume, in

whatever length of time it's going to take, are going to get word that he's been found. I knew it then, but that was kind of weird to have that kind of information and know that the people this is going to really matter to don't have it yet. I mean, certainly it wasn't the case like I wanted to contact them or anything, I can't even remember his name now. But I just remember in that point thinking about them and wondering, is this going to reopen the wounds? What does this do for them? And that was tough, that was really tough.

In some way there was a confessional aspect to this experience, yet it was shared with the community around the T. Mort. This provided strong bonds of relationship down at the site. However, it also served to increase a sense of isolation in relation to the rest of the world.

Preventing compassion fatigue after a disaster is both extremely hard and easy. It is easy in that the prevention steps involve basic self-care. It is hard in that after a disaster practicing self-care is often on the bottom of our to-do list. . . . *Practice self-care. That is the number one way to prevent compassion fatigue.*[41]

Since self-care "on the job" was such a challenge, and the site and its sights so potentially traumatizing, self-care "off the job" was even more important. Of course, the challenge of this also was that chaplains were conducting their regular ministries *as well* as the ministry at Ground Zero. This raises the question of how the chaplains handled those hard days and what they did in between. Some of the chaplains worked at the T. Mort. on their day off from their usual ministry and, therefore, did not necessarily get any time off otherwise. Others worked at Ground Zero as part of their overall ministry. One chaplain described the reality of the former, and the cost of it.

I was very tired, very tired. I mean, you put in another extra three days and I had told them in the parish that, "You're not gonna miss anything." There was still the weekday masses, the Sunday masses, all of the stuff that Christmas, Lent, and we did, lots and lots and lots and lots of stuff. It really didn't impact on me physically and it didn't affect the parish until last fall, and that was the health issues.

Almost 70 percent of the responding chaplains were in congregational ministry, and 43 percent of these were the primary leader of a faith community (church or synagogue) that ranged from fifty to two thousand congregants, with an average of about three hundred. Nine percent were hospital or hospice chaplains or directors of pastoral care who worked with death, dying, and sickness on a daily basis. Included in 27 percent that did not lead or assist in a congregation during their chaplaincy at Ground Zero were several whose ministries were also demanding, such as executive director, dean of a seminary, and provincial minister of a religious order. Others who were deacons gave of either their secular work time or worked at Ground Zero in addition to their jobs. Only one was retired. For most, therefore, intentional self-care had to be very deliberate and fitted in to existing life and ministry.

Tanya Pagán Raggio and Willard Ashley note, "We live in a time of tension, terror, and turbulence. We need healthy clergy to help us navigate a world where human evil and natural disasters grab the headlines. Self-care is not an option; it is a requirement that should start before the disaster occurs so we can give our best to our families and vocation."[42] One of the chaplains showed how an already established balanced model of self-care supported him during the disaster.

> I don't recall any, any excess feeling of stress. I know at the time I was. All the time I was going to the gym because I had had a scare, and so three days a week I was going to the gym regularly. And I don't remember going more regularly during that. I was taking care of myself and my regular habit of spending time in prayer as well as the [daily] offices and everything else. And I remember relying on those, both the prayer times and the gym times. I'm not aware of the feeling of stress. After working at night, gradually I'd come home and sleep for a while and get up again. But I'm not remembering feeling stressed out by it. But, I also know that I was *taking a different view*, while I wasn't designed for it, it would have had the effect of dealing with that stress and keeping it from building up.

The model offered by this chaplain shows attention to physical, emotional, and spiritual resources. Forty-five percent of the responding chaplains reported an increase in the amount of body therapy, exercise, massage, yoga, or other physical self-care practices. The predominant increase was in exercise and massage. Twelve percent reported a decrease in exercise but an increase in massage. A reason for this may have been the massage therapists that worked down at Ground Zero that were available to workers at the respite centers and in some other locations. One chaplain reported a decrease in all body therapy, exercise, and massage. Almost 40 percent reported no change in the amount or lack of these physical aspects of self-care.

Beyond the self-care steps to "go a little slower, time for yourself, eat well, get enough sleep, converse with colleagues, and as the months go along take some vacation time,"[43] Roberts, Ellers, and Wilson suggest Figley's prescription of supervision, connectedness, and self-focus to further prevent compassion fatigue. Where pastoral supervision may be part of the ethical expectations in some other countries, it seems rare for many clergy in the United States, beyond seminary or clinical training programs, to engage in supervision on a regular basis. However, the possibility of seeking out colleagues or other professionals to debrief during a disaster may be more common. A number of chaplains, however, showed reflective practices that Roberts, Ellers, and Wilson would include under "connectedness" and "self-focus":

Journaling was really part of it. Always making my rounds through St. Paul's and getting some encouragement and affection, making sure that I talked to people while I was down here. I mean, *connecting with people*, that was really a help to have, to have a community, *to be a part of a community* [my church], and come out because they were supportive and accepting, even though it was difficult to communicate and I think there was some degree of distance. I think that like anyone that's around death or something like that, there's a degree to which people sort of like, "Well, it's good for you to be there but . . .", you know, they take a step back. I think that some people may have found it a bit overwhelming for me every week to bring the Trade Center back into [*our community*] and the site and the recovery. *I think one of my coping skills is "Just be open to this." Come down and be open to what develops* in the experience. See what God's going to teach me.

I am much more religiously, to use a term here, doing the [*daily*] offices okay and that helps a lot. And like I said, when it comes to stuff that I can't handle, I'm really good at going into the chapel at the church and going "Listen, I can't take this. *I'm giving this back.* I'm expecting you to take care of it."

For those chaplains who, either through working in a hospital or through personal experience, were used to being around bodies it was not necessarily the morbid aspects of the work that had an impact on them and often the relationship between compassion fatigue and compassion satisfaction was high.

Death itself doesn't have the same mystique for me as it has for some other people because I grew up essentially in a cemetery, because my grandfather, his house was in the middle of the cemetery. And when I was in college, I was a volunteer fireman and we had the experience of being at a bus fire where all of the passengers on the bus had been killed and burned. So as I said, I definitely think that I probably went into it with a slightly different background than a lot of the other chaplains did who may not have had the same familiarity with thing having to do with death and dying.

Again, the chaplains' experience, self-care, interpretation of what they experienced, and the meaning of what they did could be seen to be significant factors mitigating against or contributing to a traumatic outcome of the stress of working with bodies and those grieving them. One can see how the desire and privilege of contributing, which Winnicott sees as so important, is not only identified with on an individual basis but as part of the larger whole. Just as we can identify with the destructive tendencies in humanity, in the opportunity to contribute we can see that they are *not* the end of the story.

I think on the other side of it the feelings I had were of *gratitude* of being able to be there and to see how people were giving so much of themselves. It was that side which stays with me now very much. And even at the time of being down there, going off at the end of a shift to see whoever it was coming in to take over. To see those who were going to stay there, for however number of hours still, the EMTs and the cops and the medical people and all of that. It was a good feeling in that sense to see that *mankind is good* basically. And every time I left, it happened the last time, I left knowing that whoever was there with me that, that little group in there was doing a lot of good. It was a *privilege* to be there with them, it really was. The feelings now, for those I'll remember that I spent time with down there, gratitude for their friendship and support.

Despite the physical, psychological, and spiritual cost of the ministry, it was also for many extremely life giving, something that could mitigate against long-term effects of stress. The following chaplain's reflection on the enlivening effect of ministry at Ground Zero is representative of what a number felt, although many found it had the ripple effect of enlivening their other ministries as well.

You used the word *essence* earlier, as terrible as that attack was, it brought us to our essence. It brought us right to what's important. The fundamentals, the basics, the thing that does give us life, holds us together. And I think if we understand that as a church, understand that and really try to communicate that, somehow, *God is real*. And when you walk into the sanctuary or when you walk down the street, but particularly when you walk into a sanctuary, this is important. It might be the most important thing we're doing this week and He's here. She, He, *God's here*. The Holy Spirit is real. And just believe it. It'll make such a difference in your life and not a lot of words have to be used to say that. Some long thirty-minute sermon? No, just say that. And if you want to talk about it, we'll talk about it in a class after or in studying the Scripture where we see where God reveals God's self to everyone. So the church can become very jaundiced in my view because of some of the issues that seem to center on buildings. We have to keep these buildings up and we have to have a budget for it and people have to pledge more. That is boring stuff to me. It's not life-giving stuff. It's secondary. But it's the first item on many agendas in churches. I never have liked that. But when these buildings were destroyed and there was still life in spite of that. Thank God we had those places where we could gather and talk about it and go out and serve. It just gave new meaning. As terrible as it was, it just brought things alive for me and the church and the people's faith and my own and I'm grateful for that. Very thankful. I thought I'd retire with a blasé attitude toward the church. And that was a step above bitterness, sort of. Or just, blah, just so glad to be away from that institution that emphasized the secondary. I don't feel that way at all. I know that's there and that stuff, but so is that faith and God is very real in the lives of the people.

Again, one can see that the physical and psychological stresses had to be held in tension with the meaning of the ministry and how it fit into, or developed, a new worldview. We can see here how self-care is not simply about practices of care but care for "the self." Part of self-care was having a meaningful ministry and doing it well; part of it was about what chaplains did with it when not at the site. If they did not have the spiritual and communal resources to hold, frame, and contain the ministry, it began to contain them, a risk we can see in the following chaplains' reflection five years after the disaster.

There's part of me that's clinging to it and I worry about that. That so much of my identity has become enmeshed with 9/11. I feel that 9/11 gave me a sense of legitimacy for my ministerial work. That, yeah, okay, I am a minister. I'm a good minister. Now I'm a little afraid that I'm clinging to it, [to] other people's view of me as a 9/11 chaplain, that I might use it, when people find out that I did that. And I won't offer it up, but somebody I know will offer it up in trying to impress other people with my legitimacy as a chaplain. Oh, she worked at 9/11. And I'm afraid without that, will people still think I'm a good minister? It's amazing that if somebody hears that you worked as a chaplain at Ground Zero, doors open or all of a sudden people look at you like you know what you're doing. Even though I know what I'm doing. I know I know what I'm doing. But maybe there's ego there in being attached to that. But do I want to be identified as that for the rest of my life? Or do I want to be able to let that go and see where God wants me to go?

Winnicott's Contribution to Trauma Theory

If self-care mitigates against STS, one must have a sense of "the self" to care for. Winnicott states that in early development, "The central self could be said to be the inherited potential which is experiencing a continuity of being, and acquiring in its own way and at its own speed a personal psychic reality and a personal body-scheme."[44] In another paper he notes that "The True Self quickly develops complexity, and relates to external reality by natural processes, by such processes as develop in the individual infant in the course of time. The infant then comes to be able to react to a stimulus *without trauma* because the stimulus has a counterpart in the individual's inner psychic reality."[45] A strong sense of self, Winnicott's "True Self," is characterized by an ability to tolerate what Winnicott calls "breaks in continuity" and "reactive experiences" without having to so defend oneself against others or the world that one becomes isolated psychically, and falsely compliant externally.

However, in a period where one may feel somewhat traumatized by the "too sudden or unpredictable intrusion of actual fact"[46] beyond that which we can comprehend or contain, one's defense and coping mechanisms, such as the sense of identification mentioned by the previous chaplain, can come to the fore. If we are defending our inner reality through a rigidifying of what Winnicott calls our "False Self" organization then this may exacerbate the issue of compassion fatigue through isolation. J. Eric Gentry from the Florida Center for Public Health Preparedness states:

> One of the ways trauma seems to affect us all, caregivers included, is to leave us with a disconnected sense of isolation. A common thread we have found with sufferers of compassion fatigue symptoms has been the progressive loss in their sense of connections and community. Many caregivers become increasingly isolated as their symptoms of compassion fatigue increase. Fear of being perceived as weak, impaired, or incompetent by peers and clients, along with time constraints and loss of interest, have all been cited by caregivers suffering from compassion fatigue as reasons for diminished intimate and collegial connection.[47]

Despite the normalization of symptoms of compassion fatigue, the fact that chaplains often feel like the caregivers to the caregivers, the temptation to perceive oneself as "weak, impaired, or incompetent" is constant. One must be careful, then, not simply to attend to the externals, going through the motions of self-care. Rather, care that attends to what the self experiences as traumatic and to the constitution of the self itself is vital.

The challenge for the chaplains who were coming to this disaster with less experience than others was to be able to allow themselves their vulnerability and, at times, feelings of inadequacy without being overwhelmed by those, to learn to function from the True Self, even while having to comply with all the institutional and cultural challenges.

> There were a lot of like things that happened along those lines where you found yourself just totally drawn in, like the first time I escorted remains out under a flag. My own thing is, like, "What am I doing here, doing this?" You know what I mean? This is crazy, *this is way above my spiritual awareness* and level at this point. And those were very, very powerful experiences. As a deacon I had done some preaching, you know, I had done some sermons and things and of course I taught classrooms. So I'm not nervous about being in front of people per se. But I was a basket case with this stuff. I was just a nervous wreck. And I always read from something. Only towards the end did I kind of trust the spirit to actually motivate me.

> I can remember one of the last few shifts, where they were in the lobby of the South Tower. I was on shift and there were a lot of recoveries from that lobby and they spent most of the night. I arrived at midnight and the chaplain who

had been there was like, "Oh, thank God you're here." And so I led an honor guard up the ramp for five different people, three firemen. And one of the firemen's dads came (he was also a fireman), and his brothers, and they all walked. And at that point you were on a mike and the whole site shut down. You know, I got a little church in [*a town*] and here I am, on this stage and that was anxious. And I don't know, Did I do alright? You don't get feedback for that. But I did the best I could and so go ahead.

Many of the chaplains felt a profound responsibility to "do the job well" in the face of ministry to others who had worked so hard to recover the bodies that the chaplains blessed and for the families that were receiving them, in this case literally. One chaplain said, "I think feeling adequate to the task—that bothered me most. Of being engaged and as real as I wanted to be and to be perceived as such, and recognized, and accepted as such. And I always wanted to, I think that was the thing that bothered me most, of wanting to be appropriate to the task that we were doing."

It is here self-care must especially be seen as interpersonal and communal rather than individual. This is particularly the case when the life-cycle of the disaster in general society is "out of sync" with the life-cycle of a disaster at a recovery site. One of the chaplains shared such a feeling, saying that the worst part of his experience was

When I would be coming home in the morning, because I always worked the night shift pretty much, tired and sort of full of everything that had happened during the night and walking by and some of the people there looking at me and almost, you know, "Why are you doing that?" The World Trade Center was far removed from them and there was almost a sense of hostility of somebody relating to that. And that happened a couple of times that I was going home in the early morning.

Given the potent combination of chaplains' daily pastoral work, their own trauma history, level of education and intellect, and the dis-integrating physical and emotional forces inherent in a disaster site, there is a strong need for an individual chaplain to have the resources of trusted others rather than to rely on their own assessment of how well they are doing. Winnicott cautions about defensive structures that may pertain to highly educated people such as the chaplains,[48] saying, "When a False Self becomes organized in an individual who has a high intellectual potential there is a very strong tendency for the mind to become the location of the False Self, and in this case there develops a dissociation between intellectual activity and psychosomatic existence."[49]

As noted earlier, it is this focus on existence that Winnicott adds to trauma theory. Unlike Sigmund Freud, who came to reject the reality of seduction in favor of the fantasy of seduction as the traumatic catalyst for neurosis, Winnicott's understanding of trauma sounds much more like that of recent theorists:

Trauma is an impingement from the environment and from the individual's reaction to the impingement that occurs prior to the individual's development of mechanisms that make the unpredictable predictable. Following traumatic experiences new defenses are quickly organized, but in the split-second before this can take place the individual has had the continuous line of his or her existence (as recorded in the personal computer) broken, broken by autonomic reaction to the environmental failure.[50]

Winnicott's understanding in emphasizing "unpredictability" shows that there is a relation between trauma and worldview, which he describes as the capacity to "believe in," and an "average expectable environment" that provides confirmation of that belief. He emphasizes the person's reaction to the event, which, while depending on the nature of the trauma, he describes as "hate." He acknowledges the mechanisms that help defend against the trauma but also notes that it only takes a split-second to be traumatized. The DSM-IV definition of PTSD does not seem that different: "the person experienced, witnessed, or was confronted with an event or events that involved actual or threatened death or serious injury, or a threat to the physical integrity of self or others,"[51] even if more specific. Yet it is to be noted that the DSM-IV definition focuses solely on death, threat, injury, and to the *physical* integrity of the self, and that the psychological side is simply the response to such. Winnicott sees trauma more to do with psychological threat to the *psychic existence of the self*, not simply the physical body, which is implied in current definitions. Further, Winnicott sees trauma as related to development in terms of defense mechanisms: ". . . this theory includes the idea of trauma, by which I mean an experience against which the ego defences were inadequate at the stage of emotional development of the individual at the time. . . ."[52]

When simply reading a quote from Winnicott about defense mechanisms it would be easy to focus on the mechanisms and think in terms of classic psychoanalytic theory,[53] in terms of mechanisms such as repression, undoing, sublimation, regression, reversal, and so forth. However, Winnicott indicates it is more fruitful to focus on what one is defending against rather than what the defense mechanism is itself. This brings us back to Winnicott's developmental theory and understanding of the integration of the self. We can see this in his discussion of trauma.

The result of trauma must be some degree of distortion of development. It will be seen how normal and healthy anger would be in comparison with such awfulness. Anger would imply survival of the ego and a retention of the idea of an alternative experience in which the "let-down" did not occur. Clinically, the state which is called "panic" easily becomes a feature. Direct study of panic is unproductive because panic itself is a defence. It is of value to look on panic as an organised awfulness arranged around a phobic situation whose aim (in the defence organisation) is to protect the individual from new examples of the unpredictable.[54]

These defenses are to protect against the disintegration of the ego and even the self. Such integration depends on the degree of emotional development and integration already achieved. Paradoxically, in Winnicott's thought, the greater the achievement of integration the more the person "can be *hurt* by being traumatised; hurt or made to suffer, as opposed to being prevented from achieving integration."[55] When faced with that in our world which shatters our belief system, even for a split-second, we can feel that the self which constitutes our very being can begin to "fall apart," or even cease to exist.[56] Trauma, then, is the threat of annihilation of the self, of not going on being, and perhaps also the pain or suffering of the integrated self.

Another chaplain noted the challenge that related to both his own defenses and the desire to defend that which was "sacred":

> So a lot of the stuff I just kept within and learned to cope with it that way. I think down here the same, that not being isolated in that sense, because there were people I could talk to, but maybe not trusting what they would do with what I would say. I think that fear would be there, too, somewhere in there because of what I experienced here—a lot of it was sacred: the sharing with the EMTs in the morgue, the stories I would not share with anybody. And just, you know, the time standing around or listening to some of the firefighters and cops and Medical Examiners. I wouldn't know what to do with it, it's not something I would bring up in casual conversation. . . . it's not the stuff I would talk about that way and so I would just keep it within and it just stayed there until I shared it all with [*a doctor*].
>
> I sort of realized that no, you got to work at it, too. So that whole side for me, these strongest feelings, there was a fear of rejection, of if I would be seen as sick or something like that. That's not the way I portray myself to people. That I am in control of who I am and my health and all of that but deep down I know "stuff goes wrong." And to admit to that was a big thing. So that was the big fear of opening up. . . .
>
> So I just went and asked [*a colleague*], "You go to see somebody?" He said, "Yes, every week." I said, "Oh, my God," and I said, "Can you tell me who you see?" And he gave me the name and he said, "I'll let him know that you're asking." I said, "Not too quick now." Anyways, so he gave me the number and I think I called him about four months later. It was a big, big move on my part, really big move and my first meeting with [*the doctor*], he sort of asked me, "Yeah, [*your colleague*] told me about you five months ago. What took you so long?" I said, "Actually making the call." But it was good because he's a good man. Tough man but I needed that. It was very good, very good for me. I think I saw him for ten months on a weekly basis.

For some of the chaplains it felt like it was their True Selves that could manifest at Ground Zero, and the break was with existence outside the site.

It was such a new experience and not wanting to be inappropriate, but want-ing to represent God and doing everything right. To the point where to be able to go back [to Ground Zero] because, for lack of a better word, it was "home." This was a comfortable place. And that one of the things I know was really hard at the end was that we were so used to every week leaving the trivial and the petty and the unimportant. There was a lot of good things that were hap-pening ministry-wise, it wasn't all criticism, but there was one time a week at least, where you came, I said it was the *Cheers* moment, "where everybody knows your name," where you're back with people doing a good thing. You came back here and the members at church knew I worked down here, but they probably didn't know—well, some of them knew that I worked at the morgue—but people would ask, "How can you go back week after week?" And I said, "Because in a way it was safe. It was comfortable. Because it was only in here are you with the people that really know, that you don't explain anything, you don't have to rationalize." I was talking with another worker, I said, "To me it must be what it's like when you finally can go to a nudist colony. Where at first when you go in and you've never been a nudist any time in your life. You're going to feel like you stick out, you're going to feel weird. Then all of a sudden you realize everybody's naked, everybody's vulnerable, everybody's doing the same thing." Which is kind of a very perverse way to look at what we did here. Except *we were vulnerable*. But it was very safe because there was nobody that was king of the Pile. Everybody was all about the same purpose in that. And so the hardest part was when we left, we knew we'd never be back.

In discussing schizophrenic and borderline cases, which he sees as very "sophis-ticated defence structures," Winnicott sees an aspect of the illness as "an organisation towards invulnerability,"[57] and notes "If we are successful we enable the patient *to abandon invulnerability and to become a sufferer.*"[58] Although this theory arises out of attention to psychosis, we can see in a general way for the human person suffering is an achievement. Suffering denotes a sense of integrity of the self, the feeling of 'I AM,' and 'I am in my body,' without disintegrating or depersonalizing but the self suffers in relation to traumas that the environment offers up and learns to accept and inte-grate. Such traumas for Winnicott are actual facts of environmental impingement, be it a major trauma or the "cumulative trauma" of relationships that are constantly unreliable, unpredictable, or impinging. One can see the achievement of suffering in relation to trauma, the sense of integration and personalization, in a chaplain's earlier brief comment about one of the visual images contained in the interview: "It's very much like what I saw for the first time that night. That pile. Oh, there's pain with this one. Everything's just flat, leveled on top of vehicles. This one hurts."

One chaplain spoke about his journey through to a place of accepting vulner-ability, when discussing the two-weeks paid leave his church gave those who worked as chaplains in response to the 9/11 disaster.

When we were given money to leave . . . What did they call it? I think it was called *respite*, where for two weeks we were supposed to leave the site, we were supposed to be gone. [I was] wondering, I'm going to leave here, this is where I can come and it's comfortable here. It's where I don't have to worry about being "up" or anything. That I was kind of concerned about being separated from that and what do I do if I have sadness, if I have doubts. I was anxious about that.

And I ended up taking a trip because it was so cheap. It was just very inexpensive to fly at that time. And a lot of the anger that I had, the anger, the sadness, the frustrations and stuff that I thought would come with being separated. It was nice being somewhere else where, again, people cared for me. As soon as they heard my accent and stuff, the guys [from Ground Zero] actually sent me with fire department and police department patches and they said, "Anybody you see that is kind to you, if you see a firefighter, if you see a police officer, just give them [a patch]." I had wads of these things and I came back with none of them. That is how I ended up dealing with all of the different issues for me.

The debriefing was clinical. That short of a period of time didn't help me resolve any of that. But being ready *to receive the ministry of other people*, the love that happened through embraces and through a pat on the back or a smile or whatever at Ground Zero, happened when people weren't curious, they didn't want to hear the morbid stories or anything, they were just glad that I was taking some time for myself and that I'd give them a patch and they bought me a scotch or whatever. That's what ended up taking care of a lot of those issues for me better than more of the program stuff, the debriefing and those things. It never really did it for me.

And I think that's probably another dividend from the whole experience was *being opened to being cared for*. Before I did not like to—that was vulnerability. I wasn't willing to. I probably wanted it but wouldn't express it or wouldn't seek it or allow it even. But I got pretty good at it. I felt better and also realized I think part of it was that because of my love, my ministry being so well received, how can I deny somebody else that opportunity if they sincerely want to do that for me.

Suffering and vulnerability, this chaplain realized, is about mutuality. It is about being willing to receive what one gives, and if it is a ministry grounded in love, that love does not, and should not exclude oneself, one's True Self. Another chaplain noted,

The best I can do with this is to allow things to be what they are. Everything has tradeoffs. There are no more, there are no less, they are. You deal with them the way they are and fully and completely present. Insofar as you'll repress the moment, you'll pick that up later. So that's when on a couple of occasions when I've gone to Eslan Institute out in Big Sur, there would be times when I would be able to sit or lay on the floor and have people touch me and sob. Not crying over a particular thing but just being able to, in a moment of safety, be *entirely vulnerable* without having to explain. Now, that's much better in Big Sur than in a Gator heading down to the Pit. And it's not that one's real and the other isn't. *Both are real, both are authentic.*

In another paper Winnicott speaks about "gross trauma" and "subtle trauma," but goes on to say, "In the end, trauma is the destruction of the purity of individual experience by too sudden or unpredictable intrusion of actual fact, and by the generation of hate in the individual, *hate of the good object*, experienced not as hate but delusionally as being hated."[59] This denotes another aspect to trauma. It is not necessarily the action of "bad objects" that traumatizes as they often act in predictably unreliable or reliably unpredictable ways, such as terrorists committing terrorism. Often what is most traumatic is the "failure of the good object," those people and institutions and even nations that we expect to act in a reliable, constant, and caring way toward us and others, and yet fail to do so. This is one of the reasons why both community in a disaster and community outside of it is important. The chaplains needed to be connected to those who would be external "good objects" for them, encouraging a self-care that they could not always sustain themselves. This is especially true for those pastoral caregivers whose internalized images of what it is to be a "good object" had a tendency to become split and idealized and therefore exacting psychically—in other words, a feeling like one always has to be the good pastor, always available, always in the best form, endlessly empathic, and so forth.

Several of the chaplains experienced this externalization of the "good object" in the care of their parishes or, for those who were in nonstipendiary ministry, from their employers.

So I submitted for a sabbatical to my congregation to get time, before the training began, to be able to serve regularly up here and, because of the circumstances, they granted it. But they also came up with me right after Christmas, on December 28, about twenty-four people. We were only supposed to be twelve of us but they allowed twenty-four of us to come serve at St. Paul's. They really wanted to do this so we traveled by bus up here. And the congregation came with me three times to do that.

Well, my parish, I think they were considerate. They sort of thought I was helping out and you could see the towers from [*the town where the church was*]. . . . So they were [fine]. They knew it was close. So they gave me time to sort of keep my head together. I didn't have to be there [at the church] every single day for eight hours a day. You know, enough of my work went into my sermon, so they knew I was doing something. I didn't do anything that would reveal anything that I shouldn't reveal, but they got enough of a grasp of it.

I was very fortunate. I was working at a full-time job. My bosses said, "Whatever time you need to take to do this, you take that time." And they paid me full time, never cut anything out of my salary. And supported me through the whole time.

The community was very supportive of my going. You know, when I would come home, there was always a brother there who would welcome me home and have a cup of coffee with me. You know, just to be there so I had, "Hello?" Just to be there with me. I had great community support from my [*religious*] community.

During the interviews, however, it became apparent that despite the traumatic aspects of working on the site, what was most painful was what Winnicott would describe as "the failure of the good object"—those people and organizations that the chaplains expected care and support from and community with, but which left them feeling more isolated in the task.

In Winnicott's understanding of early development, there is both the sense of the "environmental mother," the caregiver that becomes a reliable sustaining empathic presence, and the "object mother," which the child can use ruthlessly in seeking to satisfy its instinctual impulses. As we have noted, it is the survival of the mother that builds a "confidence that there will be an opportunity for contributing to the environmental mother . . . the opportunity for giving and making reparation."[60] However, what in general ministry generally feels like an integrated relationship, where "mother church" is both the reliable presence and the one actively related to in the day-to-day ministry, for many in the disaster of 9/11 this relationship split, and the church was often experienced as failing to be reliably present and caring. Psychically the reliable presence could be interpreted to become for some an almost idealized Ground Zero community, and the "good object," which may have formerly been externally represented by one's parish, bishop, diocese/synod, or denomination, became the frustrating "bad object" that then becomes split off from one's desire for reparation and consequently encourages a withdrawal of concern and a repository for anger. This could perhaps be understood clinically as compassion fatigue and burnout. Winnicott writes in his paper "Aggression in Relation to Emotional Development,"

Anger: In my description there now comes a place for anger at frustration. Frustration, which is inevitable in some degree in all experience, encourages the dichotomy: 1. innocent aggressive impulses toward frustrating objects, and 2. guilt-productive aggressive impulses towards good objects. Frustration acts as a seduction away from guilt and fosters a defence mechanism, namely, the direction of love and hate along separate lines. If this splitting of objects into good and bad takes place, there is an easing of guilt feeling; but in payment the love loses some of its valuable aggressive component, and the hate becomes more disruptive.[61]

Keeping in mind Winnicott's caution about the split of objects into "idealized and bad," compare the seemingly idealized picture of Ground Zero that follows with how many chaplains later described their relationship to their faith communities.

> There was a movie, oh, probably *Brigadoon*, where every hundred years or so this town was visible and then it disappeared again. And in a way the recovery community down here felt like *Brigadoon*, that, after the ashes this beautiful loving caring community cropped up with buildings that had nothing to do with the ones that came down. It was like the Stations of the Cross. It was like the Salvation Army and the Red Cross and whoever else was down here giving out food and Nino's and the green-tarped café and all the hazmat places to hose off, it was like a different town. And everybody there was helping everybody else. I know when I was on shift, there was these two paramedics who would always come over and make sure I had something to eat, whether I was hungry or not. But their service was picking me up in one of those little ATVs and driving me to either St. Paul's or the big bubble or something to make sure I ate.

Despite the difficulties between the uniformed services and the challenges of the work, the sense of community at Ground Zero was often experienced as incredibly nurturing and affirming. This may have been because in so many ways *it was* those things. However, the split comes when one's own community pales in comparison. We can see in Winnicott's thought that this has not to do only with the fantasy of the individual but also the response of the actual external object. For those faith communities that failed to hold and handle the "spontaneous gesture" of their clergy's chaplaincy, the result was an increased sense of isolation and disconnection between what felt real to them and what seemed real to their faith communities. What faith communities need to do is to be good-enough caregivers to chaplains, which entails an adaptation of ministry in the time of a disaster that encourages a positive response, self-care, and integrated connection to their everyday ministries. Otherwise, the cost of such a split relationship is part of the pain chaplains bear in responding to what is real need through their own capacity for concern. The prevalent response to this real or perceived "failure of the good object" was, as Winnicott indicates, anger.

> The biggest challenge I had was finding the time to do it. And the lack of understanding on the part of various, at that point, part-time employers that, "You know, rather than spending three days answering your phones, I could spend two days [at Ground Zero] this week and you could consider this a min-

istry of your parish." But they were just not at all interested in that sort of thing. I get very concerned when religious institutions are focused only inwardly. And I felt a lot of that. So it [the chaplaincy] was mostly days that would otherwise have been a day off. . . . which has a cumulative effect as well, because there isn't a day off. . . . But down here? No, there's a very, *a sense of reality here.* I remember when I was working at [*a particular church*], there's *no sense of reality there,* lovely people but it's just not real. I mean they have people, have it be a higher priority that when the phones rings once during the day, someone answers it, than the work keeps going on here. I just kind of didn't get that. But that's the church, right? "We pay your salary. You work for us."

[*And did you find yourself at any time becoming angry at all?*] . . . Well, not here [at Ground Zero], not here. At work? Yes. I think that was the carry-over from all of that. That a lot of *what people thought was important and was real was meaningless really* and putting such importance to it and not seeing what was going on or not. It was hard to say, being in the [*center of the denominational*] sanctity and getting that reaction. But that's where I found in the parish was good, very supportive. At work it was "Oh, you missed another day of work," geez, from some, until I gave them some of my choice language and settled that. The anger I think was, "Well, what are you doing?" You know that reaction and I had to catch myself on that after a while. It's not doing any good and it's not doing me any good either being angry like that. It's a waste of energy. So channel it elsewhere.

You felt like you really weren't appreciated. I mean, there was no "Thank you for taking these shifts for the last seventeen weeks." . . . It's like you're on duty and not really much of the show of gratitude for the efforts that we did there. And then my diocese, even though they knew I was doing it, it was like, "Well, that's his thing." The only time I think I felt some little respect for the fact that we were doing this as volunteers was, I called Bishop [*name's*] secretary and said, "You know, I've lost my car thing about clergy parking." And she was so kind and so considerate. That's the only person I came in contact with that seemed to have a sense that we had done something good. You didn't need much, but you needed a little bit of somebody to think, well, you know. The diocese, the clergy, the Red Cross never, never, never had anything that said that to us. I think, almost it's like you're sort of a needy person, you need to be affirmed in little bits by somebody.

Some of the chaplains found they were angry at their church bodies for lack of support; others were angry because in many cases it seemed like the *individual* clergy were making a response but this was not a concerted church effort. This feeling cut across all the denominations.

[I] still was a little bit provoked at them [the church]. Just seemed to me that we had all these resources and, it's like, "Who's minding the store?" I mean, of all times in the world that we should have been organized it just didn't happen. I mean, it's an organization that I've been a member of and served in it for the entire time of my ministry, and here we are. I've given, given, given to this organization over the years and for some reason, it just seemed as if, of all the people who should have been mobilized, it should have been members of that organization. And we weren't. And the whole thing was very strange to me. There was never any communication with the chaplains in this organization, specifically about how we could serve. And it did seem odd to me that those who were probably the most trained, except if they had a particular connection and I guess that in this church of ours, there's too much "who you know," all that kind of stuff. But if you weren't [connected], it wasn't standardized in a way that was helpful.

I initially thought that my denomination would be more supportive, more helpful. And I kind of thought that that was kind of like my fallback, that they would be there or whatever. But then I realized for one thing that I was the only one, the only [*particular church's*] guy that was over at the morgue. There was another guy that was at the family center. But it was just kind of weird because it was like being a maverick or something. It's like, "How did I end up down here?" Obviously I think my initial willingness and desire to come back was I didn't want to be left with September 11th. I wanted to be a part of the coming back. So that could be replaced. But I guess that I kind of *felt abandoned by the church*. I felt like the church, in a great catholic way, had done a good job. But the narrow focus of the church didn't do a very good job.

I got angry at [*those at my seminary*]. I got angry at irresponsibility. I got angry at denial. I got angry at what I perceived as just cowardice. I did not understand how anybody could teach at a seminary and not help at Ground Zero. What the fuck are you teaching? I mean, for all the times that seminaries and universities and colleges are wrongly accused of ivory-tower isolationism they personified it. One faculty member worked at Ground Zero and two graduate students and one seminarian. Four people out of a community of what, 350 or something like that? I was mad at them. Angry, yes, I was initially angry and then when it went on it just figured, "You're not worth my time. You're not worth my attention." I would have wanted to see every single one of them that was ordained to be a chaplain at T. Mort. What are you talking about if you can't do that? What are you talking about?

The part that I see most differently is a profound sign and sadness in the incapacity of official churchdom to have even a clue about this stuff. Of all the T. Mort. chaplains, to my knowledge, only three were [*from my denomina-tion*]. No, excuse me, there was one who came in from [*another place in the country*] who was a supervisor for Red Cross. But locally, but three. Two [*from one branch of the denomination*], one [*from another branch*]. And there's part of me that feels a tad embarrassed about that. Now that doesn't mean that there weren't [*any of my denomination's*] chaplains involved in dealing with on the wharf [at the Family Assistance Center] and out there like that. But I find that's a whole different kind of chaplaincy. The people who were out on the piers dealing with families were not doing the kind of stuff that was inside. Red Cross does not make the distinction between T. Mort. chaplains and other chaplains. I think that is a horrific and insulting thing. D. Mort. chaplains and T. Mort. chaplains, fine, I'll accept that as close, I have no problems with that. D. Mort. chaplain—peer. Chaplain dealing out with the families, not a peer. I mean, that's a fine, valuable thing. And that is not uncommon to any number of other things. I mean, I've done that myself before. [The distinctive difference] has to do with the element of danger and rawness. Dealing, *T. Mort. chaplains got a chance to deal with things without benefit of metaphor.*

This dealing "with things without benefit of metaphor" was a comment on the reality of Ground Zero. For the many who celebrated the Eucharist, the Lord's Supper, or Mass at their churches, Ground Zero, too, was a real experience of the body broken and the blood poured out. For so many, this was not *like* Psalm 23's "valley of the shadow of death," this *was* their valley. Likewise, "the pit of destruc-tion" or "desolation" spoken of in the psalms was the reality for so many who worked in the Pit at Ground Zero. This is not about the psychotic collapsing of symbolic reality and personal experience. What this chaplain described in dealing with expe-rience "without the benefit of metaphor" is that this felt "real" in a way only alluded to in much religious language and ritual. In the context of the ground of Ground Zero—where the chaplains not only said but saw the return of the earth creatures to the earth, "earth to earth, ashes to ashes, dust to dust," where they saw the "body broken" and the "blood poured out"—pastoral care was a confrontation with reality and the sense of being real that for many felt incomparable. Because a number of the chaplains felt like this was "real" ministry in a way some other ministry is often not, there was an expectation that their churches and communities would be the place that they would experience support and affirmation for themselves as pastors in this ministry. More often than not, this was painfully unrealized and there was sometimes the effect that what could have enlivened and balanced the ministry instead intensified through isolation and negation. Of note is that almost a fifth of the chaplains found their usual ministry less meaningful.

The opportunity to actually do ministry, I mean, I could expect to do ministry when I came down. On any given day at work I don't know whether I'm going to actually do what I understand as ministry. It'll probably be administration or some preparation or a lot of other stuff, which I don't really enjoy or like that much. But it was, you know, hands-on, you were there and you were available and you were recognized. The fact that you were a priest meant something on the site, in this environment. It was wonderful. It was kind of like sort of the way things ought to be, in a way. The way the spiritual community had a natural and vital connection with the secular community was recognized, welcomed, accepted, not hands-off, but in a healthy way integrated: secular/spiritual integrated.

You just had a sense of loving. Loving God and loving your neighbor. Everybody took care of everyone else. With simple acts of kindness, making sure people ate, making sure I ate. "We're going to go get something, Father. You want to come with us?" There was this whole sense of everybody looking out for everybody else. I mean, just dealing with this just felt much more life affirming than to all of a sudden kind of deal with what felt like small problems in the parish.

Symbolic of this feeling of disconnection between the church and the ministry at Ground Zero was an event that paradoxically was focused on the place many felt the most care, the threatened closing of St. Paul's Chapel as a respite center so it could function as a church.

I think it was [*a person at Trinity Church*] who felt that not only St. Paul's was in real danger, physically maybe, because of the use but the people coming there might be in danger because of the overuse of the building and the resources. Well, I was appalled as well as everyone else was appalled, because the work there was such a wonderful thing. I was in and out of there all the time during the [recovery], when I'd be down here as well as others. They'd really look to that place, and the fact that I had a connection in my work life with Trinity/St. Paul's helped with the ministry that I was doing because it was so present to the people who were working in the Pit. And so finally there was enough pressure brought to bear that they held off the closing until the end.

Do you remember them trying to close [St. Paul's Chapel]? So the week before Holy Week [*the priest in charge at St. Paul's*] told me they were going to close it on Easter. It's like, just be the worst church you can possibly be. So I helped keep it open. I went to the firefighters' union and the cops' union and I talked to the both of the presidents of that and they agreed to make some phone calls and write some letters. And then somebody got a *Times* reporter in there and I was one of the people she interviewed. And it was, in all humility, I came up with a metaphor, and it just was galvanizing. I said, for Trinity to close this place is *like rolling the stone back in front of the empty tomb.* Pretty good, huh? And so it stayed open, and I mean the public outcry was just tremendous.

Not only is this is an example of what Winnicott calls "the failure of the good object," one can also see from the chaplain's own interpretation that this was not simply about the psychology of good care but about what St. Paul's represented spiritually. For a church that was about resurrection, the apparent artificial distinction between the ministry in the church and the needs of "the world" caused a painful disconnection for those who were holding onto a sense of mission that was about the ministry of the church *in* the world but also *of* the world, which saw not only the chaplains doing ministry but affirmed the role of all the recovery workers who were engaging in what one police detective described as a "righteous cause."[62]

Trinitarian theologian John D. Zizioulas gives us insight into the theological implications of such a disconnection:

> The ministry relates the Church to the world in an existential way, so that any separation between the Church and the world in the form of a dichotomy becomes impossible. As it is revealed in the eucharistic nature of the Church, the world is assumed by the community and referred back to the Creator. In a eucharistic approach it is by being assumed that the world is judged, and not otherwise.
>
> The mission of the Church in the world is, therefore, inconceivable in terms of an attitude *vis-à-vis* the world. The relational character of ministry implies that the only acceptable method of mission for the Church is the *incarnational* one: the Church relates to the world through and in her ministry by being involved existentially in the world. The nature of mission is not to be found in the Church's *addressing* the world but in its being fully in *com-passion* with it.
>
> But precisely all this shows that the ministry of the Church *ad extra* must be an organic part of the concrete local community and not of a vague "mission" of the "Church" in general. . . . Such ministries will always be necessary to a Church that has not become unrelated to the world, but they cannot acquire permanent forms, being always dependent upon the needs of the particular place and time in which the Church finds herself.[63]

For those who were responding to the needs of those involved in recovery at Ground Zero, and for part of the concrete local community that formed in response to it, the mission was indeed to them a mission *of the* church, or whichever faith community they came from, through "being fully in com-passion" with the world at that time. The church's failure to recognize that in the immediacy of that time and place, rather than in hindsight, was, to return to the use of analytic understanding, a traumatic break in the "continuity of being," both psychologically and, one could argue, spiritually.

Paradoxically, as we have noted, it was in the community at Ground Zero that many of the chaplains experienced what felt like true community, the kind of community they preached about on Sundays or tried to live out in their daily lives. We shall explore the effects of this community in the following chapter. Suffice it to say, in their ministry the chaplains provided community and connection to the divine community as they stood alongside those in pain, and in their own bearing of the graces and challenges of the ministry what they, too, needed and found in the dust of Ground Zero was community that held them in their suffering.

One can again explore the degree of a person's integration in relation to suffering such a trauma as to whether or how long it may take to accept the situation, live with the ambivalence of the relationship, change one's beliefs about what is expectable, or instead experience isolation. One chaplain showed the movement through this process when asked about whether he experienced himself as being angry.

Only early on, when I was in the Family Assistance Center at Pier 94, where they were taking people onto the boat to go around to view the remains, wreckage, and come back. And I was just in the midst of the pain and anguish of all the people who had lost others. I was angry, but I didn't know at whom. Took a long time to figure out I wasn't angry at God. I was angry at whoever could conceive of doing this. I was really ambivalent about the feeling about the terrorists because I couldn't understand how anybody who could do this. I still can't wrap my eyes, my mind, around how anybody can be a suicide killer, don't understand that at all. But I hadn't paid too much attention to their existence in the first couple of days. And I just remember there was a point where they were giving out urns of ashes and I remember one guy said, "I don't want that." He says, "The ashes of the terrorists could be in there." And something clicked in my mind and I realized, I can't be hating them, they're dead. They're dead, it's over. There's nothing left to hate. There's nothing left to be angry about them, they're gone. So the anger that I felt periodically that would show up and my wife, God bless her, stood it and other people stood it because it would come out unexpectedly and abruptly, but it never had a focus. And so I began some therapy and talked it out and I wasn't angry anymore, just sad. Sad all the time. Sad that this had all happened. Sad that so many people had no resolution—that I found the saddest.

Winnicott's understanding of trauma, gross and subtle, connects and reconnects us to both internal and external realities, and to the understanding that suffering is both an achievement and something that can penetrate to the heart of who we are, the True Self. Whether we use the analytic language of trauma, or the more popular term of suffering, the reality is that this is painful; when one feels along with a suffering other, one suffers oneself. The paradox of pain, of suffering, however, is that developmentally it is actually a sign of health rather than of trauma.

Pain-Bearing/Suffering as Pastoral Method

As we have seen in some of the incredible work of the chaplains at Ground Zero, the art of pain-bearing is about both being and doing. For pain to be borne there needs to be a safe and trusted relationship that holds the one in pain. This space is created either by sufficient development of an alliance with an accurate empathic attunement or sometimes through the dynamics of transference, where the other may feel connected to the pastoral person through the transference of an inner relationship with an objective other. Space is also created by the acceptance of that relationship and the ability of the pastoral person to be in relationship with themselves and their own suffering, so as not to unconsciously defend against the other's pain through the dynamic of countertransference. The pastoral person working in the midst of crisis needs to be well resourced through good training and experience about what to "do" in a disaster, such as the chaplain who spoke about his "cognitive mission orientation."

Yet the pastoral person also needs to be connected at depth with how to "be," how to be their own true selves in a way that they can then respond empathically, spontaneously, and creatively as the needs arise. We can see this in the account of a chaplain who chose to read the needs of the culture around him and respond in a way that was appropriate to the situation, rather than rigidly maintaining guidelines.

Well, they discovered one night; I believe it was in February maybe, about 2:00 A.M., the remains of a lieutenant whose brother was [*a firefighter*]. . . . And so we took the Gator into the Pit to be there while they were extricating him. And it took a long time. They were trying to be gentle, but [*there were specifically difficult circumstances*].[64] There must have been forty-five people down there working on this. His brother hadn't appeared yet. His brother was coming with some firefighters from his battalion and other locations to be on the ramp when he was brought up. So meanwhile, my first experience was to ride the Gator down into the Pit and go through the smoke and protect yourself from debris flying around. I sat in the back of the Gator, which is very bumpy, and there's room to your right for a litter. It took two EMS people driving it. So [we] bumped our way down. We went about seventy-five feet down and positioning your feet, it was a good thing we had boots because there were sharp things and all kinds of building parts, no glass that I could see, but shards of metal and stone, and so positioning your feet was a bit tricky. You had to, it was like shifting, so you found one spot and had your feet planted while you're just being there with people, standing with them. And they were really working hard. And at one point a fireman walks over to me and, I think he was Irish, he had his turn-out gear on, and he says to me, "Father," he says, "you going to do the holy stuff?" I said, "Well, what do you mean? He said, "You going to use the holy water and bless him?" And I said, "Well, Red Cross training did not permit us to touch or use anything." And he took one of these out of his pocket, this Poland Spring water, and he says to me, "Father, my sainted mother would never forgive me if I didn't give this to you." So he gave me exactly a bottle like this of Poland Spring water and I said a prayer with it and when I had a chance, and they brought [the lieutenant] out in two litters. I really, I used the water. I blessed the two American flags that shrouded his body. And *that's some of the holiest water I've ever seen.* That really was special . . .

Attending to such suffering is a delicate and sometimes creative process, no more so than when the person is still "on-the-job," such as those chaplains working with first responders in the earthy instability of a disaster site in the midst of a difficult recovery with the presence of family members and colleagues of the one recovered. Often in such situations, pain-bearing is a holding of that which is traumatic while acknowledging that there is no time and space to attend to it at this time. Often the suffering is held, acknowledged, and contained by the prayer or religious ritual, such as the use of "the holiest water . . . ever." It is held and borne until it can be handed over, at times a wearying burden.

Image 3.5. A chaplain on hand at Ground Zero. (Photograph by Andrea Booher/FEMA News Photo.)

That's the end of a shift look . . . to me it is, "What do I do with this? What do I do with it? How?" Take it with you. . . . I mean, what else do you do with it? And you learn what you do with it. You learn that you have to simply give it over to God and go on. And that a lot of it you can't, I mean, what are you going to do? And you can share it with others, those who've had the same experience. . . .

She had, had a particularly rough day that day. There were thirty-some remains that came in on her. And the bags were lined up on the table from the morgue and she was like. . . . I think she had just pulled a double shift maybe.

I can relate, I don't know, it was on my face. But just that overwhelmed feeling of we're not here for eight hours, we're here for nine months. We're not here for one person, we're here for everyone. And constantly relaying that burden to God for His care sometimes left you weary.

Other times, an invitation to explore the suffering may arise formally or informally on an individual or group basis and the pastoral person needs to be able to follow the other into "the valley of the shadow of death." Again it is worth restating, to be in the valley of the shadow of death, one needs to attend to one's own suffering, without recourse to sadistic or masochistic explanations or actions, but through a grounded theology that is not only lived out in one's own actions toward others but in the community of care that holds the chaplain in his or her own suffering. However, often attending to the suffering is simply not enough. The pastoral model of Earth-making (the Holding space) and Pain-bearing (the Suffering space) may be incomplete without attention to Life-giving, which allows the person to transform the experience, to begin to (re)integrate and come to a place of wholeness in the midst of one's brokenness. The completeness of this threefold pastoral method can be seen in the ability of the person to grow through her or his suffering and be able to meet additional suffering in a new and transformed way.

chapter 4

Life-Giving
The Transforming Space

Vespers

In the artificial clarity of mercury vapor lights
Noisy whirling orange machines with
black claws reach out and worry at the wreckage of the site.
The scale of devastation is wide and open
with the weight of what was landmarked free against
the sky blue then black for
towers of lights guiding us all night and all day
now at our feet underneath us where
we saw all the city beneath our feet now
under my feet is steel, powder, dirt, bodies
of thousands; wide and open to night sky.

Vast. And still. Except the grapplers which,
constant motion, muted against the enormity,
are not heard. A noise: rushing metal down
a building on the perimeter. Heads turn instantly
Assessing, monitoring, and turn back to
wreckage below us.

At the ramp's base: two Stokes litters hold
black bags partially filled. One open and then bagged
to cover what's inside. Men in brown overalls
Firefighters, resolved and resolute uncover
their heads. Machinery stopped so
prayers can be heard in the clarity of stillness of night
in the great hush of space.

Facing the bags; strong men circle around me,
I pray.

I pray
for their souls, that they may be at rest.
Give thanks, that their bodies have been found.
For their families, that anxiety may be stilled.
For the men around me.
That they may continue.
And bless them all.

The words that I have
do not express the gratitude for the effort
of finding these bodies,
Or the goodness of all the men and women
who serve here.
Or for being present in the very best of what humans can do,
or how humble I feel
at this altar in front of me
and how I belong.
Right here.[1]

What was life giving at Ground Zero were those moments and relationships that we all need in pastoral ministry, whether as clergy or laity: that sense of community with one another and that sense of communion with God whose presence we seek to make present in our presence. The community at Ground Zero had multiple cultures, each with its own politics and the tensions between them, but it had a sense of mission that held people together for the most part and invited the chaplains into collegial, transformative relationship with firefighters, police, EMTs, and construction workers. As noted in the previous chapter, in the face of the worst that humanity can do, the chaplains by and large felt an enormous gratitude "for being present in the very best of what humans can do."[2]

The Rev. Thomas Faulkner, an Episcopal priest, who became the assistant officer for the American Red Cross overseeing the screening, scheduling, and deployment of chaplains at the T. Mort., described the experience in this way:

> We became a community of clergy who knew what we were doing. We all knew that when we were at an examination table with remains, some of which could be very disturbing and rank in terms of smell, we were dealing with the wild emotions of ourselves and other people gathered with us. We were dealing with an horrific disaster site. We were dealing with the glory of people working together and being together as God's children. We were empowered by God's spirit; we felt that we absolutely knew that this was sacred space. We all have our defenses, our ways of protecting ourselves. We put up

these defenses and that really keeps us in a safe secure controlled environment. What a disaster does, is it throws you up against a terrible reality and the defenses start to break down. All of a sudden there is a little opening. Prejudices break down, priorities change because you're up against this disaster. At that moment, there's the possibility for God to enter in, in remarkable ways, and there's a way for other people to enter in and fear to enter into the large love of people. There are remarkable moments of transformation.[3]

In what Faulkner describes as the "sacred space" of Ground Zero, we can see the relationship between those inner and outer spaces that have been described in the last two chapters as "Holding" and "Suffering" spaces. The space of "transformation" is not disconnected from those former spaces—either the externals of what Faulkner describes as a "horrific disaster site" and the "terrible reality" of the disturbing remains or the internal landscape of "wild emotions" and the erection or breakdown of defenses. Yet the sense of the life-giving nature of "the glory of people working together and being together as God's children . . . empowered by God's spirit" is not in spite of those former realities but in large part because of them. The life-giving sense of community and communion both with God and others was not a denial of the suffering or the destruction, but a transformation of it within the inner life of those involved as they risked entering into the "large love of people."

Life-Giving: A Theological Perspective

Like Faulkner, when asked about what was life giving about the ministry at Ground Zero one chaplain answered, "The sense of holiness. There was a real sense of being in sacred space." When queried as to what made the "space" sacred, the chaplain went on to say, "The space where God mattered. And that sense of the presence of God there. As I said, the overwhelming sense of being in the presence of God." Another, when asked about when he thought most about his T. Mort. experience, talked about the anniversaries as a "healthy kind of remembering," and noted, "I've never sort of focused on it or gotten depressed when I was thinking about it because it has [been] much more of a resurrection experience for me than it was the other."

Resurrection, theologically, is about being brought back from the dead, it is not about not dying. One chaplain described this well in reflecting about the differences in relation to a theological view of death and the popular psychological view of needing "closure" in relation to death.

I thought it was kind of a shame, that's all I could say about it. I thought it was a shame that so many of the cops and firefighters and EMTs talked about providing "closure" for families. I thought it was a shame because you wouldn't talk about it that often unless it was something you were hoping for yourself. And that's just so unrealistic. I mean, talk about a false hope. But theologically, it's not even something we want. I mean, are we going to cut God off from these memories of yours? You're going to cut off the Holy Spirit? You're going to cut off sanctification, transformation, transfiguration from your experience? You think it's just going to put a ribbon around it, put it in the back of your closet? I mean, come on. It's not only unhelpful, there's no such thing. Your brain isn't going to stop working. Your guts aren't going to stop, even if your brain stopped working, your soul, your heart, your stomach would know what happened to you. I mean, they did refer the "closure" to the family. Well, [there's] nothing ignoble about wanting to help the family, nothing ignoble about wanting to recover something for them to bury. Funerals, burials really are part of the healing that God wants for these people. So there's nothing ignoble about that. I just heard the word *closure* a little more often than I liked. "Closure" has nothing to do with any healthy healing process as far as I'm aware.

A resurrection mentality neither denies nor negates death but, rather, affirms that which is life giving beyond death, a resurrection life where one, at least in the case of Jesus in the Gospels, still bears the scars of death but lives with them.[4] This can be as profound as experiencing the presence of God and a transformation of self and as simple as the life-giving things one needs to do to live in the face of a disaster in the midst of a community of care.

What I enjoyed was the sense of community. You know, we were like a cloistered world that, if you weren't a part of it, you don't know what it is. And it was a world you couldn't really talk about too much with other people . . . because immediately people went from the direction of it being just sad and, yes, it was, but there was another piece to it of, in the midst of that sadness, *we had to make ourselves alive*. I have memories of driving around in the Gator and we'd all be singing songs. And *you had to do this, otherwise I don't think we could have done what we did*. I remember in particular, there was a song for Lotto back then, I can't think of it right now, but I remember there were three of us in the Gator and as we were driving, we all were like moving our heads back and forth at the same time as we were singing. And you know, nobody out there would know what we're doing and even the movement of our heads wasn't looking so much like dance movements, but it was just kind of, we're all going back and forth at the points at the time we're supposed to tilt our heads. You know, great lunches with people. *And you just felt very alive* . . .

The sense of a containing community that shared both the sadness and sense of life shows the effects of the spectrum of care for self and others. This chaplain said that "we had to make ourselves alive" and at the same time described a sense of community with humor and connectedness that was life giving in itself. This sense of being alive in the midst of destruction is an Easter Sunday image. It is not about, "Everything is alright now"; it is about finding that which keeps us alive and connected with one another, even in the midst of all that we face, be it disaster, trauma, or finding that which enlivens what can feel like dead parts of our ministry and ourselves.

As much as anything, however, what was life giving for many of the chaplains was, unlike the rabbi's reflections on the absence of God in the last chapter, was the presence of God that was there for the chaplains in what they were doing. You can hear this vividly in this vignette from one chaplain as she described a late-night incident:

> There wasn't an anxiety and then there was an anxiety all at the same time. It was one of the elevator-shaft incidents where we were called in and it was great they found at least five bodies at one time. And all these things of course happened in the middle of the night. They kept finding more in the middle of the night, I don't know why. I'm standing at the top of this hole with one of the other [chaplains], and we were watching them down there, they wanted us on site. . . . FDNY wanted us there, so we were there.
>
> And then they called down from the hole, which has got to be at least twelve to fifteen feet down, they said, "No, they want you down here." And I went, "Down where?" And the hole was not big, it was like twice the size of this table. And I said, "Well, how do I get down there?" And they said, "We'll carry you." And it was like a mesh pit, they just put us over their heads and lowered us into this hole. And my anxiety didn't come from the fear of being in the hole, it came from, "Oh God, please don't let me fall apart. Let me be strong for these men who obviously [are] looking to us to be a presence of God down there."
>
> And I went into the deepest prayer that I ever had in my entire life of "God, please help me through this." And somehow, on the way down, a calm came over me and *I felt more filled with presence of God than I ever had*, where *I just knew it was okay and that I just had to move over a bit and let God help me do this*. And after that I never felt alone down there.

One can see the anxiety about being representative of God's presence that became changed, in some way, by feeling the presence of God, which then transformed the rest of the chaplain's experiences at Ground Zero. Another chaplain described what was also an important moment that had a lasting effect.

> It's funny, it keeps coming back, the first snowfall that we had, and I think it was in November. It was early. And I was so overwhelmed by the beauty of it because there was so many lights on and it was two o'clock in the morning and it was snowing. The snow was falling through the lights and it was beautiful. And it covered up a lot of the stuff that wasn't being used so suddenly it

disappeared from view for a little while. And I said, "This is also God's work. This is all part of what's going on. And it's a bigger plan than I have to worry about because I can't wrap my head around it, so *why don't I just let it go? Let go and let God.*" *And in that moment I did*, I really did. And I literally felt myself relax and it felt comfortable walking around, and my shoulders didn't bother me, my neck didn't bother me, and from then on until June when they took that last piece of steel out, I was fine.

What was life giving about it was *the absolute certainty for me that God was in that space*. The absolute clarity that God has absolutely nothing to do with what human beings do. We've been given free will. People do what people do. God's just there to take care of us after it happens because they're not to stop us from doing whatever it is that we do. Because, otherwise there wouldn't be such a thing as free will. What would we be? So the absolute clarity every day that I was here that I was in the presence of the divine and that *the work that I was doing was holy and that was really life affirming*. And life affirming that life will go on. Even though I had heard it and been taught it and had people make examples of it. It wasn't until then that I started waking up every morning and I opened my eyes and I said, "Thank you. Thanks for another day." And there's even a Hebrew prayer that people say in the morning that basically translates out, "Thank you for returning my soul to my body. Thank you for another day of life." *I became grateful for being alive.*

Despite the potentially traumatizing experiences, one can see the sense of transformation that not only had an impact on the chaplains' ministry but, for some, their very selves. Both of these chaplains described a sense of surrender, moving over, letting go, that relates to the relaxation of ego control and rests in the relationship with the God whose presence they experienced. Another described an experience of the "presence of souls":

I remember praying [about where the globe was in the center], and we're sitting up on some beams and there was a big shelf of where the collapse had been and I just sat there, the other chaplain and I praying, and having the sense of being surrounded by souls. Not an experience that I've ever had before. And souls that were not in agony but were more present, were thankful, were at rest. Yeah, I don't know where that came from or what that is necessarily. I'm not an expert by any stretch of imagination but it was a very profound experience.

Certainly the sitting on the I-beams in the midst of, I mean, it was just like the midst of hell in a way, it was really enough. I mean, papers had caught fire on hot steel down over here as they excavated and smoke was still rising over here, and all the equipment, and the debris and the smell and just that, that moment of, *that sense of presence* was just overwhelming. And then *the*

> *longer-term transformations* that took place as a result of just the constant being here, burning out of me to some degree the arrogance and whatever you want to call it. And then the abhorrence at violence connected to my own anger. Those were really transformative.

The sense of God's presence and mystical presence of those dead in the destruction of Ground Zero transformed a traumatizing space into a sacred space, and for several transformed their ministry in a way that was life giving:

> That was transformational: different appreciation for the church and the depth of faith that God gives us, that gives a new respect for the church and its people. So, just a deepening of the relationship. I was glad that happened. I was getting ready to retire early, take the thirty-year out option that we have. And I was eligible in '01, August of '01. And I hesitated, there was this something going on inside of me that I didn't take it. I didn't take August of '01. Well, here we are a month later and what happens?!? And I know why I was thinking about early retirement because I was kind of burned out, tired, I mean, I did the thirty, I'm ready to quit. And I don't want to deal with vestry meetings anymore, or the finance campaign every year, I mean, forget it. And Mrs. So-and-So, who goes from one problem to the next to the next to the next, on the phone all the time, 24/7. No, thanks, can I get out of this? I'll just stop and do things I want to do like preach, teach, lead worship, do consulting. But this other stuff, forget it. Meetings, uh-uh [*no*]. I was ready to quit all that stuff. . . . But 9/11 happened. And I couldn't stop, I mean, I couldn't leave the folks. But I needed to be with them, too. *I needed the church. And people needed for me to be around and I needed them. We all needed God and so we hung through it.* And I retired early in '03, two years later.

This account of his own transformation in relation to the church shows the profound relationship between community and communion that can be so life giving. It shows a mutuality of need, without an abandonment of role, where both pastor and community need each other and both need God. Like the accounts in the chapter on pain bearing, this shows a recognition of vulnerability that allows a relationship within community, where the priest is not only *for* the community but *of* the community, even in the midst of ministry *to* the community.

Eastern Orthodox theologian John D. Zizioulas draws from very different roots than Augustine of Hippo; however, this interrelationship between ministry and community is vital for him:

> If . . . we do not isolate the ministry from the reality of the community created by the *koinonia* of the Holy Spirit, what "validates" a certain ministry is to be found not in isolated and objectified "norms" but in the community to which this ministry belongs.

It may be argued that the community is something that we cannot grasp and deal with and we shall therefore sooner or later arrive at the procedure of "criteria." But to arrive at a certain judgment by considering the community first is essentially different from looking at the community through the spectacles of "criteria." . . . Church structure and the ministry are not simply matters of convenient and efficient arrangements, but "modes of being," ways of relating between God, the Church and the world.[5]

Here it is that the Holy Spirit creates community from which ministry arises. Zizioulas's sense of community is grounded in ecclesiology, not anthropology. Grounding his trinitarian theology in the work of the Cappadocian Fathers, he sees the unity of the Trinity not in terms of "substance" or the "being" of God as love shared by all persons of the Trinity, but as the outpouring of love from the Father who "*out of love* freely begets the Son and brings forth the Spirit."[6] The being of God for him is thus, to use the title of his book, a *Being in Communion*, an affirmation of "relationality" being that which constitutes God. This for him is a crucial difference between Eastern Orthodox theology, grounded in the work of the Cappadocians, and Western theology, which follows from Augustine's thought. In a postmodern world, which can often seem to emphasize multiplicity as a contrast to unity, such a understanding is attractive. One can affirm "qualities" like "relationality" and "multiplicity" as primary without the qualifications that a sense of unity provides. Yet underlying Zizioulas's formulation, there is an essentially hierarchical, seemingly chronological understanding of trinitarian relations and a concrete understanding of substance that does disservice to Augustine's thought and seems once again to reinforce a top-down model of relationship so prevalent in patriarchal and colonialist mentalities. Zizioulas writes,

> Thus God as person—as the hypostasis *of the Father*—makes the one divine substance to be that which it is: the One God. This point is absolutely crucial. For it is precisely with this point that the new philosophical position of the Cappadocian Fathers, and of St. Basil in particular, is directly connected. That is to say, the substance never exists in a "naked" state, that is, without hypostasis, without a "mode of existence." And the one divine substance is consequently the being of God only because it has these three modes of existence, which owes not to the substance but to one person, the Father. Outside the Trinity there is no God, that is, no divine substance because the ontological "principle" of God is the Father. The personal existence of God (the Father) constitutes His substance, makes it hypostases. The being of God is identified with the person.[7]

Yet the affirmation of the community of the Trinity as the will of the one, even if eternally begetting, rather than the being of all, seems to negate the being in relationship that is shared by all the persons of the Trinity in the mutual communion of love. If, as Zizioulas says, the Father freely begets the Son and brings forth the Spirit, is love something that God the Father does, rather than *who* God is, and is this love shared by the other persons, hypostases, or not? Perhaps this is an essentially "substantialist" question; however, Augustine seems to come to an understanding that love is the "who" rather than "what" of God. Yet Zizioulas does affirm, like Augustine, "The expression 'God is love' (1 John 4:16) signifies that God 'subsists' as Trinity," but continues to say "that is, as person and not as substance. Love is not an emanation or 'property' of the substance of God . . . but is *constitutive* of His substance, i.e. it is that which makes God what He is, the one God. Thus love ceases to be a qualifying—i.e., secondary—property of being and becomes the *supreme ontological predicate*. Love as God's mode of existence 'hypostatsizes' God, *constitutes* His being."[8]

If this is so, then substance needs to be read in terms of "relationality," being as being-in-relationship, and that "relationality" needs to be read *not* simply in terms of multiplicity but in terms of love, that which is not only eternally self-giving but also receiving. Miroslav Volf's comments on relationality in the context of discussing the "ecclesial person" beautifully makes this distinction.

> It is not enough, however, to understand the catholicity of the ecclesial person as relationality, since this objective catholicity of person, "being from others," can also be lived individualistically. Ecclesiological individualism—as any other individualism—does not consist so much in the absence of relations that define the being of the person as in the conscious or unconscious denial of being conditioned by these relations and in the refusal to both enrich others and to allow oneself to be enriched by them. In actuality, every human being is shaped by others. The individualist lacks what I call the subjective dimension of the catholicity of person, namely, one's self-understanding *as a relational being* and the conscious attempt to live one's own relationality within a community of mutual giving and receiving.[9]

It was this mutuality in giving *and* receiving in community that was so life giving for the chaplains. Rather than a hierarchical view of ministry as that love which is dispensed by the chaplain to those receiving it, the chaplains themselves experienced being included as equals in community, whilst still retaining the differentiation of their particular role. Such a sense of mutuality and role appropriation is reflective of a model of Trinity that is perhaps more reminiscent of Augustine than the Cappadocians (as read by Zizioulas).

> **Our rule was, with the group that I kind of worked with the most, that the people who were dead and were leaving in the morgue vehicle were always accompanied and they said the people who are still alive also are accompanied out of the site every night. So every night somebody would walk with you to your car, they would walk with you to the subway station. We took care of each other. It was one of those things where you think you're coming in with the gospel of Jesus Christ and the love of God to minister to these people, but how much it was really a team and how well we worked together.**

What becomes somewhat evident in many of the chaplains' reflections is that they experienced this community as often being very different from their parish communities in the sense of inclusiveness and care. Again, theologically, this brings up the question about a too-concrete identification between church and ecclesial community. The chaplain above continued on to say,

> But then, as much as I was feeling I was trying to provide ministry to these people, to take care of these people . . . near the end of my shift, things were kind of slowing down anyway, some of the firefighters came up and as they were putting their brother in the morgue vehicle, they said, "We appreciate the fact that you have been here all day with us and that you have cared for us and you are part of our family." It was like, here I am standing there blessing the body as it was put into the morgue cart and they made sure they took care of me. I felt like we were all sitting there with this big shovel, trying to keep heaping blessings onto another person, but there's somebody somewhere else that's heaping them on you. Which, [in] parish life, you don't always feel affirmed. You preach and then thought it could be and probably what you thought was one for the record books and nobody says anything on their way out. It was just, you could almost become addicted to that kind of environment because it's effective. It's not like they were always patting you on the back, but you knew by the fact that somebody looked better when they were done talking with you or praying with you. It was just this huge paycheck that you received with each person. And that's what I would say would typify the whole time. *Always wanting to give, but always being cared for. It was such an incredible example of team ministry.*

Volf, who like Zizioulas and Stanley Grenz comes to use the term "the ecclesial person," nevertheless appears to take one step beyond the equation of that ecclesial self with the ecclesia, the church.

> The same Spirit baptizes all into one body of Christ and simultaneously "allots to each one individually just as the Spirit chooses" (1 Cor. 12:11-13). This twofold activity of the Spirit in unifying and differentiating prevents false catholicity of either church or persons from emerging in which the particular is swallowed up by the universal. The Spirit of communion opens up every person to others, so that every person can reflect something of the eschatological communion of the entire people of God with the Triune God in a unique way through the relations in which that person lives.[10]

Perhaps it is Volf's eschatological focus which calls him to say that "the Spirit of communion opens up every person to others," in a way that can be interpreted to include those beyond the walls of the church in the "entire people of God," or perhaps this catholicity extends only as far as the temporal church, where, like Zizioulas, he equates trinitarian social relations only to Christians due to the sacrament of baptism. Nevertheless, in the concrete relationships the chaplains found themselves living out in their ministry, the distinctiveness of their denominational or faith affiliations did not discount a sense of unity that was inclusive of all.

Perhaps we cannot, as Zizioulas said, grasp and deal with the mystery of community without reverting to criteria. I would pose, however, in reflecting upon the chaplains' experience, that the marks of community are *not exclusively* to do with ecclesial sacramentality but with the marks of the Triune God in God's own freedom that seemed to inspire not only Christian chaplains but the God who inspired also the interfaith and even a Muslim chaplain to minister in love at Ground Zero in the midst of a community that ministered to them. Again, it was this kind of community that was experienced as life giving, often in contrast with the ecclesial communities bound together by baptism and the Eucharist.

> The sense that there was a job to be done and I was doing it. I mean, it really needed to be done. I'm very sarcastic and skeptical by nature and I wonder if there really need to be so many [*particular denominational*] churches in Manhattan. Each of them putting on grand concerts . . . well, that's my place, we'll have thirty paid choir [members] and a 120 people in the congregation and I think, "Wouldn't these resources go to better use if you people just went across the street." But this felt like, someone needs to be here and right now that's me and there's really something that needs to be done and the people who value it. . . . There were some regulars [at Ground Zero]. You'd see them, you'll be here next Saturday, I'll be here, too, kind of. And the way that they made it clear that they, you know, if every parish could be like this, we'd all be remarkably happy because they made it very clear that they were happy we're here. We value what you're doing. I thought, gee, we should have a training session for the average vestry. They teach them just these couple of phrases they could use.

This is not to idealize the community at Ground Zero, or the chaplaincy. Part of what was life giving was working out what it meant to be there and do this ministry, with the complexities of being identified with a particular faith community, ministering to a recovery community that had a majority of Roman Catholics, at least as far as the FDNY, in the context of the death of persons from multiple nations and faiths. A few vignettes show these challenges and how the chaplains worked with them:

> By the time I came to T. Mort., there had been chaplains, I guess, that had been serving there during the course of the whole experience, versus the rest of us, for the eight, nine months. So I came there late, in the late stages of T. Mort. I know that was the source of some discussion, maybe even some dis-

agreement over chaplains. There are chaplains there who believe very strongly their own denominational theology must be applied in every chaplaincy setting. For example, some Christian chaplain I met would not in any way pray without invoking the name of Jesus, without ever knowing the victim was a Christian even. That became a source of some concern. For me it was no problem. All my prayers were nondenominational. And the other thing I think I really used was the Twenty-third Psalm because so many people know that. "The Lord is my Shepherd and I shall not want." People didn't need written text to follow them and I would use that text. Other than that it was just extemporaneous. It was totally extemporaneous. I never had a book. I never had a directory or a hand-book that people felt that I had to follow pages. It came really from the heart.

Or the time, I'll never forget, this one Medical Examiner, she was Jewish, and I asked her, I said, "I don't want to . . ." You know, I really erred on the side of those who had come from a Christian liturgical background. And I said, "When I bless these bodies, when I pray for you I feel like I'm not always min-istering to you because you're Jewish." And she said, "Because you say the same benediction at the end that we say in Temple," she said, "you do it in English, which is fine, because I'm Reform." She said that was the bond. But with her I ended up developing a great, great rapport . . .

They [recovery workers on the site] would sometimes hold back some remains near the end of a shift or whatever if they kind of had enough of a certain chaplain. Because they said, I tried to explain that we've all been told to keep it generic and so on and so forth. "But he'd just make up prayers. He never even prayed the Lord's Prayer." You could tell that they were really asking for the more formalized prayers and stuff like that, that the other chaplain wasn't familiar with. And then when they were bringing in, they brought in a sheikh. They go, "Look around here, we have one Jew and a bunch of Christians. Why do we have to have a sheikh as a chaplain?" I said, you know, "Bring that up with the people." Because I said, you know, "I can understand it. I can appreciate that." But that was hard when it was not even a Christian, that they had problems with that. Some people had issues with female clergy because they were Roman Catholic and weren't used to women clergy. But even some of them, they really embraced her, I can't remember the gal's name, but they really embraced her. They really enjoyed her ministry, even though it wasn't, they said, "It's just a little different for us." I said, "That's fine, as long as she's still ministering to you." But the same way they didn't like when the rabbis were there. They go, "He doesn't, he isn't going to mention Jesus." And so that became a definite issue. And it was kind of funny, though, when they found out that the next guy coming up was liturgical mostly. They wanted the sign of the cross. They wanted things that they were connected to.

Despite the challenges to the community receiving ministry that was not necessarily of their own faith tradition, it appeared that many in the recovery community embraced those who were different, even as different as a Muslim imam from Roman Catholic firefighters, or either from women clergy.

And we had one Muslim chaplain that I met. There might have been more Muslim chaplains, but that was the only one I met. I was glad to see him there. He really was, he was a convert to Islam, though. He was not born into the culture. And so obviously, in my little bit of conversation with him. It's a different response than I would have had, had it been an individual born in Lebanon. [He was received] I suppose with a little more distance. In New York, it's kind of like, I had a commander once that tried to tell me, he said, "Eighty-five percent of your soldiers are Unitarians or Universalists or agnostics." And I said, "No." I said, "About 85 percent of them are at best charming pagans and sometimes they are just charming. And if you scratch them a little bit, there'll be some 'Father, Son, and Holy Ghost' business in there someplace." And so the reality is that for the people who worked there, there was some "Father, Son, and Holy Ghost" business there someplace. They may not have been very closely tuned to the Almighty but our culture has got some Father, Son, and Holy Ghost business.

Unfortunately, the imam, a well-respected corrections facility chaplain who ministered as part of the chaplaincy at the T. Mort., died a couple of years after 9/11, so was unable to be interviewed for this book. One chaplain spontaneously shared:

With T. Mort., there were Jews, there were Christians, there were Catholics, there were Protestants, there were fundamentalists, there was an imam and you didn't hear, "I don't want, see, that offends me." And we were very respectful of the others as well. Like I said, it brought out the best and the worst, I think. No, no, it didn't. It was, it gave a peace that everybody seemed to get something from, or at least it seemed to me as everybody could get. But then again, nobody sat there and made fun of the imam when he did the prayers either.

When asked how the Muslim chaplain's ministry was received down at Ground Zero, one female chaplain replied:

Well, I remember him talking, he goes, "Well, in the beginning it was hard. Just think, you got somebody coming in the ministry who looks like bin Laden." I said, "Well, hopefully they realize that you're here for a totally different reason." And yeah, I tried to talk to him and walk with him but, he couldn't, even

> I don't even know if he was supposed to be talking to me, you know. I know that a lot of the Orthodox priests don't talk to women and things like that. But he was very nice.

The Muslim chaplain, according to the schedules, took nineteen shifts between December 22, 2001, and May 6, 2002. It is to be hoped that his ministry became less "hard," as perhaps can be attested by other chaplains' spontaneous accounts.

> I wonder how his family is? He brought them down one day. Oh, they're so gorgeous. A boy and girl and his wife. Oh, they were such good kids, such wonderful, just beautiful people, literally.

> I think what I remember most was the camaraderie. I never saw anybody excluded and I remember wondering what was going to happen the first day a Muslim cleric came down as a clergy. I wondered what was going to happen. And we were just as happy to see him there as the person that was going to be a chaplain. I'm sure there were people who had second thoughts or were uncomfortable ones, but they never got expressed.

We get a small window into how the Muslim chaplain made sense of his ministry through the words of another chaplain when asked about whether he had any thoughts or feelings about the terrorists.

> Well, I felt that they were wrong, but that they had to be motivated. I have to recognize that they were motivated in such a way that would enable them to do that. And they were real people. And so something was going on in their mind and heart and being and experience that enabled them to do that. And I think they were wrong. But I didn't have any feeling of retribution or anything like that with them. And one of our chaplains, I forget his name, he is a Muslim. . . . He was very helpful to me. . . . *just the fact that he was there*. I realized there was another way in the Muslim faith. There's another way, I knew. I didn't know where this other part had come from and what it was. If it was real or wasn't real to the faith, was an aspect of it, I suppose. But it was enabled by that culture in some way, as wrong as it was. But one time, I remember, the imam said, "You know, as Americans, we have no Mecca, but we can bring our hopes and our thoughts and our history and our experience and find it some[where]. This [*Ground Zero*] can be our point of reference." That was very meaningful, how he brought together and lifted up. He said, "But we do have a Mecca now and it's right here."

We can see how, for this Muslim chaplain, Ground Zero may have become a holy place for him, too, not as a celebration of terrorism, but a place where one could pilgrimage to so as to worship God in and through the action of ministering to others. One wonders, How does a trinitarian ecclesiology embrace such ministry, or does it exclude it? One chaplain described it well, as coming close to being "one":

> There were several phrases, you know that prayer that says, "In those whose faith is known to God alone." To me, of course I'm all for leaving people alone. I'm not an evangelist in the sense of going out and saving souls. Now I think I'm an evangelist for what I believe was Christ's demands of us. But as far as saving souls, I'm not into that at all. So, I think the fact I was heartened at the time about the fact that there was a lot of both ecumenical and interfaith coming together. Unfortunately, I think we blew that one nicely later on. But it was about the closest we ever got to sort of being "one."

A number of the life-giving moments were in this difficult ecumenical, interfaith, but sometimes amusing space of trying to work out what it meant to minister in such a community, both between the chaplains and with those they ministered to.

> And the first time I met him [a chaplain from a less well known church], he was sort of swooping over. I was taking over from him and he said, "Can I talk to you?" And I said, "Sure." So we went outside and he says, "You know, I'm from a faith group that has no ritual, really. So I'm really at a loss for what I can do here. Any suggestions?" And being a smartass I said "Yeah, become Catholic." But then I said, "No, seriously, we have some things that you can adapt." I said "I'll photocopy them and give them when you're here next." And I left them for him down there in the morgue. And he adapted all that to his wants and needs and so we worked that way. So it was good to be with [him], yeah.

Two female chaplains recount:

> Oh, they [the people at the T. Mort.] were wonderful. At first, of course, they have their own kind of way of communicating with each other and stuff. And yet, after a while, because every time I was there, there was a different group, I never saw the same two there, and so they had to get used to me, I suppose, as they had to get used to others and quite often they were very curious. And they wanted to know, "How did I get to be who I was" and all of that, they wanted the story and so on. And so, that's okay in that setting. They wanted to know. "Now you're who?" And I would tell them and they'd say, "You're not a nun?" "No." "Are you married?" "Yes, I am." "Really?" And then there are a lot of people who said, "I wish we could have that in our church." And probably, and I'm just guessing, probably 90 percent of the people that I saw were Roman Catholic.

Another time I was talking [to] one of these firefighters and this guy, he had to go outside, because you couldn't put him on a floor, he was just too big. And I went out and I talked to him and I did a whole bunch of things and he also hugged me. And he says to me, "Father, I love you." And I said to my congregation when I was talking, I said this is the first time I've not said to someone, "Don't call me Father."

Like the Roman Catholic firefighters who asked what to call the woman priest or here called one of the women priests what made sense to them, and the Roman Catholic priest who helped his brother from a nonsacramental church, there was a great deal of generosity of spirit that became evident as relationships and ministries were negotiated.

They didn't care, as long as you were doing what you did with some integrity. If you were a Christian, they wanted to hear your Christian prayers. They didn't want you to make up the version that you must do a lot in the cathedral because you have so many interfaith events. They didn't want to hear that because it seemed to them inauthentic. Even though as a Christian priest you wind up absolving a Jew. I don't think there's any prohibition against that.

Gender differences and faith affiliations became less important than integrity of approach and care of others in the community. Such spirit became clear when the chaplains became involved in one of the characteristic but sometimes difficult signs of life in a disaster community, its black humor and practical jokes—intentionally or accidentally. Such a sign shows a real (if sometimes unintentioned) sense of collegiality.

When we were down, when the morgue was right by the cross, there was the porta-potties, and the guys didn't see that I had gone into one, and I'm in there and all of a sudden it's rocking. It's just obvious they're just pushing back and forth. And I know that none of the guys that I know are standing by there because they had already left to go to St. Paul's, and I'm going to the bathroom. So I walk out and they were mortified, because they just messed with a priest. They thought it was somebody else because he was in the one next to me. And so they got the wrong outhouse. So there were those kinds of moments where it was just a lot of fun and laughter.

One chief I remember, he was a funny guy. We'd be over at T. Mort. and this voice would come over [the loudspeaker from the command center at the 10/10 Firehouse], "What are you doing smoking that cigarette out there?" We didn't realize, obviously, we were completely in his view. And he would rib us a lot. But, I remember going down in the Pit with him once. It was a harrowing experience. He loved to do safely risky things. We had quite a time with him. We'd get in the Gator and way down there at the north tower, and when the pile was still very high, the stuff was sticking all out of it all over the place. And the incline was just about almost perpendicular and we drove up that thing, he just drove like a mad man. We got up to the top and did we retrieve them? No, in that case we did not, we did not. He said, "Well, come on, I'll take you back." I said, "I'll meet you down at the bottom." So he knew he had done a good job.

Well, there were just some silly moments. Like when I fell off the all-terrain vehicle that [we used] when we would go down to the Pit. We had a route, when they opened Church Street again, it was always one of these things where we were trying to keep the tourists from taking pictures of what we're doing and stuff. We would camouflage everything and we would go out on Church Street and zoom down past Burger King and make a right. That was when the permanent ramp was built. And they hit a pothole and I was sitting in the jumpseat in the back and I went flying. And so it was hilarious, because at first they didn't know I was gone. And so I'm whistling but with all the noise and stuff and the vehicle itself made a lot of noise, it was just funny. So I'm walking down the street whistling and pretty soon they were probably a maybe a good two blocks down, they realized I wasn't back there anymore. So they said, "Come on, catch up." They wouldn't come back and get me or anything.

At one point I'm riding the train down to the T. Mort., right in the subway. And I catch my reflection and say, "Shit." As you know, if you button the clerical collar and you have the pin it, it feels as though the collar is attached. I look in the reflection, "Shit, [no collar.]" So I get there, there was an Episcopal woman priest and a deacon with her. I said, "Please, please, please tell me you have an extra collar, please?" "No, but you can use this one." Oh, God, a little bit of a thing. So that day the clerical collar that I wore was held together in the back by duct tape and that provided the ray of light for many a person that day.

The sense of humor, camaraderie, and lack of deference showed a collegiality that bespoke an inclusion of the chaplains as part of the community rather than seeing them as outsiders. This sense of collegiality extended to caring and hospitable acts toward the chaplains and, for many chaplains, in an acceptance of them as part of a team.

There was a time, I remember thinking how wonderful that the blessing of body parts is seen as important rather than interference. There was just sort of a sense of that T. Mort. chaplain is part of the team rather than as an unwanted extra. The chaplain was seen as a real part of the team. And that was a wonderful experience in that regard. My experience a lot of times is that if the bar association is having a dinner, they may want to have a minister there to say grace. It's a nicety rather than an integral, important part of the event. But that the teamwork, the chaplain seemed to be an important part of the team rather than just something nice they added on.

They went and they got me out of my sneakers, it was *the Port Authority cops* who did it for me. They went and they got me new boots, the cop boots, too, when my sneakers went out and melted. And they'd come back and I said, "I don't want to take this. This belongs to somebody else." He says, "They're a size 5. Nobody else is going to wear them. Put them on." So I put them on. I couldn't walk with them okay. They were so big, they were so heavy, they were so stiff, the things walked me. And they were laughing at me. They said, "Don't worry about it, they'll soften up." . . . But there was that. There was just some of the tenderness . . .

There was just a bang-up, wonderful *Medical Examiner*, a woman. Oh, I forget her name, she's an absolute delight, one of those people you just feel buoyed up in the human experience just to be with. And I think that's what I found most. And that's still the generative aspect of that work is getting to know these people and how wonderful they are.

I remember one of my first days down, *a policeman* . . . I must have been really out of it, but he insisted on walking me right to the train. Not the train station, but on to the train. Because I had done an overnight shift and he had wanted to make sure I got on the right train.

I got myself a bunch of patches. And there was one *EMS* patch and the reason I liked it was, it was a big patch and FDNY was pretty big, but EMS was pretty big and I saw it on a woman's jacket. She was standing in front of her ambulance down here when it was over on Church Street, when they moved the morgue, T. Mort., to Church Street. And I said, "Oh, I love that patch of yours because it's got the EMS is big on it." She said, "Well, here, you can have it." I said, "Wait a minute." She says, "No. I can get another one. Don't worry about it." She takes her jacket off and a pocketknife and cuts the patch off her jacket and gave it to me. I thought that was cool as hell. I said, "You didn't have to do that." She said, "No." In other words, a "We're really glad you're here" kind of thing. And those things, you're torn between laughing and crying, you know what I mean?

I have a doctorate in [--], from Harvard Medical School, a PhD, but I taught medical students for a little while. I know a lot of medical stuff. I sort of had been acclimated to it in a way. And I sort of knew stuff. Actually, I was as good as the *Medical Examiners* most of the time identifying what part of the body that was. We'd have a little choice and I'd say "Left elbow," and he'd say, "That's right." And so on, so it became, and we weren't trying to make a joke of it, but you know it was just something in common. If you could find anything in common with anybody, you could have a little connection and they knew that you knew and so that was kind of a way to connect with people.

Another chaplain spoke about the memorable connections made, in the hospitality of another, that lasted well after the incident.

Here, a cop offered to give me a cup of coffee. I got it a half an hour later. [*Cold?*] Oh, yeah, but it was wet, it was good. It was interesting, this was still at the tents. That was early on and it was cold and the weather was cold. He came by with somebody else and the Salvation Army truck was down the road further. And I didn't have a cell phone then so I couldn't move. But he was walking by with another guy and stopped and said "Hey, Padre. You want a coffee or something?" I said, "Yeah, I'd love one." He said, "How do you take it?" I said, "Black and no sugar." So he went off and I would say about half an hour later he came back with my cup of coffee and wished me all the best and thanked me for being there. And that was amazing, too, how they did that and all. But for me, even just doing that, that was something.

I met that guy again in April. I was up at a retreat center there, getting ready to present a marriage encounter weekend and I see this couple walk in and straight away I look at this guy and "I know you." I couldn't quite connect and he stood there and he says, "Black, no sugar." I thought, "Wow." You know, without even knowing it I think the people I met down here, there was a connection made without even knowing their name or anything like that. Somehow, looking back on that now, just to see all the connections that were made, even not meaning to make connections in that sense.

These connections speak of a sense of community that was intense and immediate but vitally necessary in Ground Zero not just to survive but also to *live*. Another chaplain described this life-giving sense.

Well, it was life giving, it was that you were coming alongside people with a defined role *to promote life in the midst of death*. To represent a God who is living in the midst of death. To live my vocation as a priest to the fullest, I would say it's one of the more difficult places to express that priesthood, that ministry. It was *very life giving to be part of a team*, always; never except when I was walking around by myself I was solo. But I would walk and join a group of people. Okay, I didn't do any work solo, if you will. And that was very life giving. Because I really think to me that's what it is to be part of a community.

And it was a real community of people who assembled here. Whether it was a community up at St. Paul's or in the T. Mort. itself or down on the site or when you would go to the shack, whichever.

This sense of community can be interpreted in a reductive way psychologically as that which met the chaplain's needs, the need to be needed and the need to be cared for, yet the descriptions go beyond that to a real sense of community that has to be engaged theologically. In this space of destruction so many of the chaplains experienced a life-giving community and a transforming communion with God that, despite the suffering, yielded a space for growth and life even in the face of the bodies broken and the blood poured out. This is not to say theologically that the community created by God is outside the church, but it is to suggest that the community created by the Spirit is not limited by that or reduced to it. That which was life giving was lived out in the shadow of the cross, the sign of suffering and death.

Image 4.1. The cross next to the Temporary Mortuary at Ground Zero. (Photo by Andrea Booher/FEMA News Photo.)

In a literal way it was lived out in the shadow of the cross formed by the broken crossbeams of the south tower of the World Trade Center, a cross that was highly controversial but a symbol of God's presence for many. A number of the chaplains were very ambivalent about the cross, questioning whether it was "an imposition of Christian identity onto something that really didn't proclaim it," and whether it implied a universal representation that did not apply to those many who were killed who were not Christian. However, the cross at Ground Zero was something that was discovered "laying around," as it were, a symbol that grew out of the experience of the recovery workers and not created and imposed by religious hierarchy. It felt like something that had survived the destruction and became loved by many. Soon we will explore this life-giving sense in Winnicott's thought and see how that which survives destruction can be transformative. We can see both the sense of discovered symbol and subsequent reflection present in the following reflections.

One day at St. Paul's Chapel I met a very big policeman who had been on vacation when this had happened and [was] feeling very guilty about it, survivors' guilt. So I took him out into the graveyard of St. Paul's Chapel and I had noticed on the hill of debris, that there was a cross. A girder, a cross that had just fallen in place. And so I pointed to that. And he helped me see that there were two others. So there were three crosses in the girders right in front of our eyes. And that helped both of us. It was like Golgotha, it was like a Good Friday experience. And yet the cross meaning hope for all of us and resurrection, so we talked.

Stepping out in that graveyard and seeing those crosses in the debris. Oh, that was just a mighty moment there. It was a reminder to me of *God's holy presence* in the midst of all this. And I shared it with others, took a picture of it. Interesting, it's a nighttime picture, it's not the greatest shot. But you can see the crosses. Transformational.

[I] still don't know what they're going to do with [the cross] when they finally finish rebuilding. I hope they find a place of honor for it. Yeah, they lifted it up and lifted it out. It was amazing—and obviously it isn't a symbol I [as a rabbi] connect to—in that it's *a symbol of God's presence*. And it was a symbol of hope of recovery for those that were working there, of rebirth, of beginning again. And I think it took a symbol like that to lift the incredible darkness that surrounded the site for so long. To lift it because for 90 percent of the people working there, it was their symbol and it became mystical. God must have done this. How could it come out just like this? God must have done this and God must be watching over us. And for so many people it was so important. And so as a symbol of what was going on, it was important for me, too, not as a religious symbol but as a symbol of the change of what was a feeling around the site. A change in the feeling that our hope was now to continue recovery, to help as many families complete. Some darkness went away when that cross came out and it was very powerful time. The same guy from FEMA who got us in, he and a few others got together and said, "Well, if there's going to be a cross here, there should be a Jewish star, too." And they created that. And it stayed for a while and then disappeared. I have no idea where it is. I don't know if it's still anywhere on the site. I haven't seen hide nor hair of it.

I'm going to use one word and I'll stick with it and explain it. But the word is "transparent." Transparent means to be able to see in everything and in nothing. The cross, the T. Mort. cross, the Ground Zero cross. I mean, come on, construction workers seeing in a void a piece of metal peculiar in this and finding in it sanctity. Wow, that ain't bad. That ain't bad at all. To see three firemen raise a flag, in Iwo Jima kind of ways, and then to refuse to let people play with it, to make it into their own thing. "Well, don't you think one of them should be black?" "Well, no." "Why not?" "Because one wasn't." "Well, they were all white." "Yeah, so what?" So what? I mean they could have all been black. I mean that misses the thing. So transparent is to be able to look about with clear sight to see what's there.

This sense of seeing what is there and making a response is not about either an imposition of doctrine or a theology of works but about the living out of love even in the face of death and destruction. It is well put by a rabbi:

The Kaddish became much more meaningful as I began to focus on the meaning of the words rather than just the presentation of it. And the fact that I was praising God in the face of death and the fact that I was acknowledging the glory of God and that all of this was part of God's glory. How? I don't know, but that doesn't matter. Why? Dumb question, you're never going to get an answer. The answer was what do I do with it. How do I live my life? And *I realize that I live my life by bringing more spirit and more spirituality and more loving that I can to as many people as I can.*

In the life-giving ministry at Ground Zero the chaplains both bought "more spirit . . . and more loving" and found it in the space of destruction and disaster.

Life-Giving/Transforming in Winnicott's Thought

In Winnicott's psychoanalytic thought, survival beyond destruction even in the midst of destructive elements is that which occasions love. We can see this in the mothers who love us even when we are aggressive and frustrating, in relationship with the partners who are with us "for better, for worse," the church that sees even in our sinful and broken humanity the redeemed child of God, the Ground Zero community which taught the chaplains that even in the face of the worst of what we do to one another, we can transform it through our own response and the love of God.

Near the end of his life Winnicott sought to articulate his unique ideas about a further step developmentally than "object-relating" that is intimately related to love. He saw object-relating as a coming from a place of "self-containment and relating to subjective objects,"[11] which may or may not be real in themselves, perhaps simply being "a bundle of projections,"[12] much like the Freudian view of God as an illusory projection of the Oedipal Father. The new developmental "feature" Winnicott called the problematic name of "object-usage." To the nonclinical ear this sounds more like a regression than a development. To "use" people, to "objectify" them, is seen as selfish and callous. Even, to the clinical ear, this term and Winnicott's articulation of it was not well received when he read his paper "On the Use of the Object and Relating through Identifications" to the New York Psychoanalytic Society in 1968.[13] However, Winnicott's terms are paradoxically almost the opposite of what they sound in everyday language and a number of clinicians argue that the terms should be switched, with "usage" denoting the maturationally earlier position.

However, I think there is a profound principle that Winnicott was reaching to that has to do with the maturational development of letting go, or destroying the illusions of what we want others to be and allowing them to be what they are. This is about really living creatively in response to the world as it is rather than living a magical "as if" life, as if life conformed to what we want of it. In analytic terms, it is a giving up of "omnipotent control."[14] If we continue to relate to others merely on the level of our own identification with them and our projection of our own needs in them, then the other has more to do with our own fantasy of what they are than with who they are in themselves. Winnicott states, "a capacity to use an object is more sophisticated than a capacity to relate to objects; and relating may be to a subjective object, but usage implies that the object is part of external reality."[15] Although Winnicott sees this capacity again as a very early one maturationally, primarily in the relationship between mother and child, this can also be seen to be a lifelong achievement. This may relate to one's relationship to one's "primary love object,"[16] to God, to the ability to use a "debriefer" rather than protect her from the reality of one's experience, or even, we can hypothesize, to the "objects" that were being recovered at Ground Zero, the destroyed loved ones of grieving families, friends, and colleagues. Given that so many of the chaplains referred to Ground Zero as a place where they experienced what was "real" in the context of destruction, I think it is worthwhile seeing if there is a reflection of the life-giving process we have been discussing theologically in Winnicott's psychoanalytic thought about "the use of the object."

Winnicott outlines a sequence that occurs *in fantasy* that shows the movement from subjectivity to objectivity as regards relationships with others.

> This sequence can be observed: (1) Subject *relates* to object. (2) Object is in process of being found instead of placed by the subject in the world. (3) Subject *destroys* object. (4) Object survives destruction. (5) Subject can *use* object.[17]

This terse sequence can be difficult to follow if disconnected from a real-life example. Yet it is interesting to see something of a reflection of the resurrection mentality we were pondering on earlier, where the object is both destroyed *and* survives the destruction. Winnicott, however, puts it in terms of the "I-Thou" relationship as a dialogue.

> The subject says to the object: "I destroyed you," and the object is there to receive the communication. From now on the subject says: "Hullo object!" "I destroyed you." "I

love you." "You have value for me because of your survival of my destruction of you."
. . . The subject can now use the object that has survived.[18]

There is, then, a recognition of the external reality of others, not that they are simply created by our need for them, but have a reality in themselves beyond our desires and drives. It is from here that reality becomes shared and we can "use" our relationships with others, not simply for a reinforcement of our false self structure, but can reach to that creative, even playful, and life-enhancing space where we can grow.

This, for Winnicott, is a move from what in its extreme form is the relationship to a idealized other, to the relationship to a real, objective other that may be different from what we would wish of them. Although Winnicott relates this to the relationship between the primary caregiver and infant, we can see it clearly in other love relationships. In intimate relationships, for real love to be present we must move beyond our projections and identifications with our loved one, beyond the idealization of who they are, to the reality of who they are in themselves, "recognition of [them] as an entity in [their] own right."[19] Some relationships cannot survive this loss of the romantic ideal, and yet, Winnicott would suggest, that is exactly the place where real love takes hold.

In the context of Ground Zero, how does this relate to the experience of the chaplains and their sense of what was life giving or their transformative moments? We can explore this in a number of respects: the relationship with God, with the church, with community, with those able to be used for self-care and debriefing, and with the "object" of the mission and ministry at Ground Zero, that is, the care of the dead and those who cared for them.

At Ground Zero there was this paradoxical but integrated experience of immense grief at the finding of bodies and body parts and the "joy" of finding them, particularly those known to the firefighters, PAPD, and NYPD officers on the site. In a sense you could say that what was found was that which had been destroyed yet survived. The survival, of course, was only survival of human remains, not the life of the person! This survival of a person's remains, however, which was a tangible representation of who they were, was infinitely more preferable to the failure to recover any surviving fragment. One chaplain described this experience with the recovery of the remains of an EMS technician.

> There were two EMS people that were lost. And I was there the day they found one of them. And the crew I was on with, they knew the guy, . . . so they found him and this time all the EMS people were the honor guard. And they brought the remains out under a flag and I got to do the prayers over that individual into the morgue and the M[edical] E[xaminer] doing the exams. . . . There was a sense of relief among the EMS people, because they got one of them. They felt good about that. And then they would sit around. We sat around and relayed stories about what he did and how he did it and what

> kind of guy he was and all this stuff. Kind of like purging all of this stuff out
> of their system so it made it a little easier for them, I suspect. But they were
> very happy about that.

You can see that paradox of destruction and survival, of life giving even in the midst of death, in another chaplain's comment about the best and worst of Ground Zero.

> Standing in a drizzle at the request of people, with stole and collar, to remove
> a body, a torso that was wrapped around rebar. They had to use an acetylene
> torch and they had buckets of water there because the flesh and other things
> would catch on fire. And they wanted me there in uniform so as they're doing
> this they could see me there. Some people would call that the worst. That
> also has about it some of the best. So one of the things that marks in unique-
> ness this kind of event is you're most likely to find those words together in
> what I would consider healthy. If you have people saying the best parts were
> drinking a cup of coffee and laughing and the worst parts were the things like
> I described, you've got opportunity for some dysfunction.

Here even, ministry had to survive the chaplains' desire to change things, to make things better, to survive the destruction of good feeling, and in doing so became transformative through the ministry of presence even in horrific circumstances.

Winnicott's world of the child and its mother, the psychoanalyst and the analysand, seems worlds away from Ground Zero. Yet again, Winnicott has something significant to contribute to the understanding of life-giving transformation in relation to destructiveness. Winnicott is writing in the context of seeking to formulate an understanding of "inborn aggression" that seems to have a positive function in creating rather than being simply a frustration in relation to reality. He writes, "The assumption is always there, in orthodox theory, that aggression is reactive to the encounter with the reality principle, whereas here it is the destructive drive that creates the quality of externality."[20] The difference is a subtle one but profound. The aggression in the psyche that destroys to create, rather than destroys to annihilate, is an inner destruction that is not about "anger reactive destruction"[21] but about "the destruction that is at the root of object relating and that becomes (in health) channeled off into the destruction that takes place in the unconscious, in the individual's psychic reality, in the individual's dream life and play activities, and in creative expression."[22] This point is crucial, the differentiation between aggression that is about creation and that which manifests as an angry reaction against reality is akin to the difference between a joke about a terrorist and that about a victim. The unconscious destruction that is always going on is not about destroying the external with which you are angry, but about destroying the internal image of the other as you have created it. This then enables you to see the other more clearly and have a creative aggression that mobilizes a new response again and again to an external other rather than a static relationship with an internal other.

How did this play out at Ground Zero? Perhaps the difference can be seen in the chaplains' differing thoughts and feelings about the terrorists:

> I would say unmitigated hatred. When the bombing in Afghanistan finally started, I was so relieved, I was just so impatient for somebody to do something back—revenge of some kind. The graffiti that was every[*where*], magic-markered in the port-a-johns universally sort of gave all those sentiments. But one of the things that I used, when I was down there, is that I would end whatever form of blessing or whatever with the Lord's Prayer. And I distinctly remember at the beginning that all the folks who were primarily Catholic in the fire department and stuff would be joining me and I was struck immediately by the phrase in The Lord's Prayer, "And forgive us our trespasses as we forgive those who trespass against us." And you're standing in the midst of the rubble that was still on fire, still smoking, and still you could smell the remains decaying of the people who had been killed. And it was a very, very strong statement to make. And after awhile even though I'd continued to use the Lord's Prayer at the end, FDNY folks, they didn't continue to pray it. It became the chaplain's prayer, not the prayer of the group. It's very interesting and I can't identify when that changed, but I would have to say probably in October or late October, that it began to change, the penny had begun to drop for them.

When I commented that the chaplain was not just saying a prayer that was rote, people were listening to the words, the chaplain continued on to say,

> Yeah, and they didn't want to forgive those who trespassed against them, and so they backed away from . . . I mean, by that point you'd begun to have the funerals and those guys were so deep down, just so deep down. . . . And it was such a huge burden for them. I mean, more than anybody else in the site that I saw, working alongside them, talking with guys who lost their buddies and, remember we were in the north tower or south tower in just all this powdery dust and these guys, "I'm here looking for my buddy and I wouldn't even know what he looked like at this point, because it's all just powder and all that's gone." The sense of futility and just hopelessness that pervaded so much of their feelings and their grief over and over and over repeated until just absolutely none as such . . .

Here, in the face of the reality of looking for one's colleagues that may be powdery dust in the dust of Ground Zero, the reality was for many just too painful, too encompassing to allow thought of forgiveness for the ones who had caused such devastation. Allowing the meaning of the Lord's Prayer was too close to the reality of what they were facing. For many the reaction was anger, and even, as this chaplain described his early response, "unmitigated hatred." Like the child turning away from its mother to kill off her reality, the temptation is to turn away from the object internally and not to turn back, externally to annihilate, or as with the prayer, to turn away from the symbol of transformation in anger. It is interesting that what we do not see is what it was like for this to become "the chaplain's prayer," rather than the communal prayer of the group. Perhaps in some way the chaplains could symbolically hold that which could not be held by others: "forgiveness," "mercy," "love of enemy." For others there was a different quality.

I suppose the part of my experience that bothered me most was the world and I'd include the church in this. To articulate what this was, my immediate response to this, we use words like AWOL and attack and I thought, *what the perpetrators did was absolutely such a classic image and picture of sin.* That in some way they were able to gain control of the cockpit, destroy the pilot, and they put themselves in the throne as though they were God, and acted as God. And whenever we throw God off the throne, and act as though as we were God, awful things happen. And I don't think I ever heard anybody articulate this as sin. And I still think we have to deal with it as sin. And it was a sin that was substantially different than when you have armies lined up on a border and that would attack. This was sin of specific, recognizable individuals. That I think should be dealt with as sin.

And then when we deal with it as sin, our response is not hate. Whenever you hate the sinner more than you hate the sin, you try to overcome one sin with another sin that's probably worse. And I think our response of hate is always unwise. I'm not a Pollyanna, and I'm not a pacifist. But it's a matter of recognizing this for what it was and it was sin. And I never heard any churchperson speak about that being sin. You deal with it differently when you recognize it as sin. If it is sin, then I said when they were trying to divide up the money to the people who were survivors of those who died in the World Trade Center, I said, *"It would be wonderful if we made contact with the wives or the mothers of the terrorists who perpetrated the crime and say we want them to be in the distribution."* Which I think would have made a world of difference on our dialogue. If we would have dealt with the sin we would have a dialogue. When you deal with it as a judgment, you have no dialogue. And we were very quick to deal with it. And obviously we all make judgments. I mean, you can't get a hold of these people and do anything to them, they're all atomized. So I guess my response to the whole thing was theological, which for me made it much easier to deal with. . . . *But once you take it out of the context of sin, you also remove the contents of grace, of mercy, love, and forgiveness.*

Another chaplain responded to the photo of the firefighters raising the flag by reflecting:

> Well, it's that false sense of unity. The flag to me is a demonic symbol and it works against the kingdom of God in ways much more effective than the church is. Do you know what I mean? And what it elicits is exactly the stuff that feeds the cycle of violence, you know. And that's exactly what we saw. We didn't see anybody gathering around the flag in grief or mourning. We saw them gathering around the flag yelling about *retaliation and revenge*, you know. Bush was perfect. It was perfect. He couldn't have scripted a devil any better than his shit.

When asked, "So did you experience any of that at Ground Zero? People talking of revenge and retaliation?" the chaplain replied:

> Uh-uh. No. It doesn't happen at Ground Zero. It doesn't happen in a place like that. That's the collective mind-set that has the luxury of that thought. . . . In fact, I remember a cop, I was standing on the Pile talking and this cop leaned over to me and he said, "Do you know that Bush and bin Laden have the same banker?" See, that's a cop for you. Cops don't talk about revenge. Cops are too cynical to think about revenge. . . . That retaliation and revenge stuff, that's luxury. You can't be dealing with reality and be talking with that at the same time. It's too vicarious.

When asked, "And so what was reality here that countered that?," the chaplain went on to say, "Death, destruction, and chaos. But revenge, retaliation is a move away *from the reality of chaos and death and destruction*. It's a move toward order, I mean in a false sense of human order, cultural order." This chaplain identified that there was something about Ground Zero and having to live with the destruction and the chaos which was important that in fact didn't feed the cycle of violence. "Right. I never heard, I never heard anger down there. Or any talk of revenge or retaliation. I don't think I ever did."

The responses of the chaplains to questions about the terrorists and their reading of the responses of those around them seem to fall toward both ends of the spectrum—from the chaplain who spoke of his "unmitigated hatred" and saying that the graffiti "magic-markered in the port-a-johns . . . universally gave those sentiments" of revenge, to the chaplain who "never heard anger down" at Ground Zero.

So what was the reality of Ground Zero, the former or the latter? Could it be that each chaplain's projections found a home in those whom they worked alongside, those chaplains who were angry with the terrorists finding others who were also, those who were not experiencing anger instead focused on the recovery in the midst of the "chaos, death, and destruction"? For Winnicott, one can hypothesize, it is a change in attitude or a transformation of the destruction that is the sign of life, health, growth. Are there reflections of this in the following two accounts?

> Probably, more closer to the end—and now it's kind of weird with all the health issues that are coming up now and that—but we would hear once in a while about somebody who had killed themselves. And so we actually had a pact with kind of our team, with the guys I worked with the most, and women I worked with the most, that we exchanged phone numbers and e-mail addresses, that sort of thing. But our thing is that the terrorists don't get another one. That was probably our biggest focus, was that they already did what they did. To let them win somebody by a suicide or everybody would talk a lot, especially when we were over at the respite center, you know, the marriages that, if they were fragile before, they either went completely over the edge or they kind of got cemented back together and stuff. So there was this whole thread that was woven through it that we're [not] going to be about doing, I'm [not] doing the work of the terrorists, *we're going to be about making good where we can*. So when you think about all the horrible things that they did and stuff like that, it was just like, yeah, but we're here now. *Now we are bringing about the good*. Probably the biggest discussion we had was the whole suicide thing, because we had talked about the fact that some of us go home alone and how at night that was hard. To go home and be in bed alone and not have anybody just to give you a hug when you got home and stuff like that. And so we felt that the biggest thing besides human life that the terrorists stole from us was our joy. They took away that, whatever was going on in your life, you still had your life. It was a beautiful day on September 11th, all this stuff. And they just sucked it all out of us in one blink of an eye. And the goal was not to let them have any more victories.

A chaplain quoted in the previous chapter about his not hating the terrorists again noted this feeling of change later in the interview:

> This reminded me to remember that I have an incredible gift and so does everybody else that's alive on the planet. And so it changed a lot of things. People said, you know, do you hate the terrorists that did that? I say, "How can I hate them, they're dead. If they're alive, I can be angry with them, they're dead. It's God's job to deal with them, their souls need a cleaning. They're going through a soul wash right now."

Whether these responses are about an angry reaction against the reality of destruction, or a destroying of one's own projections and predisaster worldview and a discovery of something new, perhaps only the ongoing outcome can tell. Whatever externally that survives destruction or not, in one's inner world it has to be meaning which is discovered, *not imposed*. If it is the latter it is simply an offering of the False Self seeking once again that omnipotent control. This is one of the reasons, however, why pastoral method needs to look for signs of life in the midst of the suffering, not as a denial of the suffering, but so one does not get stuck there. Where are the signs of life, growth, health that take into account the destruction and the resultant suffering, but somehow transform it also? This needs to be read *out* of each situation and not read *into* it, which is why theological principles like "forgiveness" cannot be imposed, but a turning once again to the objects of our anger to regain connection with them is a transformation that has a life of its own and in its own time.

The feel-good moments were also a survival of life in the midst of death, as can be seen in the gallows humor of the site. This is often characteristic of first responders. In some ways this can be seen as a defensive response. Ellen T. Gerrity and Bryan W. Flynn, in *The Public Health Consequences of Disasters*, see gallows or black humor as a sign of stress in first responders to disaster, "another mechanism to depersonalize the victim or survivor."[23] Much humor is indeed a sublimation of aggression, a comic representation that is unconsciously intended to dehumanize, depersonalize, denigrate, and at times annihilate; however, black humor in first responders serves multiple functions. French psychoanalyst Pascale Navvari "shows how, thanks to black humor, the ego refuses to allow itself to be wounded even by the most tragic circumstances the subject experiences."[24] Jacqueline Garrick says, "the use of black humor, therefore, can be seen as a means of allowing negative or maladaptive stress responses to become positive or adaptive and to facilitate survivor's progress in the recovery process. . . . Kuhlman described gallows humor as, 'Violating principles usually associated with human meanings and values. . . . It is an in-kind response to an absurd dilemma, a way of being sane in an insane place.'"[25]

Funny experience[s] . . . got us through. We would watch horror movies in T. Mort. at like four in the morning, because you had to have a sense of humor down there. We would also talk to the remains and the guys. One of them was doing that and "Oh, God, I'm going to go to hell." I said, "You're not going to hell, actually why not, let's all do that." [*What kind of things would you say to the remains?*] It's like, "We're glad you're here with us," and we would just have conversation like they were still there. We'd get into joking, "We're going to get something to eat, you want anything?" But it became like a normal thing to do and it made it more comfortable there. And then I remember around Christmas, one of the deputy chiefs of the fire department, I just went on rounds with him, he needed that. And I said, "Sure, I'll go on rounds with you." And he wanted to know if I sang, because I had started singing prayers for the dead, because I didn't want it to become rote. So I just started making up songs. And he says, "Oh good, let's sing." And we were riding around in the ATV and singing Christmas carols at the top of our lungs.

Perhaps Winnicott would described this as "playing," a creative and healthy encounter with reality. What is significant in this gallows humor is a shift in identification. Rather than a defensive depersonalization that annihilates connection, to gain distance from the victim, there is a move toward personalization, even if seemingly macabre to an outsider of the situation. It is this move in Ground Zero narratives that seems to signal growth and resiliency, a sense of survival in the midst of destruction that Winnicott is reaching toward in his reflections.

> The fact that people are resilient, [and] could be humorous in the situation whether they were fire department, police or even people in [grief], be humorous and carry on. Lighter? I don't know. Just the jokes, the jokes that people made, workers made, other people. Wisecracks, I mean, that was, there was a pretty constant level, pretty constant flow of humor at one level. I mean it wasn't all just grim and heavy and stuff like that.

Situations also arose spontaneously where gallows humor was used to transform humorous reversals of the moment:

> One was after we found a piece of a bone fragment of some sort, and they asked, we should have some sort of blessing, and we had a little bit of bone fragment that got sort of a very quick extemporaneous prayer. The more you got to a recognizable body, I was dragging out "The Litany at the Time of Death' and improvising, because it doesn't work. You know, it's not a litany, you kind of give them something they can just say. Anyway, so we said this little prayer and then the Medical Examiner is looking at it. I heard him whisper something and he said, "This is a pork chop." It was. We all thought it was hysterical. It's like a pork chop. It was someone's lunch. . . . And another moment was when we found the wallet of a bit of remains after I think it might have been lengthiest time of death. And they said, "Oh, his name was Silverstein. He was a Jew. You just absolved a Jew." And the M.E., whose name was something Jewish, said, "And I bet he needed it, too."

Chaplains told stories of ceremoniously transporting remains from the Pit to the T. Mort., fully aware that what they were holding was probably a chicken bone but waiting for the M.E. to identify those remains as "Caucasoid" or "KFC." The spontaneous moments that arose, however, and the creative response to them, such as that of the M.E., shows the fine line in gallows and black humor that is intimately related to the culture within which the humor finds its life and the levels of identification. Wendy Doniger, in her thoughtful and amusing article, "Terror and Gallows Humor: After September 11?" notes,

For permission to joke is granted at very different moments to the victims, the specta-tors, and the perpetrators (or those associated with the perpetrators) of atrocity or terror (even if the latter are personally innocent of any wrongdoing) or anyone who can be suspected of a lack of sympathy with the victims, for the presupposition of sympathy is the precondition for a successful joke.[26]

Permission to joke about the perpetrators, bin Laden (who was given a mythical brother, Hadn bin Laid) or, more uneasily, the Arabs in general, was granted long before permission to joke about Arab victims; and, as far as I know, no one in the national press has yet ventured to joke about the victims of our bombing in Afghanistan. Yet there were jokes about our own victims, in New York, though this sort of humor was primarily granted only to victims themselves: New Yorkers could say things about New York that no one else could say, just as only Jews can tell certain jokes about Jews, and only blacks certain jokes about blacks.[27]

Like Winnicott, who emphasizes both destruction and survival, Doniger's thought is that "Gallows humor . . . presents us with a world that is hopeless but not serious."[28] However, it is really only those on the inside of such a community like the recovery community at Ground Zero who would be able to participate in this way, and at times even understand the mentality that is so life-giving to those on the inside. It is that creative, life-giving sense that connected you to others, that transformed the death and destruction of Ground Zero into real community. Theologically, it was a way of saying, "God is bigger than this"; psychologically, "Life is bigger than all this death." Both sentiments are captured in a vignette from one chaplain:

I remember another fabulous incident where I was being driven down into the Pit by a guy who was a maniac. I mean, he was driving out of control. And we get down and we reach a point where he goes off the groomed path and hits the brakes so we kind of skid off sideways and all this. You could almost feel the force trying to pull the Gator off. And when we come to a full and complete stop, he's in the driver's seat, his partner's in the back and I'm riding shotgun and he turns to me and he says, "I scared you, Father, didn't I?" And I'm trying to keep my best poker face and before I say anything the guy in the back says, "What are you talking about? Priests don't get scared." And I said, "Well," I said, "maybe we're a little bit like firefighters. If we do get scared we try not to show it to anybody."

And then the guy said to me, "Well, you know what?" He said something to the effect of he was not afraid of the devil. And I'm thinking, this is going to be interesting, and so I said, being very polite, "Oh really? Okay." And he said, "You want to know why I'm not afraid of the devil?" And I said, "Why?" And he said, "Because," and his point was ultimately God is above the devil. And so with that, he can live. And I just thought, "Wow," who thought I was all of a sudden going to have this great little theological moment with this maniac driver, driving me down into the Pit?

This sense of transformational space—that even in the midst of the space of destruction God is above this and within this, that the bush is burning but not consumed, that we, though destroyed, are not consumed, that we can not only survive enough to laugh at the small things but can make a creative reparative response—enabled people not only to survive but to grow, to be the "I-AM" who I am, the "True Self" in Winnicott's terms, in the midst of this death and that which was life giving.

I think the first time that I saw a recovery of somebody that was pretty much intact, almost complete, there was just a moment of realization. A moment of connection with that person, with God, and with all the other people around, how we had in that small place, in that small moment, this full circle of life and death and living and dying and finishing something and moving on. And that was very powerful.

This kind of growth and development is generally spoken of under the increasingly popular term *resiliency* and the newer term *post-traumatic growth*. It is a reflection on the "glass half-full" mentality that seeks to focus not simply on those who are traumatized by disasters, but on those who are not. One chaplain showed an attitude that is a good example of resiliency which has to do with personal qualities rather than skills:

I think you had to survive and to cope. It was the ability to [say], I have to leave, go on to something else. I'll be back. But this is part and parcel of the human experience. I didn't allow it to be so encompassing that it just overwhelmed me.

Ranging from personal qualities, to activities to build resiliency, researchers are attempting to discover and name what enables a person to be resilient in the face of trauma and what enables one to grow, despite being traumatized. For those that do not come into disaster-response ministry with a natural feeling of resiliency, or who don't experience such transformational moments, intentional building of such a life-giving quality is necessary. This was one chaplain's recipe from Ground Zero:

The biggest survival one is to be 100 percent there when I was [at Ground Zero]. In that sense it's like holding a thistle. There are some things that if you do gently it's worse. And so to be in whole-heartedly is the only way to do that. To be in a way when I talked about humble and proud? Humble means to know, that even after I've been there, I don't know enough to do this myself.

And I'm not talking about me and God doing it, I'm talking about me and other people. God gets me there and sustains me through, but if I need help to go over a piece of rubble, I damn well better be willing and instantly able to ask somebody to help me with that. This is not a time for prayer, this is a time to say, "Yo. Give me a hand." That's one, full, and completely *being there*.

The other is to allow myself *calibration*. Calibration is it takes more than one try to get something. That doesn't mean you fail nine times before you get it right. That means each time you do it, you get something and you adjust from that and you get it better the next time. Does that mean the first nine times you did it, you did it wrong? Well, that's not a helpful way to look at it. To get something done satisfactorily to the people involved means a variety of wholehearted attempts and recalibration.

The third thing is to let people *be who and what they are*. So I can do some things differently and in *that* situation better, that doesn't mean doing better in *this* situation. It means I can do better in that situation. That's why we've got more than one person. Thank you. I don't have to be someone else, better than they are. I just need to be better than I am.

Again, keeping in mind Winnicott's theory, the focus is on the growth of the True Self, the "I" that "I AM." It is from this place of being that doing unfolds in an integrated, spontaneous, and creative way. Winnicott notes, "It is hardly necessary to point out that the I AM state and the state of BEING and the feeling of reality in existing is not an end in itself, it is a position from which life can be lived."[29]

Life-Giving/Transforming as Pastoral Method

Paying attention in pastoral care to what is life giving means attending to those seemingly elusive but often powerful aspects of transformation. Unlike a sense of holding, which can be intentionally created and practiced, these aspects of life, a little like the Spirit that may inspire them, "blow where they will" (cf. John 3:8). It is as subtle and profound as the difference between surviving and living, between reacting and acting, between "self-care" and the Self's care. As we can see in the chaplains' narratives, these are moments that can be discovered, captured, and delighted in but not manufactured. However, what can be created are the conditions that can contribute to this, even in the midst of a disaster site.

For one chaplain it was as simple as saying yes rather than no to things, if at all possible. For another it was about appreciating life and seeking to live from that postdisaster gratitude:

On the one hand, we need to appreciate life because it could be gone in a minute. Three thousand people got up that day and thought they were going home that night. They all had plans for that evening, the next week, whatever, and it all got taken away from them. I think in our world or society, we divorce life from death too much, in that we're conditioned we're not supposed to think about it, face it, what have you. And I think this brought home the reality of, if you love somebody, you should tell them you love them. What's the point of holding off? And at the same time it's hard to live in that immediacy. Ultimately within the social contract, we can't be. It's hard to live every moment as if it could be the last moment. But we need to appreciate life, it's the only thing that God's given us and it's a real gift. I think that probably is the most important. And the other piece to it is, it's like my tattoo, death doesn't have the final say. It's not the final answer. There is always life afterwards. Be it in this life and in what's yet to come, death is not the end. As awful as what they did in commandeering these planes and the level of destruction and what have you, the amount of goodness that came out of it surpasses the death and the evil and what have you. It's that understanding, that in the midst of tragedy tremendous, tremendous blessing, love, comfort, what have you, will be the next thing.

The Gospel of John describes this in the words of Jesus, "I came that they may have life, and have it abundantly" (John 10:10). Winnicott describes this space as that of play: "It is in playing and only in playing that the individual child or adult is able to be creative and to use the whole personality, and it is only in being creative that the individual discovers the whole self."[30] Winnicott sees in adult life that this sense of playing encompasses the whole cultural experience. We can see a symbol of this sense of life and transformation in the chaplain's reflection above, a symbol that I cannot but think would fall under Winnicott's rubric of "play."

I have the steel-beam cross tattooed on my leg with a dolphin on top of it as a symbol of the resurrection. The cross is not the final say. New life, new beginning, resurrection, what have you, trumps it in the end. . . . I got that a year ago. It took me forever. I was wanting a tattoo and at the same time wanted something of 9/11 to stay with me. But I did not want a tombstone. It does not say 9/11 on it. And you know, there was a stretch there where I had various things. At one point I thought about something that incorporated the towers themselves. I ix-nayed that, shadows of the towers behind something, ix-nayed that. I was going to have *in paradisum*, ix-nayed that. And then finally all of a sudden it was just, the cross was simple. But then the issue was, it wasn't to be just the cross and so I started to flip through a book of Christian iconography trying to find something that called to me and I saw the dolphin, liked the concept of the dolphin as savior and as a symbol of the resurrection and thought maybe I'll put that above the cross as a sign of there's death, but then there's new life, there will be. And so I did that over a year ago and am quite pleased with having done that. I tell people that in terms of things in my life, my getting this tattoo is one of the things I'm most proud of.

This symbol of death and life powerfully depicts that transformative space. As can be seen, it may take some time to get to and cannot be rushed; it has to more be trusted, or even discovered. However, this transformative space of death and life, that "resurrection experience," can be present even within such a disaster. Rather than simply staying with suffering, or denying it, suffering can be transformed through creative response, as can be seen in the request of a chaplain that sees those suffering as vulnerable but refuses to treat them passively as victims, leaving them stuck in their pain, but invites them into active response.

... going into the site and working with guys to pray with them to bless their machinery because they knew they weren't just picking up debris, they were picking up people and that was really hard. Initially, kind of a thing that ended up being, not a hallmark, but a routine for me, I realized that the guys have a lot of time on their hands, they can't listen to iPods or anything or whatever because they have to be able to hear. But it just seemed like they had too much mental time that they wanted to be prayed for, they wanted all this. They were very good about expressing their needs, but I was feeling a little bit inadequate like, I can walk down here to this terrible place, but then I leave and they're stuck there.

So it ended up being [that] I had these 3 x 5 cards that I don't even remember why they gave them to us initially, but I started putting prayer requests on the cards for them to pray for. I said, because they kept on mentioning, "All I think about is this, this, and this." So I said, "Would you pray for a friend of mine whose son needs a liver transplant and is dying? Could you pray for them?" And it just so happened that they were fluorescent colors, so they were very bright in this place. And through subsequent nights I would run into these guys again. And one guy, it was just like one of those great moments where he said, "This was really tricky," he said, "it was the first time I have not sat and thought about what's happening here but there's other people that are still going to work in the morning and still fighting with their spouse and so I appreciated being able to pray for somebody." And that was one of those God moments where I was just thankful that God inspired me to give guys a 3 x 5 card with somebody's name on it.

The transforming space can be as simple as a 3 x 5 card, as a cold cup of coffee, as profound as the cross formed by the destruction of Ground Zero and as powerful as the community that enables the holiness of God to be present. Pastorally, one needs to look for the life-giving moments and the transformative experiences. To paraphrase the founder of psychodrama, Jacob Moreno, "Look for the movement."

Like the American Psychological Association, which is not only focusing on risks, symptoms, and treatment of PTSD, but looking also toward resilience and post-traumatic growth, in the moment we can also stand alongside others and not only hear about the worst of what they are experiencing but also the best. Perhaps the most resilient of chaplains in a disaster are those who know this reality already, and therefore even in the worst of circumstances are imbued with that sense of life and hope that can contribute to the transformation of such a community of care. We can see this in the words of another chaplain, speaking about blessing human remains in the T. Mort.

> But I prayed for the people, I thanked God for his creation, this human being and for all the people who knew and loved this person, may finding these remains bring closure and peace to them knowing that now they can bury, even if it's a small portion, that they would be able to take this, their loved one, and now give them respect and final burial, whatever their tradition would be. And then thanking God for the eyes of the people, the construction workers who found them, and all that. And so when I would pray and bless and all this, it was, of course, centered on the fact that another person had been found, but it was also on the living.
>
> And one of the firefighters remarked at one time, "Not that it's bad, but," he said, "you tend to smile when you pray." And I said, "Because I have hope out of all that has happened that's evil, that good is being brought out, that people will have remains, that you've been blessed by being part of that." So I said, it was kind of a hope-filled ministry, because if you focused only on the death and the destruction and the horrible smells and that, it would always be overwhelming. Being in a community, being a part of something that was bringing about good, was very important.

Being in this community was indeed transformative for many of the chaplains, a place where they experienced their own vulnerability and ability to suffer with others, and create empathic holding relationships of care and concern that were a gift to others, in the earthy dust and destruction of Ground Zero. It was a place where many experienced God as both immanent and transcendent, with them, at times within them, and within the hands and hearts of the community in that "sacred place." The *sacred place* was less of the physical reality of Ground Zero, and more the relational reality of the *sacred space* of community and communion experienced at Ground Zero. The chaplains blessed, they hoped they were a blessing, and they felt blessed by being there. A final reflection from one chaplain about his last day captures this so well. When asked, "How did you finish in the ministry at the T. Mort?," he replied,

> With sadness, in a sense. My last night, I think I got finished at six in the morning. It would have been the fifth of May. . . . They knew I was going, I sort

of told them that night. The tour I was with and some of the regulars (you get to know them) sort of blamed me for not telling them earlier. I said, "No, it's not about me, it's about us, about what we're doing." I don't like that attention. Maybe another area I need to look at in my life. But coming to the morning time that I knew somebody else would be coming soon so said your little goodbyes tearfully and just sort of stood together and prayed together, which was really neat. *And they blessed me!*

Image 4.2. T. Mort. Chaplains' Patch.

And then I sort of said "Hi" to the new guy taking over and I walked out that door and went to the cross and said "Thank you." And walked out the gate but went back again, I found it difficult to leave. I really did. It was tough. I just went back to the cross again and I didn't go back inside. I didn't do that but I just stayed there for a moment and with determination walked out the gate to the subway. And when I got home I crashed. So many, I guess not, well, memories, yes, but painful memories, good memories, life-giving memories. The painful ones were keeping me up, from going out the first time. But thinking back on it all now I'm very happy that I was a part of that. I really am. I think it made me a much better priest, a much better man.

Trauma, Trinity, and Transformation

Earth-Making, Pain-Bearing, Life-Giving

Compline
Up the ramp walking
feeling my shoes in the dirt
in procession.
The open back of the ambulance
Litters inside, reverently, carefully placed.
Doors open for prayer.
Uncover again.

Feeling the men in a circle at my back
I pray
again for their souls
for their rest
and give thanks
for their finding
for the men.
Touching each bag,
I bless.

Firefighters cover their heads
and walk down the ramp.
To gather in more.

Forgive me dear Lord, for thy dear Son,
The ill that I this day have done;
That with the world, myself, and thee,
I, ere I sleep, at peace may be.[1]

In the beginning of this book I outlined my belief that the Trinity offers a threefold model of pastoral engagement that leads from a place of trauma to that of transformation. This thesis followed through the argument that this is so because the image of God in the human person is a trinitarian image, and that the God of love, and the love of God, can be experienced in human life in this way when we are acting out of this image inspired by the God who is with us. The analogy Augustine of Hippo used for this image of God, "which *we* are," was that of a mirror. Yet the very fact of our humanity and the world we live in makes this an obscure reflection and difficult to perceive.[2] Yet in these pages we have witnessed, in the persons and work of the chaplains at the Temporary Mortuary at Ground Zero, some clear images of the love of God in our world. Only God knows whether this is due to the inspiration of the Spirit of God, or through the action of the chaplains in "renewing" that image. However, the profound and moving stories of these women and men at Ground Zero and the community around them show, as Miroslav Volf writes, "the divine labor of love's suffering and risk . . . engaged in the transformation of the deeply flawed world that is."[3]

I have argued that this "divine labor of love," where we become what we are—the image of the Triune God—is a labor that is reflective of the *economic Trinity*, God as God is for us in the world, God in *active* relationship with the world. We, too, become like the God whose image we reflect in active relationship with others, in Earth-making, Pain-bearing, and Life-giving. Yet, these relationships are grounded in a world where we suffer and cause others to do so. In reflecting upon this world we could have used any or many different examples that are clear pictures of such suffering. Recent history has offered us the experience of the disaster of September 11, 2001. This disaster offers us not only a picture of the kind of trauma humanity can experience but also a picture of how far we are both like and *unlike* the image of God. Those that perpetrated this disaster, we can theologically argue, were also "this image which we are," and yet were not manifesting love as we know it. Augustine's point is that humanity is that image *through which* we see God, humanity is not God but only, enigmatically, an obscure reflection. The point for him is not the mirror, but that which is seen through it. This reflection, I would argue, is only manifest in us when we live and act out of love, as I believe the chaplains did at Ground Zero over those long nine months of the recovery effort.

Love is no simple thing. To love in traumatic circumstances, circumstances in which we are inflicted with fear, horror, and helplessness, is a challenge and a gift. The challenge is to build a relationship with others and ourselves, where we not only open ourselves up to them and their suffering but risk connecting with our own vulnerability and pain both interpersonally and intrapsychically. The gift is in so doing, we experience the love of God in us, and through us, and for us in the face of the other. In the end our hope is that the gift of loving is greater than the suffering often entailed in living out that love. Overall, we can see this in the experience of the chaplains at the T. Mort. at Ground Zero, who exhibited a manifest sense of life, gratitude, and growth due to their experience of the chaplaincy. Yet it was a growth that was borne in the pain and suffering of a community of both immense distress and immense care and concern. The chaplains showed many of the signs of Secondary Traumatic Stress and yet they also showed the transformative signs of post-traumatic growth. Through the lens of D. W. Winnicott we have seen that their often creative and spontaneous acts of care were most often grounded in a true sense of self, able to hold itself together without that annihilating fragmentation and to achieve the suffering that connects us deeply to each other and the depth and breadth of who we are and our being in relationship with others. Yet, we have also seen the true interdependence of relationality. These achievements were also made possible by the recovery community that created space for the chaplains, in the ways their own pain was held, and whose work gave the chaplains the privilege of discovering a meaning and mission that was so life giving, even in that space of death and destruction. This experience can continue to offer those who work in other pastoral settings an image of both care and community that can contribute to their experience of well-being.

I end, as many of these chaplains did, with an immense sense of gratitude for the chaplains, their work, their community, and the gift of their participation in these reflections. I began with what could have seemed like a theoretical model of pastoral care, where we attend to the three movements as "Earth-making/Pain-bearing/Life-giving," as we create "Holding/Suffering/Transforming" relational spaces. However, I felt like I only discovered the depths and breadth of this model through seeing it reflected in the chaplains' being and work at Ground Zero. It is essentially a simple model, as simple as the command to love is simple. This love, in all its trinitarian complexity, is both our challenge and our gift as we engage in pastoral ministry, for in it we become what we are, the image of God, the God of love: Earth-maker, Pain-bearer, Life-giver.

Notes

INTRODUCTION: TRINITY AS A PASTORAL MODEL IN THE FACE OF TRAUMA

1. Stephen R. Harding, *A Book of Hours for the World Trade Center* (Glasgow: Glasgow City Council, 2006), 10.

2. I am following the most popularly agreed on version of events, which interprets the 9/11 disaster as a terrorist attack. This version does not take into account the conspiracy theories that suggest the deliberate destruction of WTC 7 and of the North and South Towers of the WTC by other agencies.

3. This number includes 343 FDNY firefighters, EMTs, and paramedics; 20 NYPD; and 37 Port Authority PD.

4. Paul Greene, et al., *FDNY Crisis Counseling: Innovative Responses to 9/11 Firefighters, Families, and Communities* (Hoboken, N.J.: John Wiley, 2006), 102. The original text says "psychotherapists" rather than "responders."

5. American Psychiatric Association, *Diagnostic and Statistic Manual of Mental Disorders III* [DSM-III] (Washington, D.C.: American Psychiatric Association, 1980), 236–38.

6. Richard J. McNally, *Remembering Trauma* (Cambridge: Belknap/Harvard University Press, 2003), 78.

7. American Psychiatric Association, *Diagnostic and Statistic Manual of Mental Disorders IV* [DSM-IV] (Washington, D.C.: American Psychiatric Association, 1994), 427–28.

8. *The Book of Common Prayer* (New York: Church, 1990).

9. *Disaster Spiritual Care* training is offered by the International Critical Incident Stress Foundation.

10. Stephen B. Roberts and Willard W. C. Ashley, eds., *Disaster Spiritual Care: Practical Clergy Responses to Community, Regional, and National Tragedy* (Woodstock, Vt.: Skylight Paths, 2008), 236.

11. Stephen Roberts, et al., "Compassion Fatigue among Chaplains, Clergy and Other Responders after September 11th," *The Journal of Nervous and Mental Disease* 191, no. 11 (November 2003): 756–58.

12. K. J. Flannelly, et al., "Correlates of Compassion Fatigue and Burnout in Chaplains and Other Clergy Who Responded to the September 11th Attacks in New York City," *Journal of Pastoral Care and Counseling* 59, no. 3 (Fall 2005): 213–24.

13. I chose this time period as it was a time when largely accurate records were kept. This list therefore excludes the larger number of clergy who previously worked at the T. Mort., either through the auspices of the Catholic Archdiocese of New York whose clergy staffed the T. Mort. for the first two months after 9/11, or those under the Episcopal Bishop for Chaplaincies office who ministered from St. Paul's Chapel who did not continue as chaplains at the T. Mort. after mid-November. A number of the chaplains from both of those groups, however, did continue to minister at the T. Mort., so their accounts represent those who ministered in the time period of September 11 to November 12, 2001.

14. See Carrie Doehring's discussion of the trifocal lenses of pastoral care: premodern, modern, and postmodern in her *The Practice of Pastoral Care: A Postmodern Approach* (Louisville: Westminster John Knox, 2006), 2.

15. Ibid.

16. The thought of D. W. Winnicott is generally seen as part of the "'Object Relations'" school of psychoanalytic thought, although he was more of an "independent.'" J. R. Greenberg and S. A. Mitchell, *Object Relations in Psychoanalytic Theory* (Cambridge: Harvard University Press, 1983), viii–ix.

17. Stanley J. Grenz, *The Social God and the Relational Self: Trinitarian Theology of the Imago Dei* (Louisville: Westminster John Knox, 2001), 4–5, quoting Ted Peters, *God as Trinity: Relationality and Temporality in Divine Life* (Louisville: Westminster John Knox, 1991), 34, 37.

18. Leonardo Boff, *Holy Trinity, Perfect Community* (Maryknoll, N.Y.: Orbis, 2000), 49–50.

19. John Godsey in D. F. Ford, *Modern Theologians* (Oxford: Basil Blackwell, Oxford, 1990), 55.

20. Carrie Doehring, *The Practice of Pastoral Care*, 3.

21. I use "holding relationship" as a shorthand term to denote the character of relationship, in this instance between the primary caregiver and infant. Holding is, however, only one part of the relationship, which encompasses both physical and psychic holding, handling, and presenting of "objects."

22. Catherine Mowry La Cugna, *God for Us: The Trinity and Christian Life* (San Francisco: HarperSanFrancisco, 1993 [1973]), 103.

23. See Augustine, *On the Trinity*, Cambridge Texts in the History of Philosophy, (Cambridge: Cambridge University Press, 2002), 181–82. See Book 15, chaps. 8–11.

24. Of the chaplains that ministered at the T. Mort., 67 percent were male, 33 percent were female.

25. Harding, S., *op.cit.*, 5.

CHAPTER 1: THE TRINITY FROM IMMANENT TO ECONOMIC

1. Stephen R. Harding, *A Book of Hours for the World Trade Center* (Glasgow: Glasgow City Council, 2006), 8.

2. "Definition of the Union of the Divine and Human Natures in the Person of Christ," Council of Chalcedon 451 C.E., Act V. See "Historical Documents," The Episcopal Church, in *The Book of Common Prayer* (New York: Church, 1979), 864.

3. Indeed, this is an understanding shared by both Eastern and Western theology. Orthodox theologian John D. Zizioulas writes: "Another important contribution of the Holy Spirit to the Christ event is that, because of the involvement of the Holy Spirit in the economy, Christ is not just an individual, not 'one' but 'many.' This corporate personality of Christ is impossible to conceive without Pneumatology. . . . Pneumatology contributes to Christology this dimension of communion." *Being as Communion: Studies in Personhood and the Church* (Crestwood, N.Y.: St. Vladimir's Seminary Press, 1985), 130–31.

4. Augustine, *On The Trinity*, Cambridge Texts in the History of Philosophy (Cambridge: Cambridge University Press, 2002), Book 15, Chapter 17 (27), 199–200.

5. Ibid., 202 (italics mine).

6. I generally prefer to use the term *community* rather than *multiplicity*, as the focus of the former reflects relationality rather than numerical value.

7. Jürgen Moltmann, *The Crucified God: The Cross of Christ as the Foundation and Criticism of Christian Theology* (London: SCM, 1974), 267–78.

8. Augustine, *On The Trinity*, 19.

9. Ibid., 22.

10. Ibid., 24–25.

11. Ibid.

12. Augustine defines the inward side of being a person as that which is related to reason and the outward as anything the person shares in common with the animal kingdom. It is notable that he sees reason as part of the soul rather than a separate thing.

13. Ibid., 71.

14. Ibid., 87.

15. Ibid., 10.

16. Ibid., 13.

17. Ibid., 156 (italics mine).

18. Ibid., 163.

19. Ibid., 181–82.

20. Ibid., 164.

21. Ibid., 204

22. Ibid., 21.

23. Ibid., 24–25.

24. D. W. Winnicott, "Morals and Education," in *The Maturational Processes and the Facilitating Environment: Studies in the Theory of Emotional Development* (Madison, Conn.: International Universities Press, 1994), 96. It is notable that Winnicott writes, "the word *infant* implies 'not talking' (*infans*), and it is not un-useful to think of infancy as the phase prior to word presentation and the use of word symbols," 40.

25. In an interesting clinical paper, "The Split-off Male and Female Elements to Be Found in Men and Women," Winnicott speaks of his developing acceptance of a "theory [where] it is necessary to allow for both a male and female element in boys and men and girls and women." D. W. Winnicott, *Psycho-Analytic Explorations*, ed. C. Winnicott, R. Shepherd, and M. Davis (Cambridge: Harvard University Press, 1989), 176.

26. Ann B. Ulanov, *Finding Space: Winnicott, God, and Psychic Reality* (Louisville: Westminster John Knox, 2002), 77.

27. Winnicott, "Morals and Education," 96.

28. Ibid., 102–103.

29. Ibid., 95.

30. Ibid., 93–105.

31. Ibid., 97.

32. D. W. Winnicott, "Excitement in the Aetiology of Coronary Thrombosis," in *Psychoanalytic Explorations*, 35–36.

33. Stanley Grenz, *The Social God and the Relational Self: A Trinitarian Theology of the Imago Dei* (Louisville: Westminster John Knox, 2007), 331.

34. Winnicott, "Morals and Education," 103.

35. D. W. Winnicott, "'Cure': A talk given to doctors and nurses in St. Luke's Church, Hatfield, on St. Luke's Sunday, 18 October 1970," in" C. Winnicott et. al, eds., *Home Is Where We Start From. Essays by a Psychoanalyst* (New York: W. W. Norton, 1986), 112.

36. Ibid.,113.

37. Ibid., 119.

38. Ibid., 119–20.

39. Ulanov, *Finding Space*, 130–31.

40. Church of the Province of New Zealand, *A New Zealand Prayer Book—He Karakia Mihinare o Aotearoa* (Auckland: Collins, 1989), 181 (italics mine). Original prayer in John Cotter, *Prayer at Night* (Sheffield: Cairns, 1983).

41. Personal e-mail from Jim Cotter to Storm Swain, January 11, 2007.

42. David Cunningham, *These Three Are One: The Practice of Trinitarian Theology* (Malden, Mass.: Basil Blackwell, 1998), ix.

43. John Milbank, "Sacred Triads: Augustine and the Indo-European Soul," in Robert Dodaro and George Lawless, eds., *Augustine and His Critics* (New York: Routledge, 2002), 90.

44. Ibid. (italics in original).

45. Catherine Mowry La Cugna, *God for Us: The Trinity and Christian Life* (San Francisco: HarperSanFrancisco, 1973), 378.

CHAPTER 2: EARTH-MAKING: THE HOLDING SPACE

1. Stephen R. Harding, *A Book of Hours for the World Trade Center* (Glasgow: Glasgow City Council, 2006), 6–7.

2. *The Book of Common Prayer* (New York: Church, 1990), 499.

3. Ibid.

4. Gen. 1:1—2:4a: "In the beginning when God created the heavens and the earth. . . . Then God said, 'Let us make humankind in our image, according to our likeness; and let them have dominion over the fish of the sea, and over the birds of the air, and over the cattle, and over all the wild animals of the earth, and over every creeping thing that creeps upon the earth.' So God created humankind in his image, in the image of God he created them; male and female he created them."

5. Karl Barth, *Church Dogmatics* I/1 (Edinburgh: T & T Clark, 1960), 553 (italics mine).

6. Ibid. (italics mine).

7. Ibid.

8. Ibid.

9. The Rev. Joan Dalloway is a CPE Supervisor with the New Zealand Association of Clinical Pastoral Education (NZACPE), a psychotherapist, and faculty for many years in the psychotherapy program at what is now the Auckland University of Technology. "The Three Pastoral Questions" is a model she has shared in the NZACPE Supervisors conferences.

10. Genesis 3:8-9: "They heard the sound of the LORD God walking in the garden at the time of the evening breeze, and the man and his wife hid themselves from the presence of the LORD God among the trees of the garden. But the LORD God called to the man, and said to him, 'Where are you?'"

11. The second pastoral question, Dalloway suggests, is "Do you want to get well?"—the question to the man at the pool of Bethesda who had been crippled for thirty-eight years (John 5:6); the third question is to blind Bartemaeus, "What do you want me to do for you?" (Mark 10:51).

12. Donald W. Winnicott, "The Mentally Ill in Your Caseload," in *The Maturational Processes and the Facilitating Environment: Studies in the Theory of Emotional Development* (Madison, Conn.: International Universities Press, 1994), 223–24.

13. Phyllis Trible, *God and the Rhetoric of Sexuality, Overtures to Biblical Theology* (Philadelphia: Fortress Press, 1978), 77.

14. Ibid., 78 (underlining in original).

15. Ibid., 80.

16. Ibid., 85.

17. Ibid., 97 (underlining in original).

18. Ibid., 98–99.

19. Ibid., 139 (italics mine).

20. Winnicott, "The Theory of the Parent-Infant Relationship (1960)," in *The Maturational Processes*, 43–44.

21. Winnicott notes in relation to "holding" and "living with," "It should be remembered, however, that a division of one phase from another is artificial, and merely a matter of convenience, adopted for the purpose of clearer definition." Ibid., 44.

22. Winnicott, "Psychoanalysis and the Sense of Guilt (1958)," in *The Maturational Processes*, 15.

23. Winnicott, "The Theory of the Parent-Infant Relationship," 49.

24. I am using Melanie Klein's spelling of "fantasy," as it denotes (like Winnicott's use of the word *illusion*) an inner reality that is not simply fictitious but a creative imagining that has a relationship both to inner instinctual urges, outer realities, and psychic construction.

25. Winnicott, "The True and the False Self (1960)," in *The Maturational Processes*, 145.

26. Winnicott, "Clinical Varieties of Transference [1955–6]," in *Through Paediatrics to Psychoanalysis: Collected Papers* (New York: Brunner/Masel, 1992), 297 (italics mine). In fact, with one patient he sees the False Self as that which she defines as her "Caretaker Self." Winnicott, "The True and the False Self'," 142. (N.B.: The publishers of *Maturational Processes* captitalize "True and False Self," whereas the publishers of *Through Paediatrics* do not.)

27. Winnicott, "The Theory of the Parent-Infant Relationship," 49.

28. Barth, *Church Dogmatics* I/1, 553.

29. *September 11, 2001, We Were There . . . Catholic Priests, How They Responded, in Their Own Words*, USCCB Secretariat for Vocations and Priestly Formation, available online at http://www.usccb.org/vocations/wewerethere.shtml, accessed February 1, 2011.

30. Winnicott, "The Capacity to Be Alone (1958)," in *The Maturational Processes*, 30.

31. Ibid., 31.

32. Ibid., 34.

33. Lt. William Keegan Jr, in *Closure: The Untold Story of the Ground Zero Recovery Mission* (New York: Touchstone, 2006), 183–84.

34. *September 11, 2001, We Were There . . .* (see n. 31, above).

35. Russell Haber's classification of diversity, from "Diversity in the Supervisory Relationship," in Haber, *Dimensions of Psychotherapy Supervision: Maps and Means* (New York: Norton, 1996).

36. Ibid., 56.

37. Winnicott, "The True and the False Self," 148.

38. Gerald Egan, *The Skilled Helper*, 2d ed. (Monterey, Calif.: Brooks/Cole, 1982), 123–24.

39. Ibid.

40. The chaplain who shared this encounter was hesitant about this story being printed but went on to reconsider and consented as long as there were no identifying details. We both thought it important that chaplains be aware of homicidal as well as suicidal ideation but there was a great deal of respect for the cop who dealt with it appropriately in the moment by seeking sanctuary with the chaplain.

41. Stephen B. Roberts, Kevin L. Ellers, and John C. Wilson, "Compassion Fatigue," in Stephen B. Roberts and Willard W. C. Ashley, eds., *Disaster Spiritual Care: Practical Clergy Responses to Community, Regional and National Tragedy* (Woodstock, Vt.: Skylight Paths, 2008), 211.

42. Technically, rather than popularly, as defined by the International Critical Incident Stress Foundation (ICISF), "Defusings are 20-45 minute group discussions" generally following a shift at the venue of a crisis or deployment. "'Critical Incident Stress Debriefings' (CISD) are also group discussions . . . more detailed and structured than the defusing. . . . They usually take one to three hours to complete." George L. Everly Jr. and Jeffrey T. Mitchell, *Critical Incident Stress Management: A New Era and Standard of Care in Crisis Intervention*, 2d ed. (Ellicott City, Md.: Chevron, 1999), 18.

43. This is not representative of CISM debriefing, which happens in a group of peers and is a seven-stage process that leads from an introduction to questions on facts, thoughts, reactions, symptoms, and includes a teaching component and reentry strategies. Ibid., 86–87.

44. Stephen B. Roberts, et al., "Compassion Fatigue among Chaplains, Clergy, and Other Respondents after September 11th," *The Journal of Nervous and Mental Disease* 191, no. 11 (November 2003): 756–58.

45. Roberts, et al., "Compassion Fatigue," in Roberts and Ashley, eds., *Disaster Spiritual Care*, 222.

CHAPTER 3: PAIN-BEARING: THE SUFFERING SPACE

1. Stephen R. Harding, *A Book of Hours for the World Trade Center* (Glasgow: Glasgow City Council, 2006), 11.

2. T. G. Serban, "Attending to the Dead: Morgues, Body Identification and Blessing the Dead," in Stephen B. Roberts and Willard W. C. Ashley, eds., *Disaster Spiritual Care: Practical Clergy Responses to Community, Regional and National Tragedy* (Woodstock, Vt.: Skylight Paths, 2008), 255–56.

3. There are, however, some animal stories that counter this generalization.

4. Jürgen Moltmann, *The Crucified God: The Cross of Christ as the Foundation and Criticism of Christian Theology* (London: SCM, 1974), 248–49 (italics mine).

5. Ibid., 246–47.

6. Ibid., 243.

7. Dorothee Soelle, *Suffering* (Philadelphia: Fortress Press, 1975), 26–27.

8. Ibid., 32.

9. "Seven years after the terrorist attacks of Sept. 11, the remains of 13 of the 19 men responsible have been identified and are in the custody of the F.B.I. and the New York City medical examiner's office . . . which holds the remains of 4 of the 10 hijackers who flew planes into the World Trade Center buildings." Sean D. Hamill, "7 Years Later, 9/11 Hijackers' Remains Are in Limbo," *New York Times*, Sept. 20, 2008.

10. Soelle, *Suffering*, 69.

11. Ibid., 70.

12. Ibid., 102–103. Soelle quotes Sermon #79 in *Meister Eckhart*, trans. Franz Pfeiffer (London: Watkins, 1956), 200 (translation slightly altered).

13. Ibid., 146.

14. Ibid., 148–49.

15. Judith L. Herman, *Trauma and Recovery* (New York: Basic, 1997), 155.

16. Ibid.

17. Melanie Klein, *Love, Guilt, Reparation, and Other Works 1921–1945* (New York: Free Press, 1975), 311.

18. Ibid., 313.

19. D. W. Winnicott, "The Development of the Capacity for Concern (1963)," in *The Maturational Processes and the Facilitating Environment: Studies in the Theory of Emotional Development* (Madison, Conn.: International Universities Press, 1994), 77–78.

20. J. R. Greenberg and S. A. Mitchell, *Object Relations in Psychoanalytic Theory* (Cambridge: Harvard University Press, 1983), 204.

21. Winnicott, "The Development of the Capacity for Concern (1963)," *The Maturational Processes*, 74.

22. Ibid., 73.

23. Ibid.

24. American Psychiatric Association, *Diagnostic and Statistic Manual of Mental Disorders IV* [DSM-IV] (Washington, D.C., American Psychiatric Association, 1994), 427–28. The symptomatic criteria of PTSD that follow this definition cover three clusters of symptoms broadly defined under the categories of (1) Re-experiencing, (2) Avoidance, and (3) Arousal, which have the duration of at least one month and cause "significant distress or impairment in social, occupational or other important areas of functioning."

25. Diane Myers and David F. Wee, *Disaster Mental Health Services: A Primer for Practitioners* (New York: Brunner Routledge, 2005), 16–17.

26. Research on the disaster of Swissair Flight 111 has indicated that there is significantly higher risk of PTSD for local volunteers that are exposed to the recovery of human remains and this

increases with the duration of the exposure. However, the sample size of that study was small and other studies have not born out the correlation between exposure to human remains and PTSD. See Terry L. Mitchell, Kara Griffin, Sherry H. Stewart, and Pamela Loba, "'We Will Never Ever Forget . . .': The Swissair Flight 111 Disaster and Its Impact on Volunteers and Communities," *Journal of Health Psychology* 9 (2004): 254–55.

27. DSM-IV, 424.

28. Charles R. Figley, "Compassion Fatigue: Toward a New Understanding of the Costs of Caring," in B. Hudnall Stamm, ed., *Secondary Traumatic Stress: Self-Care Issues for Clinicians, Researchers, and Educators*, 2d ed. (Lutherville, Md.: Sidran, 1999), 3–4.

29. Ibid., 11.

30. B. Hudnall Stamm, "Work Related Secondary Traumatic Stress," *PTSD Research Quarterly* 8, no. 2 (Spring 1997): 1.

31. Ibid.

32. Figley, "Compassion Fatigue," in Stamm, ed., *Secondary Traumatic Stress*, 17.

33. Stephen B. Roberts, Kevin L. Ellers, and John C. Wilson, "Compassion Fatigue," in Roberts and Ashley, eds., *Disaster Spiritual Care*, 209.

34. Figley, "Compassion Fatigue," in Stamm, ed., *Secondary Traumatic Stress*, 20–21.

35. Roberts, et al., "Compassion Fatigue," 212–13.

36. Ibid., 217, citing C. A. Darling, et al., "Understanding Stress and Quality of Life for Clergy and Clergy Spouses," *Stress and Health* 20 (2004): 261–67.

37. Figley, "Compassion Fatigue," 22–23.

38. T. L. Creamer and B. J. Liddle, "Secondary Traumatic Stress Among Disaster Mental Health Workers Responding to the September 11 Attacks," *Journal of Traumatic Stress* 18, no. 1 (February 2005): 89.

39. Ibid.

40. Ibid., 94.

41. Roberts, et al., "Compassion Fatigue," 211.

42. Tanya Pagán Raggio and Willard W. C. Ashley, "Self-Care—Not an Option," in Roberts and Ashley, eds, *Disaster Spiritual Care*, 35.

43. Roberts, et al., "Compassion Fatigue," 211.

44. D. W. Winnicott, "The Theory of the Parent-Infant Realtionship (1960)," in *The Maturational Processes*, 46 (italics mine).

45. D. W. Winnicott, "Ego Distortion in Terms of True and False Self (1960)," in ibid., 149 (italics mine).

46. D. W. Winnicott, "The Concept of Trauma in Relation to the Development of the Individual within the Family" (1965), in *Psycho-analytic Explorations*, ed. C. Winnicott, R. Shepherd, and M. Davis (Cambridge: Harvard University Press, 1989), 147.

47. "Understanding Compassion Fatigue: Helping Public Health Professionals and Other Front-Line Responders Combat the Occupational Stressors and Psychological Injuries of Bioterrorism Defense for a Strengthened Public Health Response," http://www.fcphp.usf.edu, accessed February 7, 2011, cited in Roberts, et al., "Compassion Fatigue," 211.

48. Of the thirty-three responding chaplains, one chaplain held an associate degree, three held a baccalaureate degree, twenty a masters degree, and eight a doctorate as their highest degree. If generalizable, this indicates that 85 percent of the chaplains held a graduate degree.

49. Winnicott, "Ego Distortion," 144.

50. D. W. Winnicott, "The Concept of Clinical Regression Compared with That of Defense Organization" (1967), in *Psycho-analytic Explorations*, 198.

51. DSM- IV, 427.

52. Winnicott, "The Concept of Clinical Regression," 198.

53. In which I would include the theory of Anna Freud.
54. Winnicott, "The Concept of Clinical Regression," 199.
55. Winnicott, "The Concept of Trauma," in *Psycho-analytic Explorations*, 147.
56. It is interesting that for Winnicott suicidal ideation can both be a response to a self that has felt like it has ceased to exist already, or a desire to protect the True Self, even at the cost of the physical self.
57. Winnicott, "The Concept of Clinical Regression," 198.
58. Ibid., 199.
59. Winnicott, "The Concept of Trauma," 147 (italics mine).
60. Winnicott, "The Capacity for Concern (1963)," in *The Maturational Processes*, 77.
61. D. W. Winnicott, *Through Paediatrics to Psychoanalysis: Collected Papers Through Paediatrics to Psychoanalysis: Collected Papers* (New York: Brunner/Masel, 1992), 207. Note 1 reads: "I should now say 'idealized and bad' instead of 'good and bad'" (1957).
62. Lt. W. Keegan Jr., *Closure: The Untold Story of the Ground Zero Recovery Mission* (New York: Touchstone, 2006), 114.
63. John D. Zizioulas, *Being as Communion: Studies in Personhood and the Church* (Crestwood, N.Y.: St. Vladimir's Seminary Press, 1985), 224–25, under the substructures (a–d); italics Zizioulas's.
64. N. B. The difficult circumstances of the recovery do not need to be discussed and have been withheld.

CHAPTER 4: LIFE-GIVING: THE TRANSFORMING SPACE

1. Stephen R. Harding, *A Book of Hours for the World Trade Center* (Glasgow: Glasgow City Council, 2006), 13–14.
2. Ibid.
3. R. W. Franklin and M. S. Donovan, *Will the Dust Praise You? Spiritual Responses to 9/11* (New York: Church, 2003), 119.
4. Compare the resurrection appearance of Jesus in John 20:19b-27: "Jesus came and stood among them and said 'Peace be with you.' After he said this he showed them his hands and his side."
5. John D. Zizioulas, *Being as Communion: Studies in Personhood and the Church* (Crestwood, N.Y.: St. Vladimir's Seminary Press, 1985), 243, 244.
6. Ibid., 41 (italics mine).
7. Ibid. (italics mine).
8. Ibid., 46.
9. Miroslav Volf, *After Our Likeness: The Church as the Image of Trinity* (Grand Rapids: Eerdmans, 1998), 281.
10. Ibid., 281–82.
11. D. W. Winnicott, "On 'The Use of an Object,'" in *Psycho-Analytic Explorations*, ed. C. Winnicott, R. Shepherd, and M. Davis (Cambridge: Harvard University Press, 1989), 220.
12. Ibid., 221.
13. D. W. Winnicott, "On the Use of the Object and Relating through Identifications," first published in the *International Journal of Psycho-analysis* 50 (1969), and appears in *Psycho-Analytic Explorations*, 218–27.
14. D. W. Winnicott, "On 'The Use of an Object,'" 223.
15. Ibid., 227.
16. Ibid., 231.
17. Ibid., 227.
18. Ibid., 222.
19. Ibid.

20. Ibid., 226.

21. Ibid., 223.

22. Ibid., 232.

23. Eric K. Noji, ed., *The Public Health Consequences of Disasters* (New York: Oxford University Press, 1997), 117.

24. Pascale Navvari, "Humour noir, sublimation: Quelques questions," *Revue Francaise de Psychanalyse* 62, no. 4 (October–November 1998): 1163–72.

25. Jacqueline Garrick, "The Humor of Trauma Survivors: Its Application in a Therapeutic Milieu," *Journal of Aggression, Maltreatment & Trauma* 12, no.1/2 (2006), 176.

26. Wendy Doniger, "Terror and Gallows Humor: Can Life Be Beautiful After September 11th?," in Jerry Piven, ed., *Psychological Undercurrents of History, vol. 2: Terror and Apocalypse* (San Jose and New York: Writer's Showcase, 2002), 389.

27. Ibid., 392.

28. Ibid., 411.

29. Winnicott, "On 'The Use of an Object,'" 435.

30. D. W. Winnicott, "Playing: Creative Activity and the Search for the Self," in *Playing and Reality* (New York: Routledge, 1977), 54.

CONCLUSION: TRAUMA, TRINITY, AND TRANSFORMATION

1. Stephen S. Harding, *A Book of Hours for the World Trade Center* (Glasgow: Glasgow City Council, 2006), 15. The final verse is a quote from Thomas Ken, in *The Hymnal 1982* (New York: The Church Hymnal Corp., 1985), #43.

2. Citing the apostle Paul, Augustine says that we, when beholding "'the glory of God, are transformed into the same image, from glory to glory, as through the Spirit of the Lord' [2 Corinthians 3:18]." Augustine, *On the Trinity*, Cambridge Texts in the History of Philosophy (Cambridge: Cambridge University Press, 2002), 182. This transformation for Augustine is that of the obscure image that we are, into the "same image," where we clearly reflect the one whose image we are. "But this perfection of this image is to be at some time in the future" (189). Hence, the space we live in, as being "made in some manner or other" as the image of God and yet not reflecting that clearly (without the action of the Spirit), means that the human person as a personal, relational image of God, is "a likeness that is obscure and difficult to perceive" (184).

3. Miroslav Volf, "'The Trinity Is Our Social Program': The Doctrine of the Trinity and the Shape of Social Engagement," *Journal of Modern Theology* 14, no. 3 (July 1998): 413.

Index

Index

New Zealand Prayer Book—He Karakia Mihinare o Aotearoa, A, 36
Noji, Erik K., 173

O
object-relating, 165
Object Relations theory, 12, 27–35
object-usage, 165–67, 173
objects, splitting of idealized and bad, 105, 132, 133–35
objects imago, good, 104
Office of Emergency Management/OEM, 65
oikonomia, 21, 27
Oklahoma City bombing of Alfred P. Murrah Federal building, 7–8
oneness of humanity and trauma, 42
other, the, 13, 44–45
outward/inward sides of being a person, 24–25

P
pain:
    containment of emotional, 86–88
    of ministering to those in pain, 85–89
    somatization of, 84
    unbearable, 96
Pain-bearing/pain-bearing:
    described, 85–89
    holding space for, 15, 141
    as pastoral method, 141–43
    pastoral practice and, 11, 17, 83, 89–90
    suffering, 11, 17
panic, 129
PAPD, *see* Port Authority
paramedic, 65, 134, 185. *See also* emergency medical technician
parent/child relationships, 28–29, 54–55, 56, 57, 104
parenting and first relational image, 15
pastoral caregivers, roles of, 63–64, 82
pastoral caregivers and importance of introspection, 65–66
pastoral ethic of love, 19–21
pastoral method:
    Earth-making/Holding as, 57–71
    Life-giving/Transforming as, 177–81
    Pain-bearing/Suffering as, 141–43
pastoral practice, described, 45–46
Pastoral Questions, The Three, 45–46, 188n11
pastoral theology, 10–12

patriarchy and creation, 51
patriarchy and Ground Zero, 51–52
patriarchy and the Trinity, 36–37
Paul, Saint, 26
peers and informal defusing/debriefing, 73
perichoresis, 22, 23, 38, 54
personal qualities *vs.* skills, 176
personal relationships, importance of, 79
personal space and Earth-making, 42
personality, development and integration of, 29, 133, 178
personalization of trauma, 85–87
personhood:
    Augustine's conception of, 24–25
    community/communion and, 13–14
    creation and, 42
    creation of, 54–55, 56
    described, 13, 47
Peters, Ted, 13
photographs:
    chauffeur and rig at Ground Zero, A, 88
    Cross in front of the Temporary Mortuary At Ground Zero, 163
    Early days of Rescue Period, 106
    Flag on top of "The Pile," 64
    Ground Zero seen from above, 4
    Honor Guard for a Member of Service, 86
    New York, September 30, 2001: A Chaplain on hand at Ground Zero, 143
    Raking for Remains, 49
    Recovery at Ground Zero, 45
    "THANK YOU!", 181
    Why?, 95
play, 33–34, 178
playspace, 30
police:
    deceased first responders on 9/11, 5, 85, 109
    escort, 87
    patches, 131
    recovery workers, 2, 39, 69-70, 71, 73, 77, 85, 99, 112, 139, 145, 161, 164, 174
Port Authority Police Department/PAPD, 39, 60, 62, 65, 161, 167, 185
post-modern approach, 14
Post-Traumatic Stress Disorder (PTSD), 6, 106–11, 115, 128, 190n24
post-traumatic growth, 176, 179–80, 184
practical theology, 10
prayer and trauma, 79–82

Lightning Source UK Ltd.
Milton Keynes UK
UKOW05f1955040414

229417UK00006B/53/P